GOD'S MESSENGERS

FRANK S. AND ELIZABETH D. BREWER PRIZE ESSAY

OF THE AMERICAN SOCIETY OF CHURCH HISTORY

God's Messengers

RELIGIOUS LEADERSHIP
IN COLONIAL NEW ENGLAND,
1700–1750 *by J. WILLIAM T. YOUNGS, JR.*

THE JOHNS HOPKINS UNIVERSITY PRESS

BALTIMORE AND LONDON

The Johns Hopkins University Press, Baltimore, Maryland 21218
The Johns Hopkins University Press Ltd., London
Library of Congress Catalog Card Number 76–8544
ISBN 0–8018–1799–4

Library of Congress Cataloging in Publication data will be found
on the last printed page of this book.

For Linda

CONTENTS

PREFACE

The history of the Congregational clergy in provincial New England is the story of mortal men entrusted with a divine mission. The pastors nurtured the spiritual life of a community that had become, in their eyes, shamelessly secular. But even in seeking to arouse religious sentiments among their people, they had difficulty in transcending their own material interests. The ministers were actually members of two communities. They belonged to the congregations of laymen among whom they worked, and they were members of the ministerial profession. In theory, the welfare of the one affected the welfare of the other, but during the first half of the eighteenth century, many pastors appeared to care more for the prestige of their profession than for the well-being of their congregations. This development, which can be termed "Congregational clericalism," was undermined by the Great Awakening of the 1740s, which forced the ministers to revise their understanding of their own mission.

At any point in the story there are signs both that the ministers were in control of their own destiny and that they were victims of social forces beyond their control. By professionalizing they maintained a position of authority in a society that was becoming increasingly conscious of rank, but they unwittingly gave comfort to those forces that were uncongenial to traditional Calvinism. To revitalize themselves and their people they sponsored a revival that was enormously successful, but that undercut their position of religious leadership. Deprived of their claim of unique holiness they succumbed not to defeat, but to a new view of themselves that emphasized their work among their people.

I became interested in Congregational ministers because the problem of their role in Puritan society is at the heart of a central issue in American religious historiography. For several decades colonial American historians generally accepted Perry Miller's belief that one can construct a coherent picture of colonial life by relying almost entirely upon the published works of the Congregational ministers. But, subsequently, critics have argued that Miller failed to grasp what Darrett B. Rutman has called "the actuality of the man in the streets." In the past ten years historians have sought to portray that "actuality" by relying heavily upon land records, wills, and minutes of public meetings. Religion usually plays a minor role in these accounts.

The new social history raises the question of the relevance of the Puritan ideology to the individual colonists and of the relationship of the ministers to the rest of New England. Did clergymen articulate the common feelings of all New Englanders? Or was their own spiritual life more pure and intense than that of other men? There are many ways of exploring the relationship between ministers and laymen. For example, the topic deserves, and is receiving, intensive scrutiny from historians who are interested in demography and social structure. My own emphasis, however, lies elsewhere. I have attempted here to construct an "inside view" of the ministers' experience, to discover how they perceived and shaped their own reality. Accordingly, their diaries and sermons have supplied the most valuable evidence for my argument.

The exploration of these sources has led me to a series of questions that could profitably be asked of other clergymen in other periods of time. How did a man become a minister—what besides his office distinguished him from other men? What was the nature of the minister's work among his people? How did he understand his profession and his relationship to his colleagues? And, finally, what was the impact on the clerical profession of a religious movement that seemed to come directly from God? In studying these problems, I have been impressed by the parallels between the development of clerical and civil leadership in colonial New England. Between 1700 and 1750 the definition of the good ministers evolved from an elitist notion based upon English norms to a more democratic concept based on the American experience. A similar change in political consciousness came to fruition during the American Revolution.

It should be noted that in the period under consideration there were other ministerial groups in New England. The Baptists and Anglicans, for example, had made many inroads in the Puritan colonies of Connecticut and Massachusetts by 1740. Although clerical histories of these and other denominations would be useful additions to our knowledge of early American religious and social history, I have limited this work to the story of the Congregationalist ministers. The Congregationalists were the strongest denomination in most of New England throughout the colonial period, and, hence, to a degree untrue of other groups, their history is interwoven into the history of the society as a whole.

The preparation of this study has been facilitated by the help of numerous scholars and institutions. I am indebted to the University of California, the Ford Foundation, the National Endowment for the Humanities, and the American Philosophical Society for their financial assistance. The staffs of the libraries listed in the Abbreviations (preceding the notes at the back of the book) were helpful in directing me to pertinent manuscripts. As a graduate student at Berkeley, I benefited from the prompt, incisive, and generous criticisms of Robert Middlekauff, Larzar Ziff, and Henry F. May. Subsequently, Richard H. Dunn, Philip J. Greven, Jr., Richard Johnson, and Michael McGiffert have offered valuable suggestions. I am grateful for the encouragement of the Brewer Prize committee of the American Society of Church History. And I am deeply indebted to my wife for her perceptive editorial assistance. As to my children, Hope and Teddy, twins who were born while I was revising an earlier version of the manuscript, they taught me better than any pastor's diary the fine complexity of striving to lead a full intellectual life in the midst of pressing domestic obligations.

GOD'S MESSENGERS

CHAPTER I

THE MINISTERS AND THEIR TIMES

In the early eighteen century the New England ministers lived in a society that was becoming increasingly secular. Although a sense of spiritual decline can be discovered in almost any period of American history, it was particularly acute in provincial New England. The seventeenth-century Puritans had displayed an unusual commitment to the belief that all aspects of life should be governed by religious principles. And so it was with some justification that pious New Englanders of the early eighteenth century regarded their community as more materialistic, selfish, and fragmented than the world of their Puritan forebears.

As heirs of the early Puritan divines the eighteenth-century New England ministers had a peculiar responsibility to reverse the course of history and to remind a secular people that the fulfillment of life comes from beyond the present world. They tried to stand outside of society, "to discern the Face of the Times," and to warn their people that the present world was vain and transitory.[1] But, like their parishioners, the pastors too had worldly interests. Even as they sought to shape the eighteenth-century environment, they were shaped by it.

THE SEVENTEENTH-CENTURY BACKGROUND. New England's founders sought to establish a close relationship between religion and the life of the community. Their initial ideas on doctrine, worship, church polity, and morality had been developed by English Puritans in the late sixteenth and early seventeenth centuries. The leaders of the early New England settlements came to the New World largely in order to create a society in accord with these ideals. The ministers, as religious leaders of a community explicitly devoted to religious ideals, were men of great importance.

Puritan theology clearly defined the relationship between God and man. The divinity was sovereign, incomprehensible, and abso-

1

lute—the fit object of worship and adoration. Man, on the other hand, was sinful, contemptible, and helpless—deserving only to suffer hell's eternal torments. But, despite the vast distance between the creature and the creator, God had predestined some men and women to enjoy the blessings of salvation. These were saved, not because of their own merit, but because God imputed Christ's righteousness to them.

This view of the nature of God, man, and salvation may properly be characterized as Calvinism. Some historians have argued that the God of the seventeenth-century Puritans was less awesome than the divinity worshipped by early Reformers. But the difference has been exaggerated, and most historians today would agree with David Hall that Puritanism and Reformed theology "were essentially congruent, if not identical."[2] Seventeenth-century Puritans and sixteenth-century continental Reformers both held that God had limited himself by entering into covenants with man, and both noted that even without grace fallen man could behave in a moral fashion and even prepare himself for salvation.[3] At the same time, however, both stressed the inability of man to find salvation without divine grace. In John Cotton's Boston, as in John Calvin's Geneva, the convert's path to heaven began with the abject realization of his own unworthiness.

The Puritans developed a system of worship and ecclesiastical polity that was consistent with their understanding of the relationship between God and man. They deplored the condition of the Anglican Church, where, they believed, men and women could easily avoid the knowledge of God's wrath and of their own fallen condition. Elegant priestly vestments and stained glass windows soothed their eyes; melodic hymns lulled their ears; and elaborate rituals drew their minds away from God. The Puritans sought to remove these abominations from the Established Church. In their own meeting houses in England and America the windows and clerical vestments were plain, hymns were abandoned, and communion was a simple ceremony. The service focused on prayers, scriptural readings, and above all, the sermon. Thereby the word of God came directly to the communicant, reminding him constantly of his perilous relationship to the Deity.

The Puritan ecclesiastical structure, as well as Puritan worship, was influenced by the Protestant perception of the relationship between God and man. From the time of Martin Luther, there were Protestants who had argued that all Christian converts were equal in the eyes of the Lord and that the religious status of the minister was no different than that of his fellow Christians. Reformers in the Protestant mainstream rejected this brand of spiritual leveling, and argued that the minister had a double calling from God—that of a Christian convert, and that of a religious leader. But, nonetheless, the ministers' sense of the fundamental importance of conversion as a shared experience of ministers and laymen led them to emphasize the common ecclesiastical work of both. Puritans tended to give laymen an important role in the choice and creation of clergymen and in the government of the church. And they abandoned the hierarchy of bishops and archbishops that the Anglicans had continued from the Catholic Church.[4]

Puritanism involved also a set of assumptions about human behavior. Although man was saved by faith rather than by works, Calvinism provided the incentive for strenuous moral endeavor. The daily life was an act of worship. Sanctification, which followed justification, led the Christian to treat all his activities as holy occupations. The Puritan saint's moral stance has been aptly described by Edmund S. Morgan as the "Puritan Dilemma."[5] In pursuit of a moral life, the believer could neither withdraw from worldly temptations, nor could he freely indulge himself in them. The merchant should work hard at his trade, but must not place his desire for profit ahead of his duty to serve God and his fellow man. The husband should love his wife, but must not prefer her to God. Each act that subordinated human inclinations to the will of God was an act of piety. Hence, in a famous saying, wine was from God, but drunkenness was from the devil.

It was natural that individuals who adopted Puritanism as the rule of their own lives should be distressed by the behavior of other Englishmen who ignored Puritan precepts. Ideally, God should be made manifest in human affairs, but many Englishmen in the seventeenth century ignored the restraints that Puritans advocated. They swore, became drunk, played games on the Sabbath, and otherwise behaved as though there were no God. Worse still, such individuals interfered with the Puritan's pursuit of their own religious goals. They scoffed at Puritan moral scruples and refused to allow Puritans to worship according to their own beliefs. In the 1620s, as the Puritan movement gathered strength in England, the Anglican Church came under the direction of a monarch and archbishop who sought universal conformity to a religious system that was sharply at variance with Puritanism.

Eventually, Puritan hostility to King Charles and Archbishop Laud would lead to civil war in England. But in the 1620s and

1630s many Puritans, despairing of the possibility of reforming their own land, sought to create a more perfect society in the American wilderness. There, beyond the control of English authorities, they could build a "City upon a Hill," an exemplary community based on Puritan ideas about theology, ecclesiology, worship, and behavior.

The community that they established in American can properly be described as a "Puritan society." It is true that in New England as in Old England there were many individuals who appeared to care more for economic profits and worldly pleasures than for Puritan grace. Many business dealings and political controversies in early New England are indistinguishable from secular activities in England.[6] But to suggest that for most men and women religion was merely a formality is to overlook the pervasive Puritan influence in New England. The governments of Massachusetts, Connecticut, and Plymouth colony protected the church from heretics and saw to it that the ministers were well maintained. Suffrage in early New England was restricted to church members. The laws reflected Puritan standards of moral conduct in business and in private affairs. The ministers and magistrates presided over a community generally characterized by order, deference, and cohesion. The New England town has been described as "a cohesive social organism."[7] The families, too, were tight knit, even to the extent that many sons lived on their parents' land until they were well into their middle years.[8] The deferential pattern of social organization is apparent also in provincial politics, where the governors were assumed to have a commission from God.

In this society Congregational ministers enjoyed a position of unusual distinction and respect. They were responsible for the religious life of the whole community. They catechized the children; they led their communities in worship on the Sabbath; they initiated disciplinary action against those who transgressed the moral law; and they published sermons and religious tracts dealing with every aspect of the Christian life. As religious leaders in a society that honored both religion and leadership, clergymen were highly esteemed and well paid for their work. Many colonists made the hazardous journey to American primarily in order to accompany a favorite pastor. In the early years the settlers enjoyed the preaching of such famous English divines as John Cotton, Thomas Hooker, and John Davenport. Recognizing the importance of good ministers, the Puritans sought to secure a continuing supply of able and orthodox religious leaders. This was one of the reasons, perhaps the foremost, for the establishment of Harvard College in 1636.[9]

But in spite of the strength of Puritanism in early New England, the system was unable to survive intact into the eighteenth century. An important challenge to Puritanism came from New England's commercial interests. The right-thinking Puritan merchant subordinated his economic aspirations to the welfare of the community. Regarding his work as an act of worship, he cared more about providing goods for his fellow Christians than about maximizing his profits. But as the seventeenth century progressed, trade began increasingly to operate according to its own rules, and despite the ministers' objections many merchants made money at the expense of others. Moreover, the leading merchants challenged and eventually supplanted the ministers as the dominant professional class in New England.[10]

The Puritan hegemony was also weakened by events in England. First, New England's confidence in its own global importance as a model of the ideal Christian commonwealth was undermined during the Civil War, when England adopted a policy of religious toleration, thereby indicating that Congregationalism was but one among many valid religious systems. A few decades later the close alliance between church and state was undermined when England insisted that suffrage in New England could not be restricted to Puritan saints. And in 1684 she abolished the Massachusetts charter and replaced elective Puritan governors with royally appointed executives.

In these ways the close affinity between Puritan theology and New England politics and society was seriously undermined. The new society was less cohesive and more secular, and it was shaped by the values of the English aristocracy and the impact of the colonial frontier as much as by the ideals of Puritanism. Its ministers, lacking the sense of cosmic purpose that characterized their antecedents, were often perplexed by the community they sought to serve.

A PROVINCIAL SOCIETY. In the eighteenth century, wealth and social prestige assumed a far greater importance in New England than was evident in the early years of settlement. In comparison with other parts of the contemporary world, New England was relatively prosperous. In 1704 Madam Knight described Connecticut in terms that could also be applied to the other New England colonies. "It is," she said, "a plentiful country for provisions of all sorts and its [sic] Generally Healthy. No one that can and will be diligent in this place need fear poverty nor the want food and Rayment."[11]

As the eighteenth century progressed, the fruits of such diligence multiplied. Between 1697 and 1750 New England's imports from England increased by 500 percent.[12] In 1740 Benjamin Colman, minister of the Brattle Street Church in Boston, described New England's metropolis as "a place of great trade and business, finery and dress."[13] Colman regarded this wealth with mixed feelings. Five years earlier he had lamented the effects of English trade upon New England's currency. "There is no way to recover ourselves . . . ," he wrote, "but to live upon our homespun and to send for no more silks, calicos, and fine cloth and linen to London. . . . We must correct our own views, our pride and profuseness in clothing, furniture, etc."[14]

As Benjamin Colman suggested, the increase in trade was accompanied by the development of new attitudes. In many cases the wealthy merchants adopted a life style that was unaffected by traditional Puritan restraint. Samuel Sewall's oft quoted description of an episode in Boston in 1686 shows that a cultural schism was already developing at that time. In his diary he recorded: "Friday, September 3. Mr. Shrimpton, Captain Lidget and others . . . come in a Coach from Roxbury about 9. oclock or past, singing as they come, being inflamed with Drink. At Justice Morgan's they stop and drink Healths, curse, swear, talk profanely and baudily to the great disturbance of the Town and grief of good people. Such highhanded wickedness has hardly been heard of before in Boston."[15] Excessive drinking was not limited to the upper classes. By 1750 there were 150 taverns in Boston alone, and almost every village in New England had at least one public house.[16] John Hancock, minister of Lexington, complained that by allowing customers to take more than "a proportionable amount to drink" and by remaining open after nine o'clock tavern keepers failed to "prevent the mischief of quarrels, loudness, and thefts, midnight brawls, the diseases of intemperance and venery, and a 1,000 other evils."[17]

In the early eighteen century, the movement toward a more worldly society was also reflected in a change in attitudes toward sex. Puritans had never been sexual ascetics and had heartily approved of the physical relationship between man and wife. But they did not condone sex outside of or before marriage. In the 1720s, however, there was enough diversity of opinion on this point that a religious society at Harvard could debate the question, "Whether it be fornication to lye with one's sweetheart (after contraction) before marriage?"[18] We do not know what the society concluded, but in some churches during the next decade, 20 percent of married couples confessed to premarital intercourse.[19] In the town of Long-meadow, Massachusetts, Rev. Stephen Williams complained that there was "a notion advanced by some of its being lawful to persons that have made private promises to one another to have carnal knowledge of one another."[20]

Another sign of the secularization of New England was the pride that many people took in worldly possessions. Josiah Cotton, justice of the peace for Plymouth, was one of numerous eighteenth-century colonists who carefully maintained a family coat of arms. Many colonists coveted fine clothes and jewelry. Richard S. Dunn's description of two of John Winthrop's grandsons shows how even the descendants of one of New England's patriarchs had become obsessed with material possessions. Dunn writes: "Fitz John and Wait Still Winthrop were men of the Glorious Revolution, narrowly secular and parochial, half-humorous and half-ludicrous, uncertain of their values, and always chiefly absorbed with fashion, status and the accumulation of real estate." Both men were petty and cantankerous. "The accumulation of real estate was their main object, and the conduct of lawsuits over disputed land claims was among their main occupations. The brothers also displayed an acute awareness of their status as gentlemen and the necessity of living in style. They were always exceedingly anxious to hear about the latest London fashions in waistcoats and wigs."[21]

The love of ornaments also found its way into the churches. The "Lord's barns" of the seventeenth century, which had been plain edifices, were often replaced by more elaborate structures in the eighteenth century. One of these was the new meetinghouse in Guilford, Connecticut, built in 1726 with a 120-foot steeple.[22] Inside the churches, new and old, the practice of assigning pews to reflect each parishioner's wealth was becoming the normal custom. Hymns were also sung in a "New Way" in many churches. By the "Old Way" each man sang his own tune, giving voice to his individual piety. The new method, singing by note, though less individualistic, was more decorous.

Even the gravestones of New England, many of them still standing, reflect these basic changes in attitude. Most of the stones from the late seventeenth and early eighteenth centuries bear the figures of skulls. But the stones from the middle of the eighteenth century are adorned with the fleshy faces of cherubs or even with the lively

countenances of the men lying beneath them. The awesome fact of
death, which drove many early New Englanders to seek their ref-
uge in God, was muted by these comforting images.[23]

Theological developments also reflected eighteenth-century culture. Although most men continued to believe in a universe ruled
by God, many New Englanders tended to place more emphasis
than their forebears on man's intrinsic ability and worth. Some
began to suggest that man could earn salvation through his own
works. This position, known as Arminianism, was especially con-
genial to wealthy New Englanders, who tended to identify their
worldly success with God's approval.[24] Although few colonists
became outright Arminians before the middle of the century, many
attended Congregational churches that had abandoned evidence of
conversion as a criterion for membership, and some even became
members of Anglican churches, which were slowly gaining adherents throughout New England.

As the Puritan influence over the culture declined, other forces
gained importance in shaping the New England mind. In particular, English customs affected many colonists. In politics, the eighteenth century saw the development of a "court persuasion,"
which stressed the political leadership of New England's upper
class and the superiority of English fashions and manners. In the
same period, a contrary sensibility, "the country persuasion,"
gained many supporters. It stressed the political legitimacy of the
leader who "remained close to his constituents" and "defended
those provincial customs and values which the Court had come to
reject."[25] Both philosophies had their origins in England and were
rooted in secular rather than religious considerations.

In addition to becoming increasingly secular, New England in
the eighteenth century was more fragmented and contentious than
in the previous era. The early Puritans had urged men to subordi-
nate their selfish desires to the needs of the community. But life in
the eighteenth century was characterized by a thirst for self-
aggrandizement. As the population grew, pressure on available resources left some men wealthy and others impoverished. Families
were broken apart as sons left home to seek new lands. Town
and provincial politics were increasingly characterized by factional
struggles revolving around such issues as the creation of new towns
and the printing of paper money. Each of these changes undercut
the religious, communitarian ideals of the founders and "put one
portion of the populace out of harmony with another." In the early
eighteenth century, "a person's total attachment to any community
whatsoever diminished."[26]

Historians generally agree that the loyalties that had once bound men to communities and institutions larger than themselves had been replaced by commitments to narrow individual and group interests. In a study of Connecticut, Richard L. Bushman writes: "After 1690 the close-knit, tightly controlled, homogeneous community of the early period steadily became more open and heterogeneous." Timothy H. Breen and Stephen Foster argue that by the 1680s "Massachusetts had changed from a peaceful to a relatively turbulent society." Perry Miller's chapters on the period in *The New England Mind: From Colony to Province* are appropriately titled "The Splintering of Society." And H. Richard Niebuhr has described the eighteenth century as a time when "Absolute individuals had replaced absolute kings and absolute churches."[27]

But although the social structure of New England has been ably described by historians, we know little about the clergymen in this period. Inevitably, the ministers were troubled by their times. As merchants assumed greater importance, as politics became more secular in orientation, as Puritan restraint was challenged by eighteenth-century worldliness, the clergymen lost the central position they had occupied in early Puritan society. The ministers were keenly aware of the worldliness and fragmentation of their society, and they often complained that their people did not show any serious concern for religion. But although they criticized worldliness, the ministers were often as sensitive about their own social position as they were concerned about the decline in religious fervor. Thomas Prince, for example, was pleased when in his first days in London he was mistaken for an Englishman. He reported that people he met "wondered as much at my carriage and deportment, as at the trueness and accuracy of my language."[28] A satirical poem written at the time of Benjamin Colman's settlement as minister of the Brattle Street Church indicted the clergymen for their materialism. The poem alleged: "Our parsons grow trim and trig, with wealth, wine and wig."[29] The ministers were acutely conscious of their own professional status. After 1690 they began to join together in ministerial associations, permanent organizations that, unlike synods and councils, included no laymen. In the same period, ministers frequently published works about their profession. Between 1700 and 1740 more than one hundred and fifty ordination sermons, funeral sermons for clergymen, and tracts about the ministry were published in New England. In many of these the ministers emphasized the importance of their calling and urged laymen to recognize and honor their status. In 1720 Daniel Lewes summarized what many of his fellow clergymen felt. In the world there are many "Offices and Employments," he said, "but among them all there is none of more Importance . . . than that of the *Ministry*. Nay, it may with Truth be asserted that it is the *most* weighty, awful, and important Work that ever mortal Man was employed in."[30]

During this period when the clergymen were becoming highly conscious of their professional status their real economic and social position was far from secure. Most of the country ministers had to divide their time between religious duties and menial farm labor. Often their salaries were low and in arrears. In Boston, where the ministers were usually well paid, laymen such as James Franklin and the supporters of his *New England Courant* published criticism of the clergy's worldly pride. Other critics challenged the religious leadership of the clergy and questioned the Congregational ideal of a well-educated professional ministry.

Thus, it was in the midst of many complex circumstances that the New England ministers carried on their work in the first part of the eighteenth century. The ideal they upheld stressed religious rather than secular values. It emphasized the transitoriness of life and the vanity of earthly pleasures. And yet the ministers, like the laymen, were increasingly attracted by earthly rewards. Worse still, the clergymen began using the ministerial office itself as a source of worldly prestige.

The tension between the ministers' self-interest and their religious mission led to a crisis in clerical leadership in the 1740s. The Great Awakening, a religious revival that swept through the colonies, was a fulfillment both of the ministers' greatest hopes for a spiritual renewal and of their worst fears of popular disrespect. Awakened laymen showed a lively interest in religious affairs, but they did not always follow their traditional religious leaders, and many even removed ministers whom they disliked or joined new denominations.

In the turbulent years of the Great Awakening the ministers developed a new understanding of their relationship to the people they served. The new concept was largely a recognition of a situation that had already existed, and so in order to understand it fully, we need to begin by exploring the distinctive genesis, activities, and aspirations of the clergy. How did a person become a minister? What did ministers do? How did they attempt to enhance their position? How did they seek to increase religiosity in their communities? The answers to these questions will lead us to a better comprehension both of the ministers and of American society in the late colonial period.

CHAPTER II

THE MINISTER'S CALLING

The Congregational clergymen frequently reminded their people that the first Christian ministers were the apostles whom Jesus Christ had appointed to preach his gospel. They were proud that their profession was of divine origin. But at the same time, however, they were uncomfortable with the knowledge that Christ had chosen uneducated fishermen as his first ministers. Their own position was dependent on many years of formal training rather than an immediate sense of God's calling.[1] Certainly it was desirable that a pastor should have experienced conversion, but divine grace alone did not qualify a man to become a minister. The Congregationalists had inherited the Reformation ideal of an educated preaching clergy. They rejected the notion that unlearned men could preach successfully. "It is a glaring *impudence* and daring *presumption*," said Thomas Foxcroft, "to dream of immediate irradiation from above. The deep things of God must be digg'd out, and fetch'd up from the mine in the *common* way of study, reading, and converse."[2]

Men became ministers as a result of a complex process that had little to do with "immediate irradiation from above." Their intellectual talents, social backgrounds, and college educations enabled them to become clerical candidates. A systematic apprenticeship prepared them for their work. The politics of Congregational election produced their call to a particular parish. And finally, ordination by their fellow ministers actually elevated them to the clerical profession. Thus, before a young man even began his pastoral work, he underwent a series of experiences that distinguished him sharply from his fellow New Englanders.

EDUCATION.   A college education was the essential prerequisite for the Congregational ministry. Ninety-five percent of the clergymen had a college degree, and most studied for three years after receiv-

11

ing their A.B. in order to earn an A.M., usually in theology.[3] The content of their educations, then, and the factors that placed potential ministers in the small minority of New Englanders who became college graduates are important ingredients in the character of the eighteenth-century clergy.

The two most important determinants of whether a person would go to college were social background and intellect. Simply because of their parentage some children had a much greater chance than others of becoming clergymen. Among Harvard graduates between 1700 and 1740 who became ministers, 63 percent were sons of merchants, physicians, sea captains, innkeepers, clergymen, and other relatively well-to-do New Englanders. The proportion of Yale students with prominent parents in the same period was somewhat lower, but still substantial. These affluent fathers were a small fraction of New England's total population, but they were the parents of many of the clergymen. In addition, a substantial proportion of the pastors were relatives of other clergymen. In the early eighteenth century 17 percent of the Yale graduates who became ministers had clerical fathers, and 18 percent of Harvard's ministerial graduates were the sons of clergymen.[4]

Some ministers had family ties to a large number of their fellow pastors. Several families, such as the Williamses, the Rogerses, and the Woodbridges, produced as many as ten ministers. Moreover, in relation to their numbers it is possible that clerical sons exercised a disproportionate influence on the religious life of New England. Many of the most important New England pastors were second-, third-, or even fourth-generation ministers. Jonathan Edwards, Cotton Mather, and Experience Mayhew, for example, were from families that produced many clergymen.

It is true that an important group of clergymen arose from nonministerial backgrounds. Benjamin Colman's father, for example, was a merchant. John Wise was the son of an indentured servant. However, if a boy were born of clerical parents, it was far more likely that he would become a minister than if he came from any other background. And if his parents were poor there was very little chance that he would become a clergyman.

In addition to affluence, parental encouragement and intellectual talent greatly influenced a youth's chances of becoming a minister. Many children were encouraged by their parents to enter the clergy. For example, it was said of Thomas Clap, the president of Yale College, that "from childhood he was 'devoted and dedicated to the work of the ministry' by his pious and worthy parents."[5]

But a parent was most likely to be successful in urging a young man to become a clergyman if the youth had some native talent and inclination for his studies. Even Cotton Mather was unable to persuade his son, Increase, to become a minister, because the youth lacked an appetite for study. But the father of Nicholas Gilman was more successful. He decided to give his son a liberal education only after the youth had impressed him by repeating part of the Latin accidence by heart each evening after school.[6] Nicholas graduated from Harvard in 1724 and later became minister of Durham, New Hampshire.

Thus, a combination of social background, parental encouragement, and intellectual promise helped determine whether a young man would set out on the path to the ministry. None of these factors was a sign of piety. Being able to memorize Latin with ease was an indication of intellectual rather than religious promise, and a father's piety in "devoting" his son to the ministry did not assure that the son would himself be pious. But without the benefit of these qualifications, it was unlikely that a young New Englander, no matter how pious he might be, would acquire the education that was an essential ministerial prerequisite.

The actual training that distinguished potential clergymen from ordinary New Englanders was not designed solely for ministerial candidates. A grammar school education was part of the common experience of ministers, lawyers, merchants, and even of many farmers. Children learned to read and write in "dame schools" and then entered grammar school, usually at age seven. The curriculum of the grammar schools varied form place to place. In some towns the "Latin master" was also responsible for teaching reading and writing; in others the masters taught mathematics along with the classics.[7] But the candiate for college admission was chiefly required to learn Latin and Greek.

Although formal religious training was not always a part of the grammar school education, religion did play a role in the early education of New England's youth. The catechism, containing basic religious principles, often served to drill the students in reading and writing. In addition, many teachers gave informal religious counsel to their students. In the early eighteenth century, grammar schools were often taught by young ministerial candidates awaiting a call to a particular church, who were anxious to gain experience in teaching religious principles. Such teachers often sought to introduce religious training into the curriculum.[8]

In grammar school a student also acquired a tool that he would use frequently in his ministry: his knowledge of Latin and Greek allowed him to study the Bible in the original tongues. Many ministers maintained their linquistic skill and continued to study the Bible in the classical tongues long after they left college. Joseph Baxter, minister of Medfield, Massachusetts, maintained: "We should carefully consult the original tongues to find out the meaning of the texts we insist on."[9] Reverend Simon Bradstreet of Charlestown was once introduced as a man who could "whistle Greek."[10]

Upon completing his grammar school preparation the prospective minister entered either Harvard or Yale College. During the eighteenth century Harvard was, according to Samuel Eliot Morison, "a religious college, but emphatically not a 'divinity school' or a seminary for the propagation of Puritan theology."[11] The atmosphere of Harvard was religious, with prayers twice daily, catechism on Saturday, and a Puritan observance of the Sabbath. And a large number of Harvard graduates did become ministers: 50 percent in the seventeenth century, and more than one-third in the early eighteenth century. The college curriculum, however, like that of the grammar schools, was suited to lawyers, doctors, and merchants as well as to ministers. "Prospective parsons," according to Morison, "were given exactly the same Liberal Arts course as other boys who had no such ambition."[12]

In 1701 a second college, later named Yale, was established in Connecticut. This institution, like Harvard, sought not only to educate prospective clergymen but also to train young men for other professions. In the early eighteenth century, Yale graduated more than two hundred young men who became ministers, but in the same period it produced an equal number of students who chose other vocations.[13]

In both schools the curriculum was broad, including the "seven liberal arts" and the "three philosophies" of the medieval universities and also belles-lettres and languages. Students at both Harvard and Yale could read works that contradicted orthodox Puritan ideas, and in the early eighteenth century many supporters of Harvard took pride in the college's "liberalism." In 1712 Benjamin Colman wrote: "No place of education can boast a more free air than our little college may for these last twenty years."[14] Although some of the early supporters of Yale hoped that the college would be less liberal than Harvard, students there also were given the opportunity to read unorthodox works.[15] The Yale library included a large assortment of books that had been assembled by Jeremiah Dumner in England. This collection included an extensive selection of both orthodox and latitudinarian religious tracts.[16]

But although college students in the early eighteenth century were exposed to diverse religious ideas, there were limits to the colleges' liberalism. While it is true that Leverett may have changed the tone of Harvard and encouraged his students to consider unorthodox ideas, he did not actually espouse any heretical doctrines. In 1722, when Edward Wigglesworth was appointed to the Hollis Chair of Divinity, Leverett accepted the overseers' request that Wigglesworth should prove his orthodoxy by declaring his adherence to William Ames's *Medulla Theologiae*, the Westminster Assembly catechism, and the thirty-nine articles. In the same year the trustees of Yale reaffirmed the orthodoxy of their school after the rector of the college, a tutor, and five local ministers declared that their reading in the Dumner books had persuaded them that their Congregational ordinations were invalid. Although this episode, known as the "Great Apostasy" shocked all of New England, it did not usher in a new era of liberalism at Yale. Instead it persuaded the trustees to be more cautious in seeking their next rector. Four days after Cutler and his associates had announced their conversion, the trustees declared that thereafter Yale tutors and rectors would be required to assent to the orthodox Congregational positions on doctrinal and ecclesiastical questions before being installed in office.[17]

In spite of the diversity of ideas to which an undergraduate was exposed, the student who attended Harvard or Yale in the early eighteenth century was less likely to be led away from religion by unorthodox ideas than by the more subtle temptation to abandon the studious, disciplined life of a ministerial candidate for the more earthly pleasures of student frivolity. At Harvard and Yale there were frequent cases of drunkenness, thievery, dancing, and a variety of other misdemeanors. At Yale, tutor Jonathan Edwards testified that in 1721 his college was beset with "monstrous impieties and acts of immorality . . . particularly stealing of hens, geese, turkies, piggs, meat, wood, etc., unseasonable nightwalking, breaking people's windows, playing at cards, cursing, swearing, damning, and using all manner of ill language, which never were at such a pitch in the college as they now are."[18] Samuel Eliot Morison asserts that in this period many students came to Harvard from seaports, "which reaped the first harvests from land speculation and West India commerce, and the rum business; and where the influence of Court manners was most quickly felt. The new crop of young men came to be made gentlemen, not to study."[19] For such youths there was a broad road ahead to other professions than the ministry. At the 1712 commencement, John Leverett proudly noted that Harvard produced scholars, judges, soldiers, physicians, and farmers as well as ministers. Significantly, most of his examples were of men who belonged to a social as well as an intellectual elite. Richard Warch concludes that Yale too served the provincial upper class. He notes that the college served "as the intellectual core of a Connecticut and interior New England societal establishment; its members sent their sons to the college and Yale's graduates served it."[20]

Because social background was as important as intellect in determining who would receive a college education and graduates tended to enter the provincial elite, it was natural for intelligent, but self-educated colonists to question whether the colleges did, in fact, improve their students' intellects and souls as much as they raised their status. Ideally, those young men who were most distinguished for intellectual and religious qualities would be promoted by the educational system. But as we have seen, the schools tended to train only those children whose parents could afford the cost of their education. Some colonists complained that this system simply gave special advantages to wealthy children, instead of educating the best intellects for religious and political leadership.

In 1722 a bright young Boston youth who did not attend Harvard wrote a scathing denunciation of the college. Writing under the pseudonym of Silence Dogood, Benjamin Franklin argued that in spite of Harvard's fame as a "temple of LEARNING" most parents who sent their children to college "consulted their own purses instead of their Children's Capacities" with the result that most of the students "were little better than Dunces and Blockheads." He alleged that only a few youths actually worked at college and that when they graduated many students were "e'en just as ignorant as ever."[21] Benjamin Franklin was one of many eighteenth-century New Englanders who refused to equate intellectual talent with a college degree. No doubt he exaggerated the role of wealthy parents and personal ambition in the early lives of the ministers, but it was mainly the sons of the well-to-do who became ministers, and, as we shall see, the ministers themselves were not indifferent to questions of social status.

In statements about their profession the ministers liked to suggest that any man with a good mind and a pious heart could become a minister. In practice this was not the case. It is true that in order to enter and to graduate from college a young man did have to show some intellectual promise, and the education he received did involve a degree of religious training. But it was much more difficult for a child of poor parents to attend college than for a child of wealthy parents, and the educational system tested and enhanced a young man's intellect more than his piety.

CLERICAL APPRENTICESHIP. In eighteenth-century New England men became Congregational ministers by acquiring a skill rather than by possessing superior spiritual qualities. We have seen that only a small group of New Englanders were even qualified to enter ministerial training and that these men were distinguished from their fellow colonists more by social background and intellect than by superior piety. It was the actual training prospective ministers underwent after receiving their A.B. that fitted them with a knowledge of Christian doctrine and practice in the arts of preaching and counseling. In essence the minister was established through proper training.

Ministers' diaries suggest that it was common for a candidate to develop a sense of piety only after graduating from college. The undergraduate's intellectual knowledge of religious truth was carefully developed and tested. But there was no effort by his teachers to determine whether the scholars had experienced God's grace and had undergone conversion. Surviving diaries of ministers who were deeply concerned about religious matters while they were in college suggest that their experience was exceptional.

For pious youths college life sometimes seemed inhospitable. John Cleaveland, a Yale student who later became a famous New Light preacher, complained that having to run errands for older boys made serious thought and work difficult. He once lamented: "I think I run further and further and grow colder and colder in things of religion."[22] Some young men at Harvard and Yale reacted against the temptations and diversions of the secular world by forming religious clubs at college. In the early eighteenth century several societies for pious worship and discussion were established at Harvard. For example, David Jeffries, a graduate of 1708, formed a student prayer group in his undergraduate days. Jeffries became a merchant, but the society included Joseph Sewall and Thomas Prince, who were to become notable clergymen. Another society, formed in 1721, produced seven ministers from its eight members; among them were Charles Chauncy and Ebenezer Pemberton. A typical meeting of this group included a twenty-minute discourse by one member "on any Subject he pleaseth." Then followed a dis-

putation on two or more questions with one part of the group holding the affirmative and the other the negative. The members also
discussed recently published books and agreed "if we see or hear
of any Extraordinary Book, we will give the best account we can of
it to the Society." The topics of discussion included, "On a Future
State," "On God's Wisdom and Power," "On Regeneration," and
"Upon the Unity of the Church."[23]

A similar organization, the Philomusarian Club, was formed at
Harvard in 1728. Only those who were "adjudged to be Philomus,
i.e., a lover of learning," were admitted to the group. The club's
florid preamble reflected the members' view of their college con-
temporaries. The subscribers joined together to "stem that monstrous tide of impiety and ignorance which is like to sweep all before it." They agreed to meet four nights weekly and on each occasion to discuss "some point of learning." The club had an elaborate
set of laws and penalties. Cursing, for example, was punished with
a fine of six pennies, liquor was forbidden, and a student who
scoffed at another's performance must pay two pennies to the club
treasurer. Every second week a court was to meet in order to penal-
ize miscreants. The original members of the club were ten students
in the classes of 1729, 1730, and 1731. Apparently, the organization
had a strong appeal for young men who were interested in the ministry. Of the original members eight lived long enough to choose
careers, and seven of these became clergymen. Thus, almost 90 percent of these students became ministers at a time when only 40
percent of the student body as a whole entered the ministry. Like
the earlier pious societies the Philomusarian Club must have provided a haven within a more secular society, where interested students could discuss religious questions and lead a moral life.[24]

It is evident from the formation of such societies that some ministers became serious Christians before embarking on their ministerial training. But the comparative isolation of these students and
the diaries of other students suggest that many young men became
serious Christians only after entering clerical apprenticeship.

It was only after he received his A.B. degree that the student
began a course of studies designed exclusively for ministers. Intel-
lectually his next hurdle was the college A.M. examination, which
was usually taken three years after the A.B. was granted. Most
graduates received the Masters degree even if they did not enter
the ministry. However, the subject matter of the examinations
varied with a student's professional ambitions. There were no formal courses for the A.M., and there were a variety of circumstances
under which men prepared themselves for the degree.

Some young men lived with ministers and learned about pastoral labors as well as theology. This course had a long Puritan tradition. In the early seventeenth century, many Puritan ministers in England had trained ministerial candidates in their homes. John Cotton, for example, instructed students from Cambridge University at his home in Boston, England. In her study of *Ministerial Training in Eighteenth Century New England,* Mary Latimer Gambrell describes a typical course of studies at one of these "schools of the prophets."[25] Students would compose and answer lists of questions that they built into the framework of a systematic or didactic theology. They read theological treatises setting forth opposing points of view, and they wrote compositions and engaged in discussions.

Other candidates lived at home while pursuing their studies and when possible, met to study with other ministerial candidates. Cotton Mather describes one such gathering. The members carried on "a course of *Disputation* upon the Body of Divinity." They carefully discussed the important church controversies and prepared papers on "every Head of Divinity."[26]

Other young men had to find steady employment in the years between receiving their A.B.'s and becoming settled pastors. For such students teaching school was a common occupation. Here a ministerial candidate had the opportunity to refresh his Latin and Greek. He might also practice religious instruction. As we have seen, religious training was not a formal part of secondary education, but prayers and catechizing were often included. For example, Joseph Green gave religious counseling to his students in Roxbury. The first eighty-two pages of Green's commonplace book contain his notes for almost three months of catechizing.

A fourth way of preparing for the ministry involved remaining in residence at college and reading theology. Some students were fortunate enough to receive a Hopkins scholarship at Harvard or a Berkeley fellowship at Yale, which subsidized their studies. While in residence the graduates read theology. They paid no tuition and received no formal instruction. Often the resident A.B.s roomed with undergraduates and were probably expected ot help them with their studies.[27]

The general emphasis in graduate training was naturally upon religious knowledge. Although there was no uniform syllabus, two guides for ministerial candidates were published in New England before the Great Awakening. In 1726 Cotton Mather published *Manuductio ad Ministerum Directions for a Candidate of the Ministry.* Nine years later Joseph Sewall and Thomas Prince collected Samuel Willard's notes on preparation for the ministry and published them as *Brief Directions to a Young Scholar Designing the Ministry*. Although Mather's book is much longer and more detailed than Willard's, the two are similar in intent. Both urge the ministerial candidate to embark upon a course of study designed to improve both his intellect and his piety. Willard's *Brief Directions* begins by urging the candidate to reflect that "every good Gift, and every perfect Gift is from above, and cometh down from the Father of Light." A man must recognize his dependence on God, says Willard; he must "put off high Opinions of himself."[28] The first three chapters of Mather's *Manuductio ad Ministerum* have to do with Christian piety. Mather tells the candidate: "*My Son,* I advise you to consider yourself as a *Dying Person.*" In order to be a "true liver," Mather says, you must seek a higher end than carnal satisfaction. A young man should abase himself in order to behold the true glory of Christ. If God is with him in this, he will have the "principle of piety" in himself.[29]

Both books contain a number of suggestions for a proper course of studies. Willard recommends that the candidate begin with an intensive study of the scriptures; he should arrange them under "practical heads" for the purpose of applying them to particular human circumstances. Then he should study polemical divinity to learn what doctrines are in opposition to the truth and how to oppose them. The underlying assumption of this course of studies is that the candidate will master a fixed body of truth. He is introduced to opposing viewpoints only in order to confute errors. Willard warns that the student should not be exposed to dangerous new ideas until he is well grounded in orthodox truths: "let him read the *most approved Systems* and Common-Places, and get them well digested, for till he is soundly principled in the Fundamentals of Theology, he is readily exposed to be led about by every Wind of Doctrine, and baffled with the cunning Sophisms of Impostors, against which this will be a Defence."[30]

Cotton Mather's *Manuductio ad Ministerum* also encourages the ministerial candidate to be well grounded in the fundamental truths of Christianity. Even though he devotes several chapters to secular books, he continually directs the student to religious lessons. The chapter on "sciences," for example, is devoted mainly to rhetoric, logic, and ethics, each of which, according to Mather, has a religious dimension.

It is apparent from these formal treatises on ministerial preparation and from candidates' diaries that there was a wide variety of books that students could study in preparing for the ministry, but it is equally apparent that the basic reading course consisted of books that would be most likely to educate the candidate in doctrinal orthodoxy and religious piety. Undoubtedly, John Barnard described the intellectual progress of the typical candidate when he noted that his studies led him "insensibly into what is called the Calvinistical Scheme."[31]

The study of theology was followed (or sometimes accompanied) by a period of practical apprenticeship in the work of the ministry. Although a young man could not administer baptism or communion until he had been ordained, he could preach sermons, offer public prayers, and make pastoral visits.

Many opportunities existed for the ministerial candidate to develop as a preacher. Often a man began by "commonplacing," speaking on a religious topic, at Harvard or Yale, or by preaching at a private religious gathering.[32] John Barnard preached his first sermon "to a society of young men meeting on Lord's day evening for the exercises of religion."[33] John Burt preached to a similar society within a year of his graduation from Harvard.[34] A candidate often used as much care in composing these informal sermons as he would later expend on important discourses for large congregations.

As a young man became more proficient in preaching, occasions would arise for him to deliver sermons to settled congregations on a regular basis. A candidate might be called upon to occupy a pulpit in the minister's absence, or to preach temporarily to a congregation that had not yet settled a regular pastor. Since the pay for this sort of work was often irregular, a candidate sometimes supported himself with other jobs. John Burt, for example, divided his time between preaching and surveying. In one two-week period he preached four sermons and at the same time "went out to survey and lodged in the woods," and "ran Dr. Toppan's line for him."[35]

Before his ordination a young man could also gain practice in other aspects of the minister's work. One of the most important duties of the minister was to give counsel to the members of his parish when they experienced spiritual problems. Many candidates performed this function informally, even as undergraduates in college. Joseph Sewall, for example, ministered to the problems of several of his classmates at Harvard. He persuaded one friend, who was full of "doubts," not to refuse to take communion. He helped another to confront his sense of sin.[36] Other opportunities existed to give religious counsel to those whom one met while preparing for the ministry.

Some young men actually acquired formal ministerial positions before being ordained. Often chaplains on military expeditions or at forts were ministerial candidates. (Castle William, in Boston Harbor, was a favorite post for young chaplains because of its proximity to Boston and Cambridge.) One of the most famous of New England's eighteenth-century clergymen, Thomas Prince, began his ministry by serving as a chaplain on board a 450-ton merchant vessel, the *Thomas and Elizabeth*. In his journal he reports that "we lived very merrily," but even while he was enjoying the excitement of his first long sea voyage, Prince offered religious and moral guidance to the ship's crew. He preached, conducted religious services, and on the Captain's orders he drew up "some laws for the good government of our ship." On the voyage Prince gained experience both in conducting religious services and in setting forth standards of behavior. These same duties were to occupy much of his ministerial life.[37]

During the course of an apprenticeship, a young man had the opportunity to decide from experience whether he definitely wanted to commit himself to the ministry. A youth could be eminently well qualified to become a clergyman, but still decide he preferred some other calling. Most men who studied theology for their A.M.s and became ministerial candidates did eventually become pastors, but a significant number of men set out on the path to the ministry and then chose other occupations instead. For example, John Denison, of the Harvard class of 1710, preached for a time, but turned to public life and became sheriff of Essex County and a deputy in the Massachusetts legislature. Adino Bulfinch, of the class of 1718, attempted to become a minister, but then opened an apothecary shop in Boston instead. Usually it is difficult to know why a particular person decided not to become a minister. But there are some explanations on record. It was said of Joseph Baxter that he intended to become a pastor, but "the organs of speech in him proving weak, and his voice low" he turned to medicine.[38] In the early eighteenth century, several other men abandoned the ministry for this same reason; perhaps this was a convenient way for a poor preacher to excuse himself.

In theory, a candidate determined that he had a call from God to enter the ministry before seeking ordination. Rev. John Hancock made this process seem simple. "The choice left to us as to our callings," he said, "is no other than a conscionable enquiry which way God calleth us, and a conscionable care to take that way."[39] But God's call was not always clear, pressing, or easy to discern, and it was not unusual for ministerial candidates to have to overcome doubts about their suitability as pastors. Nicholas Gilman, in a time of uncertainty about his own vocation, was encouraged by reading in John 1:31, "men called of God to the work of the ministry, must not stand back because of the conscience [sic] of much inability."[40] Ministers were not expected to be perfect. It was enough if a young man could be reasonably certain that he was qualified to be a clergyman. Samuel Dexter of Dedham expressed the modest hopes about his vocation that most candidates hoped to achieve. Before settling as a minister he examined himself on the character of his calling. As to the principle he acted upon, he said: "I hope it is of faith—I am concerned that it should be so for whatsoever is not of faith is sin."[41]

It is probable that leaving college heightened the religious feelings of many students. The graduate who was interested in the ministry was nearing the time when he would have to assume the actual responsibilities of a pastoral career. This must have caused many to wonder whether they were worthy of becoming ministers and must have encouraged a mature consideration of religion. Joseph Green reports that in college he "roistered" until he had received his first degree. But then, he said: "When the Commencement was past I began to be in some want and especially I wanted a settled employ [sic]: And this put me upon some serious thought of my fitness to doe God service, and did somewhat restrain me and make me a little studious and diligent; and I think made me to live constantly in the practice of secret prayer." Green said that it was at this time that "God began to work saveingly upon my heart."[42] Jonathan Pierpont wrote in his diary that while he was teaching in Dorchester, "It pleased God to awaken me by the word preached."[43] John Barnard noted that after his graduation in 1700 he humbled himself "before God with fasting and prayer, imploring the pardon of all my sins, through the mediation of Christ." He sought God's help in becoming a suitable minister, "begging the divine Spirit to sanctify me throughout, in spirit, soul and body, and fit me for, and use me in the service of the sanctuary, and direct and bless my studies to that end."[44]

Comments like these by ministers who grew up in the late seventeenth and early eighteenth centuries indicate that their conversion experiences were gradual and subtle rather than sudden, overwhelming psychological changes. A typical instance is John Hancock's description of his religious life. He wrote: "Though I cannot tell the exact time when, or the manner how, or the means and instruments by which the work of grace was wrought in me, yet I think I may draw the conclusion, that the Lord has made me his, I hope I am not deceived in this important matter. . . . I have felt and experienced many of the blessed influences of the spirit from my youth to this day."[45]

In general, men who became clergymen in this period did not enter the ministry as the result of dramatic conversion experiences. Men like Samuel Dexter were undoubtedly sincere in their commitment to their vocation, but their sense of calling came only in part from an emotional yearning to serve the Lord. Their decisions were generally made after a long process of reasoning over alternatives and confronting serious doubts. The candidates were not, like Paul on the road to Damascus, overwhelmed by the voice of the Lord, pressing them into his service. But proper ministerial training was usually considered a sufficient guarantee of a candidate's worthiness to become a minister. A young man displayed at least a formal commitment to religion by embarking upon a course of theological studies. These studies did equip him with a wealth of valuable theological knowledge. In addition, his clerical apprenticeship developed his competence to deal with the practical aspects of a minister's work. It was generally assumed that young men who had prepared themselves through these endeavors were now fully qualified to become Congregational ministers.

The formative experience, then, that distinguished men as ministers consisted of education and clerical apprenticeship. During the process ministers frequently experienced religious feelings, but social background, a better than average intellect, a proper education, and clerical apprenticeship were the primary qualifications for the ministry.

CONGREGATIONAL ELECTION. By the time a ministerial candidate was ready to become an ordained clergyman, his training had set him apart from ordinary New Englanders whose formal education was in most cases limited to a few years of rudimentary schooling. Nonetheless, at this time ordinary men, and sometimes women, exercised considerable influence over the candidate's career. Except under rare circumstances, a minister could not be ordained before having been chosen by a congregation to be its pastor. And although ministers tried to control the process of election, the actual choice of a pastor remained under popular control throughout the eighteenth century.

However, the ministers often played an initial role in the process of settling candidates simply because they were most familiar with the young men who were available. In part, this was a result of the difficulties of communication in early New England. In order to secure a candidate, remote towns often had to send messengers to Boston to obtain recommendations. For example, in 1692 the town of Springfield, on the Connecticut River, needed a minister and sent three representatives to the provincial capital to ask the President of Harvard and the Boston pastors for suggestions. On the ministers' advice the messengers issued an invitation to Daniel Brewer, who returned to Springfield, was ordained in 1694, and remained the town's minister for almost forty years.[46]

Individual clergymen often had some influence on the choice of ministers in nearby towns. Daniel Perkins of Bridgewater, for example, believed that he could help settle a candidate he favored. Isaiah Dunster, a young Harvard graduate, noted in his diary that Perkins "invites me to come and keep Sabbath with him and encourages that he will help me to one of the vacancies which are near him."[47] In Boston, where the ministers were in constant contact with one another, clergymen frequently influenced the choice of local pastors. So, when Cotton Mather concluded that Boston's first church was declining because of the youth and inexperience of its sole pastor, Benjamin Wadsworth, he persuaded Samuel Sewall and others to call Thomas Bridge from New Jersey to be the young minister's colleague. At first Wadsworth objected, but eventually Bridge was installed as his colleague pastor. But despite such examples of clerical influence, the ministers' advice was frequently ignored, and in most cases laymen plainly controlled the process of settling candidates. A young man's invitation to a particular ministerial office was issued by the people of the congregation. Before a town called a pastor it usually listened to him preach for several months on trial. During this time the townspeople had the opportunity to measure the candidate against their own criteria for a good pastor.

The settlement of Thomas Prentice as a colleague pastor with Hull Abbott in 1739 in the town of Charlestown, Massachusetts, exhibits the common pattern in the selection of a new minister. First, on May 21, 1739, the town meeting, the body that was responsible for voting salaries to the town's clergy, approved the idea of settling a new minister. A week later the church met, concurred with the town, and voted "to set apart a day for solemn prayer with fasting," to seek God's help in their choice of a pastor. On June 13, after the fast, the church met again and voted to invite a single candidate, Thomas Prentice, to preach for two Sabbaths. On July 2 the church and town met together and chose Prentice as pastor.[48]

In this case the settlement of the minister had involved close cooperation between a congregation, a town, and a candidate. But frequently candidates were the victims of circumstances that clearly reflected the political nature of their settlement in the ministry. In their election the people were said to be issuing a divine call. "In ordinary cases," one minister argued, "the regular Vote and Desire of a Christian People, is look'd upon as the Voice of God, by which He calls forth to Service those that He hath competently furnish'd for it."[49] But although the call was considered to be the essential act in enabling a man to become a minister, it frequently did not take the form of a unanimous invitation.

One possible source of trouble was the administrative difference between the town and the church. The church consisted only of those who were full communion members. The town included these "saints" and the noncommunicants as well. The latter group, while not entitled to take communion, was required to attend church and to help pay the minister's salary. Hence, everyone in the town took an active interest in who became the minister. Although the town could legally only concur in the church's choice of a pastor, in fact, the town meeting exercised a great deal of control over the choice, since it paid the minister's salary. If the church elected a candidate whom the town did not like, the town would simply refuse to vote the man a salary.[50]

Although the church and town could usually concur in the choice of a minister, there were occasions when each put forth its own candidate. In Middleborough, Massachusetts, for example, in 1744 the church nominated a New Light candidate, Sylvanus Conant, and the town chose another man, Thomas Weld. Both groups ordained their man. The town used the old meetinghouse for its services, and the church built a new structure for its own. For three years, from 1745 to 1748, the town sought to tax the Conant church for the support of Weld. The issue was finally resolved by the General Court, which ruled that the Conant group could form their own separate "poll parish."[51]

Sometimes both the town and the church were divided in their choice of a minister. When only a few citizens opposed a candidate's election, he would usually accept, but if the number opposed to him was as large as one-quarter or one-third of the whole, he would have second thoughts. This was particularly true in situations where the minority were obstinate in voicing their opposition. The political nature of the ministerial elections was also apparent in the influence often exercised by powerful coteries or individuals in the church. Although the choice of the minister belonged formally to the whole town and to the whole church, a few important people could often influence the rest. In describing the election of Joshua Gee as pastor of Old North Church, William Waldron, pastor of the New Brick Church in Boston, noted, "tis certain, that the men of post, substance, and influence are for Mr. Gee." Waldron believed that in another town, Portsmouth, New Hampshire, women had great influence. "Tis a pity," he said, "that our pulpit is so much swayed by the petticoat, but some men are born to obey, while women rampant assume to rule and govern."[52]

The political character of clerical election reveals an important feature of ministerial life in New England. Despite their superior social background and education, ministers were dependent upon their people for support in their work. In many cases during the selection negotiations, this dependence was made painfully apparent to candidates and settled pastors, for some towns treated applicants more like prospective servants than potential religious leaders. In a series of letters written in the 1720s, Richard Waldron described several ways in which churches and towns offended clerical pride. Waldron noted disdainfully that Ipswich was "running wild" when the town nominated eight candidates for their pulpit, with the intention that each man would preach to them for a three-month period. Such a competition crudely revealed the dependence of the clergy on the congregation. Waldron was even more critical of the proceedings at Portsmouth, New Hampshire, when the town sought a new minister after Nathaniel Rogers's death in 1723. In a series of letters to his brother he gave advice on how Portsmouth should conduct itself. On October 14, 1723, he urged his brother to see that the town chose a pastor soon because "men's minds will grow wanton and vagrant, which will cause disputings and differences." Two months later, when the town still had not chosen a minister, Waldron concluded that the people thought too highly of themselves and expected to awe their candidates. He wrote his brother that the town failed to attract William Welsteed, one of the better potential candidates, because it had not paid him proper deference and had shown him "a mean contemptible way of treatment." He criticized Portsmouth for putting "such a valuation and estimate upon yourselves as to imagine that the best would jump at a settlement among you" and criticized their "preposterous management" of the affair. Waldron facetiously recommended John Hancock, of the Harvard class of 1719, as a man who would be sufficiently humble for the town. "He could make a very handsome bow," wrote Waldron, "and if the first did not suit, he'd bow lower a second time."[53]

The clergymen believed that the popular choice of pastors frequently meant that churches passed over highly qualified candidates because these men failed to win the support of the multitude. William Waldron claimed that Edward Wigglesworth, whom he greatly admired, was neglected as a ministerial candidate simply because of his "small still voice" and high intellectual attainments. According to Waldron, "the rabble which makes the majority" failed to appreciate his qualities; "They disgust every thing but noise and nonsense and can't be content to sit quiet unless their auditory nerves are drummed upon with a voice like thunder."[54]

Naturally, the tensions in the choice of the ministers and parishes also affected the ministerial candidates themselves. Young men generally tried to avoid parishes that were politically divided, preferring the universal approval of a potential congregation. In 1736 John Hovey rejected a call to Woodstock, Connecticut, because "a minority protested the 'mobbish principles' used to obtain the vote."[55] Jonathan Cushing rejected a call to Haverhill in 1717 because the minority, which had not joined in his call, remained firmly in favor of another candidate.[56] Sometimes a minister accepted a call only on the town's promise to avoid contention. For example, before going to Salem Village, the home of the witchcraft trials, Joseph Green insisted "that they continue in love; and if once they begin to quarrel and contend, I should look upon myself to be free from any obligation to tarry with them."[57]

The negotiations between candidate and town did not end with the minister's acceptance of a suitable post. The town and the pastor had also to discuss the financial terms of the settlement. Sometimes the minister was able to increase his salary over the town's initial offer. But if he seemed to be asking too much, he might lose the support of the town. In his negotiations prior to settling in Longmeadow, Stephen Williams feared that the people had been convinced that he was too worldly because he did not give an immediate answer to the precinct. He admitted, "they think I am desirous of too great things."[58] However, if there was a danger of offending a town by asking too much, there was at the same time the risk that if the minister was not careful about his salary, he might have years of quarreling with the town when he wanted to raise it later. The town's effort to improve its side of the arrangement was also a touchy matter. As the eighteenth century wore on, candidates often had to promise to uphold the Cambridge Platform and, perhaps, to allow ruling elders to be installed. Conservative congregations hoped that such provisions would prevent the ministers from introducing radical innovations into the church.

It is apparent that in many ways the settlement process tended to place candidates and laymen in an adversary relationship. Nonetheless, a great majority of ministers were able to settle in posts that they would hold for the rest of their lives. In the eighteenth century the average minister served his congregation for a term of more than twenty-five years.[59] This indicates that despite the abrasiveness of the settlement process, candidates were generally able to locate themselves in suitable parishes. An important ingredient of this suitability was the tendency of ministers to settle in cultural and geographical regions that suited their background and temperament.

Accordingly, John Callender, a native of Boston, and one of the few Baptist ministers who received a Harvard education, may have declined to settle in Swansea because of the lack of educated company there. In 1731 he settled in the more sophisticated town of Newport, Rhode Island.[60] Boston-born John Barnard admitted that he favored settling in Roxbury in 1711 "because it was within five miles of Boston."[61] On the other hand, a young man who had been raised in a "country town" might feel uncomfortable in a large pulpit. Samuel Dexter of Malden disliked preaching in Charlestown because, he said, "It is exceedingly exercising to me to Appear in such great Congregations. It is contrary to my Disposition. I abundantly rather chuse Retiredness, and if I might be my own Carver, an Assembly in the Country, though it were but small, would abundantly more gratify me."[62]

The candidate frequently became a minister in the area of his upbringing. John Barnard received a call to Yarmouth, but rejected it because his "honored father . . . seemed to be backward in consenting to the motion, partly because of the distance of about 85 miles, and partly . . . [because] it would not be a comfortable settlement to me."[63] Another Boston man, Joshua Gee, declined an invitation to preach in Portsmouth, New Hampshire, in part because "here [in Boston] is his mother who used strong entreaties with him, [and] here lies his estate." Along with other considerations these "fixed" him in Boston.[64] Rowland Cotton chose the more humble of two available parishes because of family ties; "Being willing to live near his parents, who were then at Plymouth, he accepted a call at Sandwich; when, at the same time, he might have been at Dedham; which, upon several accounts, was preferable."[65]

The geographical bias in the ministers' settlements is nowhere more apparent than in the case of the ministers who served in Boston in the years between 1690 and 1740. In all there were twenty-two ministers serving the Congregational churches in Boston during these years. Of these, thirteen were raised in Boston and another four within ten miles of Boston. Two of the remainder were from England. Thus, of the twenty-two Boston ministers in this period, only three were from remote New England towns.

We can only conjecture as to the probable effects of ministers settling in their native regions. But one important conclusion does suggest itself. As we shall see in later chapters, the clergy sometimes tended to regard their profession as a separate community and even to believe that the ministerial profession was more important than the secular communities in which they worked. This tendency must have been muted by the attachment of many ministers to their local regions. If a man settled in the area of his upbringing, he would be bound to his community by many shared experiences and by the ties of kinship and affection.

All in all the process that left the selection of ministers under the control of local congregations emphasized the dependence of the pastor on his people. Neither social background, nor intellect, nor superior training enabled the candidate to overwhelm his prospective communicants. At its worst, the selection process resulted in towns seeking to overawe young candidates. At its best, where there was a natural affinity between the minister and the people, it produced a sense of mutual respect on the part of candidate and parish.

ORDINATION. In the eighteenth century ministers appear to have been more sensitive to the difficulties than to the benefits of popular election. They became increasingly dissatisfied with a system that appeared to establish clerical legitimacy in election rather than in the judgment of the established clergy. Incidents such as those described by William Waldron offended clerical dignity. Although the ministers did not deny the people's right to elect their ministers, they did develop a rigorous system of clerical licensing,[66] and they continued a process, already begun in the seventeenth century, of modifying the ordination service to stress the candidate's relationship to a professional ministerial community. Ironically, within less than a century of the Puritan flight from Anglican persecution, the New England clergymen were increasingly attracted to an Anglican conception of clerical legitmacy. This development is most apparent in the evolution of the ordination ceremony.

Ordination in the early seventeenth century was a simple service in which a congregation formalized its appointment of a minister. It emphasized the minister's close attachment to his congregation rather than his special role as a clergyman. The best surviving account of an ordination ceremony in early New England is found in the records of the First Church in Dedham. The members of the church, including the future minister, John Allin, considered the creation of their congregation far more important than the installation of its pastor. The church was formed on November 8, 1638, after nearly a year of preparation. On this day eight men in Dedham made a public profession of their faith and entered into "sollemne covenant with the lord and one another."[67] The following day John Allin, one of the members of the new church, "was deputed by the church to exercise his gifts received ev'ry Lord's day to the edification of the Church till officers might be chosen to teach by office."[68] By this simple act the church appointed Allin to preach. Although no officers of the church had been formally ordained, the church met during the following winter, admitted new members, and listened to Allin's preaching. Only after the winter was over did the church set about choosing and ordaining a minister. The formation of the religious community was of primary importance; the formal installation of its pastor, although desirable, was less consequential.

In 1639 the church elected Allin as its minister and, after careful deliberation, decided that since the members had the power to choose their minister, they also had the authority to ordain him, "ordination being but a declaration of the same and installing into that office."[69] Upon reaching this conclusion they asked the advice of the elders of the church in Roxbury, who "confirmed our judgment in that point that the power of the whole worke did belong to us alone under Christ."[70] On April 24, 1639, the ordination ceremony was carried out. Members and ministers of other churches were invited to attend, but they had little to do in the proceedings. The essential steps were taken by members of the Dedham Church. Allin preached the sermon; he and two laymen ordained John Hunting as ruling elder; finally, Hunting and two other church members ordained Allin as pastor. The visiting clergymen played no part in the laying on of hands, whereby Allin was made minister of the church. Their participation was limited to a favorable testimony made by their representative, Samuel Whiting of Lynn, of "their love and approbation of the proceedings of the church by giving to the officers chosen the right hand of fellowship."[71]

This service was typical of early New England ordination ceremonies. The presence of representatives from other churches indicates that they approved of Dedham's practices. In 1648, moreover, the procedure was endorsed by the Cambridge Platform of Church Discipline. The ninth chapter of the Platform, entitled "Of Ordination and Imposition of Hands," declared that the power of choosing church officers belonged to the particular congregations and recommended that ordinations be performed locally:

In such Churches where there are Elders, *Imposition* of hands is to be performed by those Elders.

In such churches where there are no Elders, *Imposition* of hands, may be performed by some of the Brethren orderly chosen by the church thereunto. For if the people may elect officers which is the greater, and wherein the substance of the office consists, they may much more (occasion and need so requiring) impose hands in ordination, which is the less, and but the accomplishment of the other.[72]

The records of the Dedham Church and the pronouncements of the Cambridge Platform indicate that in the early years of the settlement the minister's official standing was entirely dependent upon his relation to an assembly of covenanted Christians. A church could be formed before its minister was chosen; the minister was selected by the congregation; he was given the official character of a clergyman in a ceremony performed by members of his own congregation; and the ordination sermon was delivered by the new pastor himself. These procedures emphasized the minister's place within a brotherhood of Christian believers, rather than his membership in a sacred priesthood of religious leaders.

Within a few years after the drafting of the Cambridge Platform this emphasis would change. By mid-century in most churches the ceremony of ordaining the new minister came to be performed by other ministers rather than by laymen in the congregation. As late as 1696 the practice of involving laymen in the ordination ceremony had not been entirely abandoned in New England. Samuel Sewall reports that when William Brattle was ordained in Cambridge on November 25, 1696, he had to persuade "the Church to order that Elder Clark should not lay his hand on his head when he was ordain'd." Deacon Gill, who accompanied Sewall on his return home, "said he liked all very well except the Bill of Exclusion."[73] But by now such "exclusions" were common practice.

This development radically altered the character of the ceremony. By placing their hands on the minister's head the representatives of the people had symbolized the congregation's choice of one of its members to guide their religious lives. Ordination by other ministers, however, emphasized the young man's initiation into a clerical order. The fact that by the late seventeenth century laymen were generally excluded from the ordination service suggests that the ministers were no longer willing to base their legitimacy so exclusively on their relationship to the congregations they served.

Although the ministers now played a more active role in the creation of new ministers, this modification of earlier practice did not immediately set them apart as a formal professional class. Ministers were still chosen by the congregation, and the ordination ceremony itself was often treated as a time for merriment rather than as a sober occasion when old ministers created new members of their order. Although there are few records of the ordinations of the late 1600s to give us a complete picture of the ceremony, the surviving entertainment bills for the ordination day balls suggest that the occasion was not particularly solemn. For example, the provisions for Timothy Edwards's ordination in 1698 included fourteen pounds of mutton, eighty-eight pounds if beef, four quarts of rum, and eight quarts of wine.[74] This suggests that New Englanders still believed that it is the people's election of a minister "wherein the substance of the office consists." Since the creation of a minister consisted in the church's election of a candidate, the less important act of ordaining him could be an occasion for levity and recreation.

In the early eighteenth century, however, the ministers began to claim that clerical status was bestowed by the ordination ceremony, rather than by the people's election. In 1718 Thomas Prince, preaching his ordination sermon, declared that when ministers are ordained, "The Power of taking Care of Your Souls is actually committed to Them: and They do actually receive it, and lay Themselves under the most Solemn Vows and Obligations to take Care of Them."[75] In 1729 William Williams, preaching at the ordination of David Hall, declared: "The Election of the Church or People does not Constitute them in their Office or Authorize them to act in it."[76] The people's role in choosing the minister came to be so little respected that in 1738 Nathaniel Appleton could warn that "this Privilege or Liberty of electing their own Pastors, has, on occasion of the Abuse of it by the Churches themselves . . . been taken away from many of the Churches of our Lord Jesus Christ."[77] Such statements tend to suggest that the ministers believed they should have primary authority in determining who would be admitted to their number.

In most cases the people continued to choose their own ministers, but under exceptional circumstances the clergy began to ordain ministers "at large," men who were deemed worthy to preach, baptize, and offer communion, but were attached to no particular congregation. In 1698 Nathaniel Clap was ordained by ministers in Boston to carry on "the work of the Gospel" throughout Rhode Island, which had only one Congregational church at that time. In the early eighteenth century, several other men were ordained ministers at large before setting out as preachers to Indians or to backcountry settlements. Although ordinations of this sort were unusual, the introduction of the practice gives further evidence of the shift in clerical consciousness. A man could now become a minister without having been so designated by any group of laymen.

The new importance of the ordination is reflected in the candidates' preparation for the event. Ebenezer Parkman's description of the days before his ordination is probably typical. A graduate of Harvard in the class of 1721, Parkman received a call to the ministry in Westborough in February 1724. In June he accepted the invitation. In the next few months he received his Harvard A.M. and married Mary Champney of Cambridge. He settled in Westborough and began preaching. As the day of his ordination drew near he devoted much of his time to reading books on the ministry. In October he records: "My Business about this time was reading Ordination Sermons and wherever the Minister's Duty was explained, Especially Van Mastricht, *De Ministaris Ecclesiastico*."[78] Two weeks before the ordination he dedicated a day "to humiliation and prayer to prepare myself (by the grace of God) for the awful time approaching." Finally, on October 28 he was ordained. In his diary Parkman called the occasion "the Greatest Day I ever Yet Saw—The Day of my Solemn Separation to the Work of the Gospel Ministry and my Ordination to the Pastorate in Westborough."[79]

As the ceremony of consecration by the ministers came increasingly to be regarded as the most significant step in the creation of a clergyman, the ministers attempted to make the occasion more formal and sought to end the festivities that the service had sometimes occasioned. In his ordination sermon for William Gager in 1725 Eliphalet Adams noted: "I have often seen offensive disorders upon such occasions as these, People seeming to Imagine that it was a Time when they might allow themselves more Liberty." He urged that there "be no rude, Light or Unseemly Behaviour in this Assembly this Day." Of the ordination ceremony itself, he said: "The Solemn Separation of any Person to the work of the Sacred

Ministry . . . is a thing so weighty, that Every one who are present as witnesses at such a Solemnity, should come Prepared with the spirit of Piety."[80] At another ordination service in the same year John Graham scolded those who might have come to the service "out of a vain Curiosity, or to get an Opportunity of a Frolic." He lamented that this is "too too Common with Young Persons on such Occasions."[81] There was a celebration after Stephen Williams's ordination in Longmeadow, Massachusetts, in 1716, but Williams later regretted his behavior, noting: "I fear we were too merry together."[82] Although large banquets accompanied many ordinations throughout the eighteenth century, objections against frivolity were a natural concomitant of the desire to heighten the dignity of the service.

As ordination came to symbolize the solemn initiation of a novice into a formal profession, the practice of preaching one's own ordination sermon fell into disuse. When clerical power had been thought to flow from the congregation, it had been natural for the new pastor to address his people in his moment of consecration. Thus Allin and other ministers of his time had preached their own sermons. But in the early eighteenth century, in accordance with the idea that authority passed from minister to minister, this practice became exceptional. Of the first twenty-five sermons that were published after 1716, only five were preached by the new minister himself. In his ordination sermon for John Lowell in Newbury in 1726, Thomas Foxcroft declared that he preferred the old practice. "Truly glad shou'd I have been," he said, "if (pursuant to the Custom, which hath so long obtain'd among us) he cou'd have been prevail'd on to take up the Book at this time, and preach to us his own devout Thoughts and Purposes." But Foxcroft had to admit that the former practice had fallen into disuse; he referred to the "plea's usually advanc'd in this case, against the common Custom."[83] The "common Custom" was, in fact, no longer common. In 1728 John Adams preached his own ordination sermon in Newport, Rhode Island, but between 1728 and 1740 all the published ordination sermons were preached by someone other than the new minister himself. In 1729 William Williams said: "The Objections against the *Person* to be Ordained his Preaching his *own Ordination Sermon,* have prevail'd very much against the *late Custom.*"[84]

With the growing emphasis on the professional significance of ordination and with the spread of the custom of having experienced ministers do the preaching ordination sermons acquired new importance. In 1709, for the first time, a New England ordination sermon was published, to be followed by another in 1716, still another in 1717, and seven more the ensuing year. In the quarter century from 1716 through 1740, seventy-eight ordination sermons were published.[85] Characteristically these sermons were discourses on the ministry—its necessity, authority, and responsibility—and the tenor of the sermons was strongly sacerdotal, quite in contrast to the pastoral emphasis of Allin's ordination text of 1639 (I Corinthians 3:9): "For we are laborers together with God: ye are God's husbandry, ye are God's building." The actual sermon does not survive, but we may reasonably suppose that Allin dwelt on the community of the faithful, himself included as co-laborer with his fellow saints, rather than on the sacred "separation" of the ministerial office.[86] Although it is impossible to date the change precisely, most of the ordination sermons published before 1740 not only dealt primarily with the ministry, but stressed the peculiar importance of ministers. Benjamin Colman argued that the "minister's office distinguishes him from other men," and as "it is the chief End of a *Christian* to glorify God, so it is of a Minister to magnify his Office."[87] Many other preachers echoed these sentiments.[88]

In keeping with the new sense of the centrality of the ordination of the minister to the life of the church, it became customary not to form a new congregation until a candidate could be ordained pastor at the same time. In the seventeenth century many churches had been formed and held services for months or even years before a minister was ordained to serve them. But in the eighteenth century the formation of a new parish and the ordination of its pastor usually occurred on the same day, suggesting that without a minister there could be no church.[89]

Within a century of the settlement of New England the ordination service thus underwent a series of gradual but significant changes. Congregations were not formed before their minister was installed; ordination came to be performed by ministers rather than by laymen; ministers were occasionally ordained without having been chosen by the people of any particular congregation as their pastor; the ordination sermon was preached by older ministers rather than by the man being installed; the ordination ceremony rather than election by the people began to be regarded as "conveying" the ministerial office; the sermons came to focus on the ministry rather than on the Christian community and were often published, calling attention to their significance; and, finally, in keeping with these other changes, the ministers began to insist that the ordination day should be regarded as a solemn occasion. All of these innovations emphasized the importance of the ordination ceremony.

These remarkable changes in the minister's role in creating new pastors reflect a movement toward a sacerdotal conception of the clergy. In *Faithful Shepards,* David Hall has argued that the early Puritan ministers began to abandon customs that established clerical legitimacy in congregational ordination when the Antinomian crisis revealed that popular religious judgments could not be relied upon to provide stability. As we have seen, the movement toward a redefinition of clerical legitimacy was continued into the eighteenth century. Proud of their rigorous training, uneasy about the popular basis of their authority, they were attracted to a view of clerical legitimacy that stressed the independent objective character of the clergy.

The desire for a stable basis of leadership was so intense that it actually drove a number of Congregationalists into the arms of the Anglican church. The most notable conversion to Anglicanism occurred in 1723 when the president of Yale, Samuel Johnson, and six tutors and ministers announced that they doubted the legitimacy of their Congregational ordinations and indicated that they would seek ordination in England by Anglican bishops.

Congregational New Englanders were shocked and frightened by this event, which they labeled the "Great Apostasy." The episode was especially disquieting because the converts had acted from a premise which most Congregational ministers shared, that ministerial validity was derived from other ministers rather than a congregational election. Ironically, the Puritan reaction to the Apostasy tended to stress the similarity of Anglican and Congregationalist ordinations rather than the unique qualities of the New England Way. Upon returning to Boston after being ordained in England, Timothy Cutler preached a sermon that William Waldron described as "full of raillery and bitter invectives." Waldron reported that Cutler "insists, it seems, upon the invalidity of our ordinations." The Congregationalists had a chance to respond five months later in the course of the ordination of Joshua Gee in Boston's Second Church. William Waldron's description of this ceremony suggests that the Congregationalists wanted their ordinations to be as impressive as those of the Anglicans.

On Wednesday last the ordination of Mr. Gee was proceeded in. The affair was carried on with so much seriousness and awful reverence that if I had been wavering about the validity of our ordinations before I should have been then fixed and established by the solemnity and religious devotion visible in all parties at the sacred action. Every man's soul seems to be in it.[90]

That Congregationalist ordinations were becoming increasingly similar to Anglican services is apparent in a letter White Kennett, bishop of Peterborough, wrote Benjamin Colman after he received a copy of Colman's sermon delivered at William Cooper's ordination. "By your ordination sermon," he said, "I perceive you have changed an irregular custom into much more decency and order, by not suffering the young candidate to make then his probation sermon, but to have the preparatory discourse made by a senior more apt and able to teach."[91] It is doubtful that Colman was disturbed that a Congregational innovation should be complimented for moving toward an Anglican ideal. He probably agreed with Kennett that the new practice had more "decency" and "order."

It is ironic, but not surprising that the Congregational ministers had adopted a notion of clerical legitimacy that reflected Anglican ideas about church government. As we have already noted, there was an important element in New England that regarded the English aristocracy as the proper model for social grace and stability. By intellectual training and frequently by social background, the ministers did belong to a colonial elite. The courtly view of their profession reflected in the ordination ceremonies was consistent with their view of their proper status in provincial society.

Their concept of themselves conflicted, however, with the nature of their elections and their day-to-day relations with their people. This conflict is the subject of later chapters. For the moment it is important to note the humane, indeed secular, character of the process by which a man became a minister in the eighteenth century. In the exhilaration of this moment, when a large crowd of ministers and laymen had gathered to observe and participate in his ordination, the new clergyman may have often concluded that the Lord, himself, had chosen him as one of his ministers. For example, on the day of his ordination, Thomas Prince traced the hand of the Lord through all the stages of his calling to the ministry. Christ, he said, "rules on Earth by His Omnipresent, Alwise, and Almighty Spirit. By This He inclines and qualifies particular Persons for Divine Imployments, and gives Them Opportunities of Laboring in them. By This He makes Them successful, approved, esteemed, and disposes the Hearts of His People to Them. By This He influences and directs Their Choice and Acceptance and Solemn Consecration to Their Sacred Office."[92] Other clergymen would agree with Prince that the ministers received, in effect, a call from God. But in contrast to the "illiterate usurpers" who sometimes appeared in early New England and claimed that the call of God was the only preparation they needed to preach, the established clergy of New England believed that God's call was always accompanied by years of formal training, a regular election, and an ordination carried out with "decency and order."

Religion did play an important role in all of these processes. The candidate learned religious doctrines in grammar school, college, and particularly in graduate training. He became acquainted with the techniques of pastoral leadership through ministerial apprenticeship, and (it was hoped) he grew in piety as he matured. Each of these experiences reminded him of the divine being who ruled the world, but it is apparent that other factors were involved in the creation of ministers. The candidate's social background and intellectual ability, the relationship between men within the towns, and the professional aspirations of the settled ministers all played important parts in the ministers' calling.

In theory the ministers stood apart from their times and reminded men who were caught up in temporal concerns that the real purpose of life lay beyond the world, and in many ways their training did direct them to this divine mission. But at the same time, it is evident that the process by which men became clergymen in colonial New England was intimately related to the worldly society in which they lived.

CHAPTER III

THE MINISTER'S WORK

A pastor's education and ordination tended to set him apart from the average man. His ministry, on the other hand, forced him into close association with the people of New England. Most ministers lived in small towns, where their domestic life and pastoral labors brought them into daily contact with their parishioners. Like other men the clergyman took a wife, raised a family, and ran a farm. The minister's pastoral duties required him to associate closely with his people and attend to their individual religious needs. His sermons were conditioned by the particular requirements of his audience. The ministers' work exhibits a fundamental, but frequently neglected, characteristic of Puritanism. We often tend to regard religious history primarily as a series of doctrinal and ecclesiastical developments. Certainly these formal aspects of religion are important, but Puritanism was a way of life as well as a system of thought. It was a set of attitudes that was interwoven into all aspects of life. In the ministers' careers we can observe the multiple interrelationships between doctrine and life.

DOMESTIC LIFE. The minister's formal education had equipped him with a knowledge of theology; his secular life was an education in its practical applications. The clergyman's religious ideas gave meaning to his domestic responsibilities. They, in turn, contributed to his spiritual growth and further qualified him to minister to other Christians.

Once he settled in a parish, a clergyman was immediately involved in a series of secular relationships that contributed to the course of his ministry. Ministers usually married soon after they were ordained. A few married before their ordinations, and some waited until long afterwards, but few remained single. As a rule, a clergyman felt that with his ordination and the beginning of his work in the ministry he was ready to assume the responsibilities of marrying and raising a family.

40

In itself, the fact that Puritan clergymen took wives tells us a great deal about their conception of the ministry. Early Protestant reformers had rejected the Catholic idea that the priest was "married" to God alone. This attitude seemed to the reformers to suggest that the minister was more holy than his fellow Christians, a position the Reformers rejected. The Congregationalists of the early eighteenth century took it for granted that pastors would take wives and experience with other men the joys and trials of domestic life.

The ministers regarded marriage as both a sacred and a secular relationship. Frequently, they justified their marriages in terms of the religious advantages to be gained from wedlock. John Cleaveland, for example, used religious ideas in persuading Mary Dodge to marry him. He believed that he and Mary were well suited to one another because they were "heartily agreed in the great things of religion." Reflecting on the purpose of marriage, he said, "the chief and main thing of all is to be helps to one another in our progress heavenward."[1] Widows who had been married to ministers seem almost to have been sanctified as clerical spouses. In almost every case where a minister died leaving a young widow, she married her husband's successor.[2]

The proper Puritan marriage, however, was not simply a religious alliance. John Hancock expressed a common idea when he argued that ardent love for one's spouse was an essential ingredient of marriage. "To love even with some passionateness the person you would marry," he said, "is not only allowable but expedient. Love seldom suffers itself to be confined by other matches than those of its own making."[3] Even after many years of marriage another minister, David Hall, could lament that he had become "idolatrous" in his "carriage" toward his wife.[4]

Just as religious ideas were important ingredients in familial relationships, religion also played a part in the minister's dealings with his servants. Slaves as well as indentured servants were catechized along with the minister's children. Benjamin Colman, for example, spent long hours giving instruction to his slaves. A New Englander generaly believed that a man should exhibit a Christian spirit in his dealings with all the members of his household. "Be sure," said Cotton Mather, "*if a* person *seem to be Religious,* but is not by *Religion* made a *Better* Husband or Wife, a *Better* Parent or Child, a *Better* Master or Servant, that persons Religion is vain."[5]

With marriage and parenthood the minister became vulnerable to an experience that tested the faith of many Puritans—the death of a loved one. Although the life expectancy of men in colonial New

England who reached maturity was comparable to the life expectancy of twentieth-century males, death in childhood or childbirth bereaved many New England families. So many wives died in childbirth that William Waldron believed the perils of giving birth should "sanctify the soul of any woman that had been once carried through them if rightly remembered and improved."[6]

Like his wife, the minister's children were susceptible to sickness and death. Marston Cabot, the minister of Thompson, Connecticut, lost four children in rapid succession and in the process exhibited the proper Puritan attitude toward death. Cabot's sense of despair is apparent in his diary. On November 30, "a raw cloudy day," he went about his work "full of grief." Two weeks later he admitted: "I am sometimes tempted to infidelity; question God's power and goodness; doubt whether I shall hold out or no." But, being a good Puritan, Cabot was able to see the vastness of God's majesty in the depth of his own loss. He concluded, "God is able to do for us exceeding abundantly above all that we can ask or even think."[7]

The doctrine that prepared men for tragedies such as the loss of wife or child was the Calvinistic belief that man should love God more than any creature on earth. The ministers had learned this doctrine in their childhood from their parents and at catechism. Later it was reinforced by their theological training. But until this idea was tested by real human suffering, it is doubtful that it had a deep impact on any clergyman's life. Thus, their close ties to wives, who were constantly endangered by childbirth, and to children, who were frequently the victims of disease, tested and strengthened the ministers' faith. Moreover, it was an experience they shared with their parishioners. When they sought to give spiritual comfort to a bereaved parishioner, they were often able to speak from a shared experience of loss.

In addition to running a household, a minister frequently had other worldly tasks to perfrom. Many of the daily events of the minister's lives are aptly summarized by David Hall's statement: "I was some busied in my seculars."[8] The clergyman's secular routine varied considerably from parish to parish, often in relationship to the minister's salary. Those who were well paid could spend a considerable amount of time studying, preparing sermons, and engaging in pastoral labors. Others, less fortunate, spent much of their time in worldly employments. But no matter how well their congregations provided for them, most ministers outside of Boston had to spend part of their time working on their farms.

Pastors were usually provided with land at the time of their settlement. Sometimes the salary ararngements included provisions for the inhabitants of the town to help with farm work, and often the minister had at least one servant, slave, or hired hand to help. But in most cases he still had to spend some of his own time on farm labor. Their diaries contain innumerable references to this work. In the winter of 1750 Ebenezer Bridge was "very much engaged with workmen at my meadow." The following summer he was "exceedingly engaged and fatigued in haying."[9] Even old age did not end the ministers' farm labors. In his seventy-fourth year David Hall spent a full day plowing. When he was sixty-four, Job Cushing of Shrewsbury died in his field while gathering rye.[10]

The minister's farm work was usually an integral part of his daily life. He could not simply turn the work over to a servant if he expected to produce the food that was needed to support his household. Along with tracts on theological and ecclesiastical subjects, which occupied much of his time, he had to read books on agronomy.[11] The clergyman's commonplace books, which were primarily for religious notes, often contain extensive entries on agriculture. In Ezra Carpenter's book, for example, one may read: "Mow grass that is full of polly-pod and brakey-stuff, the second week in July. Cut about this time cattle will eat it best and it will go furthest."[12] Sometimes the minister mingled his pastoral and farm labors. Ebenezer Parkman reports that on one occasion he was raking in his fields when two members of his congregation, Mr. and Mrs. Jonas Brigham, came to report their religious experiences. He first recorded the husband's "relation." Then, he reports: "Mr. Brigham took my Rake whilst I wrote for his wife."[13]

Being both a farmer and a clergyman often complicated a minister's relations with his fellow-men. At harvest time and in other periods of intense farm activity, the minister was dependent upon aid from the men in his congregation. At the end of July 1726, for example, Ebenezer Parkman's grain was lying in the field; a storm was approaching, and he needed help to rescue the crop. One neighbor, a man named Maynard, was at work in his own field with five sons. He refused to help Parkman, saying: "When my Grass and Corn will move into my Barn without hands I'll leave to Help Mr. Parkman—not before." Another neighbor, one Clark, was at work with only one son to help him. He was lame, the son had an injured ankle, and he had some ten loads of hay of his own to gather in. Clark hesitated, and then, Parkman reports: "He answers what shall I do? My own is really Suffering and Everything is backward for want of a Team, for I have none and can get none. But he is Laboring for our Souls and why Shall I refuse?"[14] During another period of need Parkman addressed his whole congregation at the end of a service: "My Help being taken away I must depend upon you to help me." He pointed out that he could not be both a full-time minister and a full-time farmer. "I must depend upon you respecting my Temporals," he said, "if you would have me attend to your Spirituals."[15]

Like his family, the minister's farm played a role in his religious life. When the farm prospered, the minister had occasion to be thankful for God's blessing. Stephen Williams frequently made entries in his diary such as the following: "We are this day killing our hogs—how good is God to us in granting us other animals for our support and comfort."[16] But farms were often sources of trouble. Just as the loss of a child could remind the ministers of the transitoriness of life, so too could some minor farm tragedy. When bears killed several of Stephen Williams's sheep, he wrote: "Thus we are made to see the vanity of our comforts. The Lord grant our affections may be weaned from the world."[17]

Farming was the most time-consuming secular employment of most clergymen, but other types of work as well occupied many of the ministers. Some towns could not afford to hire both a schoolmaster and a minister, and they persuaded their clergymen to take both positions. John James worked at both jobs in Derby, Connecticut, and Richard Jaques probably did the same in Gloucester. Other ministers, such as Ebenezer Parkman and James Bridgham, did not actually teach grammar school, but did give youths the advanced training necessary for college.

Sometimes the ministers performed secular tasks simply because no one else in the area was capable of performing them. The primary example of this type of employment was in medicine. Many ministers throughout the colonial period were physicians of the body as well as of the soul. Some, like James Noyes of Stonington, Connecticut, liked to offer spiritual and medical counseling simultaneously: "He always chose to pray with his patients and had so much the less hope of them when they did not desire it."[18] The grand period of the minister-as-physician was the seventeenth century. By the middle of the eighteenth century most of New England's doctors were learning medicine through a system of apprenticeship, and the age of the "amateur" clergyman-physician was passing. But although it was uncommon for a minister in the eighteenth century to practice as a doctor, most had enough medical knowledge to attend to minor ailments. Their commonplace books contain remedies for such prosaic ailments as worms, burns, the stone, and loss of hair.[19] One book includes a suggestion for inducing vomiting; another has a way to prevent scarring by smallpox.[20] Often remedies required apothecary skills. Ebenezer Carpenter's formula for cough medicine included spermicetti, ground ginger, conserve of roses, sweet oil, and Westia rum and molasses. Nicholas Gilman's salve for a burn consisted of a mixture of horse dung and grease.[21]

One reason that the ministers continued having some influence in medicine was that there were relatively few educated men in early New England. Even after 1700 almost 50 percent of the men with college degrees were ministers. There was certainly no necessary connection between religion and medicine, but in the early eighteenth century, many ministers, being educated, had some medical knowledge. A similar situation existed in the relationship of ministers to civic affairs. Normally, a minister did not fill any public office. But in many towns the ministers were the only men capable of performing certain civil functions, such as drawing up wills and other legal documents. For example, Thomas Hawley, minister of Ridgefield, Connecticut, was a town clerk and "performed all of the town business that required writing." In some cases these legal duties of the ministers actually carried them into public office. Solomon Lombard was a justice of the peace at the same time that he was preaching in Provincetown, Massachusetts. Andrew Gardner, a frontier preacher, was the moderator of several town meetings. And Josiah Cotton was a justice of the peace and an Indian missionary simultaneously.[22]

One can find many other examples of nonreligious activities that engaged individual ministers. John Burt knew how to survey. Jeremiah Condy, a Baptist minister in Boston, was a bookseller. Eleazar Mather of Mansfield ran a saw mill and a cider mill. John Tucke of Gosport was a shopkeeper. And John Avery of Truro was a blacksmith. Many other ministers invested time and capital in such enterprises as iron works and land speculation.[23] In each of these activities the ministers participated in the various kinds of work that engaged laymen.

It is difficult to assess the overall importance of the ministers' secular tasks. The most positive result of their having families and engaging themselves in nonministerial work was that these activities involved the ministers in the day-to-day experiences of their congregations. As such, when they preached about families or worldly activities, they could draw on their own immediate knowledge of these things. Certainly, there were many times when secular diversions were simply a nuisance. David Hall, for example, complained that harvest time was "a dreadful hindrance to me in my work as a minister."[24] And Ebenezer Parkman noted the difficulty of having "the affairs of the ministry and of a farm to manage together."[25]

But if there were some disadvantages in the demands of the world on the minister's time, there were also compensations. In fact, the work of raising a family, supervising a farm, and meeting other worldly responsibilities probably contributed greatly to the strength of the New England clergy. As Ebenezer Gay remarked in a sermon entitled *Ministers are Men of Like Passions with Others,* God's messengers were not angels; they were "frail men" who had to find religious meaning in the midst of a secular world.[26] Men of God they might be, but they participated in the common domestic and worldly concerns of their fellow Christians. In these activities they found practical application for their religious beliefs, and, equally important, they shared common experiences with their fellow Christians. In their pastoral work and in their preaching they frequently used these valuable resources.

PASTORAL LABORS.   Because clergymen have generally been known by their printed sermons, we tend to forget that for every hour that the minister spent in the pulpit, he spent many more hours giving individual religious counsel to the members of his parish. The preacher did not simply pronounce doctrine on the Sabbath and then wait for the people to apply religion to their own lives. Instead he reinforced his sermons with four kinds of pastoral instruction: setting a good example, catchizing, giving counsel, and reprimanding. Each of these was frequently mentioned in discourses on the ministry and was regarded as a formal part of his ministry. The pastor's handling of these duties was often the key to his success or failure as a minister.

The first of these tasks, setting a good example, was the *sine qua non* of the minister's work. If he failed in this and led a degenerate life, then even the best of his sermons would be received as the teaching of a hypocrite. As Solomon Stoddard observed: "Men can hardly be patient to hear a Drunkard speak in commendation of temperance, and a wanton Man enlarge in commendation of chastity."[27] Most New England ministers would have agreed with Joseph Baxter that, "If any were born without original sin it should be the minister."[28] Just as the clergyman could undermine his position by leading an immoral life, he could reinforce his preaching by being a virtuous man. "If they give a good Example," said Solomon Stoddard, "Their words will sink more into the hearts of Men."[29] Thus, the behavior of the minister was actually regarded as a mode of clerical instruction.

Because the minister was deeply involved in the secular life of his community, the necessity of setting a good example sometimes placed him under an unusual strain. As a man who needed to make a living and support a family, he was always tempted to maximize his income. But as a pastor he was expected to be charitable to his neighbors. On one occasion, after an argument with a neighbor about a cow, Ebenezer Parkman complained that people applied stricter standards of ethical behavior to ministers than to themselves and required of a clergyman "a peculiar preciseness and Exactness in making up the minutest part of an account."[30]

In the small towns of colonial New England the clergyman's moral life was a matter of public knowledge. If he were intemperate, committed adultery, or cheated his neighbor, the whole community would be aware of his transgression. Relatively few clergymen were actually involved in moral scandals, but those who were often ruined their ministerial careers. This was especially true of intemperance. In a study of four hundred Congregational ministers who settled in New England between 1680 and 1740, Clifford K. Shipton found that only 3 percent became involved in scandals. But of the six ministers who were charged with drunkenness, all were dismissed. A farmer or blacksmith might drink heavily and still perform his tasks, but a clergyman's private and public life could not be separated. If a man were intemperate, he could not be a minister.[31]

A second and less troublesome form of religious instruction was catechizing. In the mid-seventeenth century the legislatures of Connecticut and Massachusetts had passed laws requiring heads of households to instruct their families in the principles of religion.[32] Although some parents faithfully carried out this obligation, many did not. So by the eighteenth century it was customary for the minister to have to conduct special meetings for the children of the community to teach them religious principles.

Joseph Baxter explained why catechizing was necessary for children. Like their parents the children heard weekly sermons on Christian life and doctrine, but such addresses were usually aimed for above their heads. "When they hear long and continued discourses," said Baxter, the children "soon forget what they hear."

Baxter believed that the young people, as well as their parents, needed religious instruction. Sermons could not fill this need, but "by catechizing," he said, "things may be so beat into them as that they will be likely to stay with them and stick by them." Baxter argued that many people were "grossly ignorant" of Christianity due to the failure of ministers to instruct young people properly.[33]

So in the eighteenth century one of the regular duties of the ministers was to catechize the children in the parish.[34] Often the ministers conducted these meetings in various parts of the town to make it easy for all of the children to attend. The frequency of the meetings varied from parish to parish. Marston Cabot and David Hall catechized as often as twice in a single week, and Jonathan Townsend planned to catechize "once a month, more or less" at six separate locations. But usually the meetings were held only sporadically. They were often announced from the pulpit in the Sunday service a few days before they occurred, which gives the impression that they were called on an ad hoc basis. Before Jonathan Townsend made plans for regular catechizing in 1737, he admitted that the practice had been "discontinued for some time."[35] In Plymouth in the late seventeenth century periods of catechizing by the First Church were interrupted by long intervals of from five to ten years when there were no regular classes.[36]

There were a variety of ways in which these catechizing meetings were actually conducted. The catechism itself was a book that described Christian doctrine through questions and answers. There were many such books in colonial New England, some by local ministers, others imported from England. The pastors usually based their instruction on one of these works. Jonathan Townsend says that in his meetings he began with a short prayer then proceeded to catechize. In presenting questions to the children he must have either used one of the published catechisms or else made up his own set of questions. Townsend then read "part of Mr. Vincent's explanation of the Assembly's Catechism (or some other instructive book)" and then made a "somewhat longer prayer" to conclude.[37]

In addition to holding meetings for children, the ministers sometimes held special catechizing meetings for the older people of their parishes. Frequently these were held a few days before the communion service and the whole church was expected to attend.[38] Sometimes too the ministers catechized individual families. Rev. Israel Loring of Sudbury made a number of suggestions for properly conducting these family meetings. Loring said that the minister should ask his audience questions about faith, repentance, and other points of doctrine. He noted that some men may "have thought in their

minds, which is not ripe for utterance, and through ill education
they won't be able to speak well." The minister should adapt his
instruction to the "capacities" of such men. He should "frame the
answer into the question, and demand this be a yea or nay." He
should not push his audience "too hard."[39]

It is significant that men like Loring sought to adapt their catechizing to the needs of their audiences. In his book *Peaceable
Kingdoms,* Michael Zuckerman argues that the catechism was not
adapted to children's understanding: youngsters "had to tag along,
managing as well as they could." He believes that children were
expected to master a fixed body of religious truth and that the
teacher sought to suppress the corruption that was native to childhood: "Little else was required of a teacher than a strong right
arm."[40] Zuckerman is correct that the basic lessons of the catechism
were unchanging, but he overlooks the fact that ministers varied
their approach to the catechism considerably to meet the needs of
different adults and children. One reason that catechism classes were
held at all was because it was assumed that this method of instruct-
ing children was better adapted to their capacities than sermons,
which they had to attend, but probably could not comprehend. In
their pastoral labors the chief goal of the ministers was to speak to
different kinds of people on their own level. If a minister was as
diligent as Ebenezer Parkman and as sympathetic to his pupils as
Israel Loring, his catechizing could contribute considerably to the
religious instruction of the community.

Sensitivity to the condition of his pupils was an important ingredient in effective catechizing; it was even more essential in a third
area of the pastoral ministry—counseling. By discussing the catechism the minister sought to make the people understand the ab-
stract principles of Christian doctrine. By giving counsel to the
individual members of his parish he helped men and women actually put these doctrines into practice in their daily lives.

If the minister was diligent in making pastoral visits, this could
be one of the most time-consuming parts of his work. Thomas Clap,
who later became president of Yale, kept careful notes on the spiritual condition of each of his seven hundred parishioners while he
was minister of Windham, Connecticut. James Pike, minister of the
scattered frontier parish of Arundel, paid a yearly visit to each of
his people, even though such visits often required him to be absent
from his home for many days at a time.[41] At the height of an early
revival in Windsor, Connecticut, Timothy Edwards counseled as
many as thirty people in a single day.[42]

In pastoral visits the minister's objective was to discuss with his people the condition of their souls. Such conferences acquired a particular urgency if a person was dying. Often the parishioners would send word to the minister when a member of the family was ill. During visits to the sick, ministers came into close contact with the miseries of their people. Ebenezer Parkman referred to such meetings as a time "wherein my Heart has often Trembled within Me." Parkman sometimes took his wife with him on these visits— perhaps to give additional encouragement to the afflicted.[43] Many ministers must have left such visits with the thoughts of Israel Loring after he visited "Old Mr. Nurse grievously afflicted with a terrible cancer." At home he recorded in his diary: "Lord by such sorrowful affecting spectacles, make me more truly thankful for the mercy I enjoy, his case might have been mine."[44]

Undoubtedly, some of the most important pastoral visits that the ministers made were these sojourns with men and women who were facing death. Such people were likely to be particularly concerned about the state of their souls. But pastoral counseling was intended to benefit the living as well as the dying. During these visits the minister could clarify puzzling points of doctrine and help the parishioner know the state of his soul. Although the Congregationalists had no formal practice of confession that would allow the church member to unburden his soul in the presence of a clergyman, the pastoral visit sometimes served a similar purpose.

The nature of these interviews varied greatly from one ministers to another. Some clergymen made direct inquiries about the religious condition of their people; others were probably less formal. Cotton Mather recommended the first approach. In 1723 he published a pamphlet entitled, *A Brief Memorial, of Matters, and Methods for Pastoral Visits,* which contains directions for ministers on how to conduct these visits. The minister should first inquire into the state of a person's soul. He should then counsel him with "Lessons of Piety," which would be applied to the communicant's particular circumstances. Before leaving, the clergyman should counsel all the children and servants, making certain that young people were learning their catechism and counseling the servants to a "Suitable Contentment in their Station." At the end of his visit the minister should leave "Little Books of Piety" for the residents of the house.[45]

During these inquiries into the spiritual condition of his people the minister would encounter men with many types of problems. Sometimes he had to encourage those who were dismayed by personal tragedy, such as the loss of a child.[46] Often the minister tried to help men decide whether or not they had been converted. Since the minister had to fit his counsel to the needs of each individual, the differences between men made these pastoral visits particularly difficult to handle. Some men needed to be encouraged, and others to be chastised. Thomas Clap argued that if in counseling someone a minister "should mistake their State, and misapply Remedies and Directions, it might prove fatal to them." Clap gave two examples of the mistakes a minister could make. First, in dealing with a man who is "under the beginnings of real conviction," the unwary minister might give encouragement too soon, before the man had experienced deep sorrow for his sins. This would set him "upon a false and dangerous peace." The uninformed minister could also err by being too harsh. Clap mentioned the case of the man who is "truly humbled and converted, but under spiritual Darkness." In this case the minister should offer encouragement, for "to set before them the awful Terrors of the Law, may drive them into Despair, and swallow them up with over much Sorrow."[47] Ministers' comments in their diaries about their parishioners often indicate that they were extremely careful in seeking to understand the spiritual problems of each individual.

It is difficult to assess the actual impact of these visits on the lives of the people. Many parishioners encouraged the ministers to visit and appreciated the comfort and assurance they brought to troubled minds. Joseph Baxter said that the ministers' object on such occasions should be "to pour the balm of the gospel into the wounded souls, preach comfortable and encouraging truths to those who are dejected and disconsolate. They are to set broken bones, to heal wounded consciences, and bind up broken hearts."[48]

But although most pastoral visits were appreciated, there was always the danger that the minister's probing into the individual spiritual life of a parishioner would be received as an unwarranted intrusion. Ebenezer Parkman was once rebuffed by a man who believed that Parkman was improperly counseling his sister. Parkman's account of the episode is a good example of the difficulty and subtlety of the art of spiritual counseling.

Parkman reports that one evening Samuel Forbush, a member of the Westborough church, came to the parsonage and asked him to attend his sick wife. Parkman immediately came to Mrs. Forbush's bedside. After she told him that she believed she was dying and "could not but be under fears on So great an Occasion," Parkman proceeded to inquire into the grounds of her fears, telling her "that I should endeavor to remove them." He asked whether she had freely repented all her known sins, whether she found satisfaction and comfort in being a communion member of the church, and whether she loved "the Godly"? Parkman says that he asked all of these questions in front of the small crowd of people gathered in the room because he knew that Mrs. Forbush was a godly woman. If a dying person had private sins to confess, it was Parkman's practice "to desire the Company to withdraw." But he was confident that Mrs. Forbush had nothing to hide. "Here," he says, "I apprehended would be such things spoken as might be very profitable and suitable for all that heard." In fact, the dying woman did give affirmative answers to his questions, and Parkman fully expected the audience to be edified.

But in the middle of his proceedings, the woman's brother-in-law Thomas Forbush, angrily interrupted Parkman. As the minister was asking his sister whether she loved Christ's disciples, Thomas Forbush protested: "Sir, We are grown folks." Parkman reports, "I turned about in great Surprize and calmly looked upon him and then as calmly Speaking asked what he had said. He repeated the same words as before. I asked him what then? (Now rising my Self up in my Chair) why then (says he) we understand these things already, have read in the Bible and Some other Books, and our selves know these things being grown folks and come into years." The others in the room, who were "astonished" at this outburst, sought to quiet Thomas, and the dying Mrs. Forbush protested that Parkman's questioning had been "much to her Comfort and benefit." But the old man was not easily quieted. He felt that Parkman had insulted his sister-in-law by dealing with her as a child and a sinner.

For several minutes Parkman sought to justify his proceedings. "I have been endeavoring," he said, "to assist this person in preparing actually to give up her account to the great Judge, and though she may have view'd it numberless times and we may have review'd and examin'd it together, yet now at the awfull juncture before delivering it into his hands, we act most wisely to look all over as carefully as possible to find out whatever escapes or flaws there might be, Since it can never be done after, throughout Eternity, and Eternity depends upon this account." He assured Thomas that the questions he asked Mrs. Forbush were not a reflection upon her, since they were asked even of "the most advanc'd Christian that is on Earth."

Eventually Forbush asked the minister to forgive his bluntness, saying "that he knew not how soon he should need me on the Same account," but he remained unconvinced that such inquiries were necessary. At this point Parkman returned his attention to Mrs. Forbush, whose death's bed had been the scene of this heated encounter. "We came into So amicable a Composition," says Parkman, "as to go to prayer and we parted Friends." But on returning home, he says, "my Head and heart were full. . . . I went to bed, but could not Sleep for a long time."[49]

This was undoubtedly an unusual episode. Parkman's parishioners were often anxious that he give them spiritual counseling and generally appreciated his efforts.[50] But this encounter was symptomatic of one of the difficulties the ministers faced in their careers. The pastors' ability to give useful counsel to their people depended upon their individual skill in dealing with human beings and upon the people's receptiveness to their inquiries. The ministers' formal status was established in his education and ordination. But his day-to-day effectiveness depended upon his ability to maintain a sympathetic and understanding relationship with his people.

If there were difficulties in properly handling pastoral visits, a fourth aspect of a minister's work was even more troublesome. On certain occasions the minister had to admonish erring members of his church. Stephen Williams recognized the difficulty of such affairs when he wrote: "abundance of discretion and prudence is required of a minister—he having many persons of different persuasions and tempers and dispositions to treat withal."[51]

There were actually several types of disciplinary action available to the minister. If a sin was of a personal nature, such as a man's mistreating his wife, the pastor would first speak to him in private. If necessary he could get two or three members of the church to help him. If the offender did not immediately promise to cease doing wrong, or if his offense was public, he was admonished, and the elders and brethren of the church were informed of the offense. They and the minister could then cut the offender off from church privileges. If he refused to read a confession to the church, the recalcitrant sinner was often barred from communion or from having his children baptised. When the minister and congregation could not agree on a proper course of action, an ecclesiastical council was sometimes called to resolve the difficulty.[52]

One of the most frequent offenses that concerned the ministers was quarreling. Contentions could be particularly difficult to handle because there was always the danger that the minister himself would become embroiled in the argument. In the case of an offense such as drunkenness, the offender was clearly recognized by all. This was not always true during village quarrels. Joseph Baxter pointed to the difficulty of such situations when he said, ministers "have never more need to manage themselves wisely and prudently than when they see strife, and contention is prevailing amongst their people, for when they are in these feuds and contentions, they are besides themselves and if they be not then wisely and prudently managed things will grow worse and worse." Baxter argued that the minister must avoid siding with any party and should preach on the danger of strife.[53]

Often a minister tried to avoid strife by having private conferences with the aggrieved brethren. Ebenezer Bridge, for example, made visits to Jonathan Hildreth and Peter Prockter and advised them "to make up a difference between them, and not go to the law." The minister occasionally intervened to prevent problems within a family, as when Bridge "visited Colonel Stoddard, and discoursed with his mulatto servant, Hagar, who seems to feign herself ill."[54]

There were many difficulties a minister could fall into simply by carrying out church discipline. Sometimes the minister and congregation disagreed about disciplinary policy itself. After John Cotton of Plymouth was dismissed in 1697 in a particularly bitter episode, his son Josiah suggested that his father's being "somewhat hasty and perhaps severe in his censures" may have occasioned "some of the hardships he met with, and the violence of some people against him."[55] In other incidents the congregations actually demanded greater satisfaction from the offender than did the minister.

Just as a minister could offend his people by being too harsh or too lax in administering discipline, he could also encounter difficulties by failing to treat all sinners equally. Often it was tempting to overlook the transgressions of the powerful. Joseph Baxter warned his colleagues at a ministerial meeting against neglecting to to do their duty toward "great ones." They must carry out discipline "without respect to persons, rich or poor, friends or foes."[56] Solomon Stoddard said that there were many occasions when a minister is tempted "thro' a Spirit of Fear to neglect his duty" because he knows that his reproofs "will be taken hardly by some Men, they will stomach it that they are reflected upon."[57]

One final problem that often troubled ministers was the vagueness of the moral law itself. Many offenses were not so clearly recognizable as intemperance or adultery. There was, for example, no clear boundary between lawful entertainment and sinful revelry. Ebenezer Parkman has left a detailed account of his feelings on one such occasion. He had attended a barn raising and a supper that lasted until ten o'clock, which he considered a late hour. Parkman reports: "I manifested so much uneasiness that we were detain'd that I concluded everybody would retire home as Soon as they might." He went home, but then learned that "there were many yet behind and among them Some Heads of Family." So he arose and returned to the company. Having "acquainted" the host "with what Time of Night it was," he interrupted the revelers "and admonish'd them, and sent them home." Parkman reflected: "This Exerting my Authority gave me great uneasiness, but I was resolute to Show Impartiality and not be partaker of other Men's sins, as likewise to discharge my own Duty as Watchman in this Place and as having Care of their Souls."[58]

Being a faithful "watchman" and handling all of his pastoral duties well was probably the most difficult part of a minister's work. It is significant that in each kind of pastoral labor the minister's influence over his congregation was more persuasive than authoritarian. He did not teach men to apply Christian doctrine to their own lives simply by making ex cathedra pronouncements about religion. Instead he sought to show the relevance of Puritan theology by applying it to the day-to-day circumstances of the human beings in his parish. In his secular life he sought to set a good example by conducting his business dealings in a spirit of honesty and charity. In offering instruction in the catechism he attempted to make his message comprehensible by pitching it to the intellectual level of the children (or adults) whom he was teaching. During his pastoral visits he listened to people's religious thoughts and sought to help them confront their individual problems. Finally, in offering admonishments, he frequently acted with reluctance and more in a spirit of humility than of authority.

In each of these areas the clergyman's success depended upon his skill in dealing sensitively with his fellow-men. This awareness of the needs of his people was also an essential ingredient in his sermons.

PREACHING THE GOSPEL. Like the minister's pastoral labors, his preaching was a public performance and was heavily influenced by his relationship with his audience. The good sermon was both a practical discourse and a theological treatise. Its style and content were adjusted to the capacities and interests of the average man, and it was relevant to the day-to-day problems of the parish. In the sermon, above all else the minister sought to make manifest God's presence in the world—in current events, in the passing of the seasons, and in the spiritual history of each man's soul.

To be able to preach, the young minister was expected to have studied hard in preparation for the ministry and was encouraged to continue his studies after he had left college. "Ministers should keep close to their studies," said Increase Mather, "They may not wander from house to house, and then come into the pulpit hand over hand."[59] The method of composing sermons varied from minister to minister, but all started with a Biblical text. Often the ministers knew much of the Bible by heart. For example, John Cotton of Plymouth was said to know the book so well that "if some of the words of almost any place of scripture were named to him, he could tell the chapter and verse—or if the chapter and verse were named, he could tell the words."[60] In preparing their sermons, the ministers usually read the Greek, Latin, or Hebrew version of the Biblical text in order to ascertain fully its meaning.[61] In addition to the Bible, the ministers drew on theological works that they had often summarized in commonplace books for handy reference.

The composition of a sermon was usually a time-consuming task. It was considered unusual that John Adams could write a discourse in seven or eight hours.[62] Since ministers preached two sermons on each sabbath and other discourses on special days of fasting and thanksgiving, a preacher often composed more than a hundred sermons each year. In his lifetime the clergyman might easily preach several thousand sermons.

Theoretically, a minister would have most of his week free to work on his discourses, but in reality there were many diversions that could keep him from his study. The cares of his own family, his secular business, ministerial meetings, and pastoral labors generally consumed far more of the eighteenth-century minister's time than composing sermons. The ministers' diaries contain many confessions that "little matters will divert me" and that the preparation of the sermon has been neglected until the last day of the week.[63] When the demands of pastoral labors and secular concerns diverted the minister from his studies, he sometimes had to repeat old sermons. But this was a step ministers took with reluctance. Such discourses would lack the immediacy of purpose and context that was deemed ideal in a sermon.

The sermons varied from minister to minister, but there are certain general patterns that are apparent. Sermons were not merely exhibitions of scholarly knowledge. They were directed toward an audience of ordinary men and women. So the ministers sought to preach in a "plain style." They believed that the minister should not use an "exotic or strange tongue in the pulpit,"[64] and he should avoid, "FLIGHTS of Wit, petulant Satyr, exorbitant Strains of Rhetoric, fabulous Metaphors and Abstruce Allegories."[65]

Such statements bring to mind Thomas Shepherd's famous seventeenth-century dictum: "God's altar needs not our polishing." Shepherd suggested that such preaching is an insult to the Lord. In the case of the eighteenth-century ministers, however, the argument for a plain style is based upon a perception of the intellectual limitations of the congregation rather than upon God's sovereignty. John Hancock, for example, believed that a minister must level his preaching to the understandings of his whole audience; he asserted: "a minister has nothing to say in the pulpit but what concerns all the congregation, and he may if he will express it in words easy to be understood."[66]

Despite these statements about the limitations of the average man, the preachers did not conclude that they should adopt the common language of the streets. If the miniser was not expected to indulge in complex rhetorical flourishes, neither was he expected to preach without dignity. So Ebenezer Turrell was critical both of "flourishes of Rhetoric" and of "the other Extream of using indecent and homely Phrases, such as savour of the Mobb or Playhouse."[67] In finding a balance between these two extremes, Thomas Paine advocated a preaching style that was restrained and graceful. Ministers, he said, must "be careful not to deliver their Message in a too mean and homely dress"; they should avoid crude phrases, base metaphors, and sordid epithets and not become "a stranger to good Language." Altogether, they ought to "speak as becomes the Oracles of God."[68] This statement suggests that an eighteenth-century version of Thomas Shepherd's dictum on preaching might read: "God's altar should be polished with the utmost care."

This tendency toward decorousness in the language of the sermon was also reflected in ideas about sermon delivery. Thomas Foxcroft recommended that ministers give great care "to tune, and moderate the voice to a pleasing utterance." The ministers' pulpit gestures, he said, "must be compos'd to a decent gravity." They should "compose their looks and form their behavior to the utmost decency and most solemn air."[69]

In content as well as in style and delivery, the sermon was expected to be reasonable. Isaac Chauncy, for example, urged the minister not to preach "A Rambling Discourst . . . like a Rope of Sand, whose parts have no Connexion." Instead, he said, the minister must "discourse Deliberately, that the People may weigh the Truths you Deliver with the Balances of Reason, and the Sanctuary."[70]

In general, all of these statements about preaching point to a form of discourse dignified in style and at the same time adapted to the intellectual capacities of the average man. Ideally, the preaching should not be too flowery or clever, neither should it be too base or disorderly. The delivery should be graceful, the style polished, and the method reasonable.

Such preaching was undoubtedly suited to the needs of an eighteenth-century congregation. The people respected elegance and rationality, but in most towns one church served both wealthy merchants with college degrees and common farmers with only a few years of education. The plain graceful sermon was suited to both groups.

Equipped with a preaching style thought to be suited to all manner of New Englanders, the ministers sought to adjust the content of their sermons to the current circumstances of their audiences. Benjamin Wadsworth declared that ministers should "observe the Dispensations of Providence, remarkable Occurances, the Circumstances of their People, and should endeavor to suit their Preaching to such Occasions."[71] In part, seasonable preaching was a matter of preparing sermons for a number of special occasions. Along with the regular morning and afternoon services on the Sabbath, there were many religious services held to recognize notable events. A military victory or a good harvest was often celebrated by a day of thanksgiving. A drought or an earthquake, on the other hand, was usually followed by a fast day, during which the ministers sought forgiveness for the people's sins. There were also special sermons preached at lecture days and on the Thursday before the sacrament. In addition, the ministers sometimes preached sermons for particular groups within the community, such as young men's or young women's societies. Sometimes ministers delivered sermons to family gatherings and at public events. Ideally, the preachers would deliver different types of discourses to each group. Cotton Mather, for example, cited with approval Dr. Owen's argument that ministers should "deal with their Hearers according to what they are persuaded, that their Spiritual State requires," and that "A general preaching at random without a special Scope directed by such a Persuasion, turns the whole work . . . into a useless Formality."

Mather even encouraged his congregation and private groups to suggest topics for his sermons.[72]

The preachers also tried to adjust their sermons to the immediate circumstances of their people. Sometimes they simply used their sermons as vehicles for news, as when Stephen Williams "endeavored to declare some of the great things God had done for our army" during King George's War.[73] Such prosaic events as changes in weather could also suggest sermon topics. William Cooper, one of the pastors of Brattle Street Church, preached a sermon on winter on a cold Sunday in January 1736/37. He argued that men are too apt to understand seasonable changes "from second causes only, and to overlook the first; forgetting that God keeps the direction and government of all causes in His own hand, and that all the springs of nature are turn'd by Him as he pleases."[74] Cooper warned the people to stand in awe of this powerful God, to be thankful for the comforts of warm houses, clothes, and beds, and to avoid spiritual coldness by loving God and their neighbors. In sermons on the seasons the minister's chief object was to point out the spiritual significance of a common occurrence. Cooper argued that the winter was such a regular experience that we can take it for granted.

There were, however, many events in the lives of New Englanders that compelled them to seek some explanation from religion. This was particularly the case when a town was afflicted by disease or violent death. New England's Indian wars were a frequent source of tragedy. In a small encounter in Rutland, Massachusetts, Indians killed Rev. Joseph Willard and two of his neighbor's small children. Israel Loring, the minister of Sudbury, preached in the afflicted town and tried to explain how such misfortunes could occur in a world ruled by God. He recalled Job's loss of his children and said: "Let any one that knows what it is to be a parent, lay his hand upon his Heart, and consider his own Bowels, and he will acknowledge that the loss of Children is one of the sorest outward afflictions that a man can meet withal in this world." But Loring warned his congregation that men should not allow themselves to fall into despair, no matter how cruelly they may be afflicted. "Indeed," he said, "to be excessively dejected, and cast down under Afflictions, so as to impair our Health, and incapacitate us for the Duties either of our particular or general Calling, is what Christians should endeavor against, and earnestly beg Grace of God to overcome."[75]

Frequently, sermons topics were suggested by ministers' observations of moral problems in their parish. Ebenezer Parkman, for

example, preached one sermon "occasioned in part by the growing
extravagance of Velvet and scarlet among people of low Rank" in
his village.[76] Matching the proper sermon with the immediate needs
of a congregation was often a subtle problem. At one point during
a controversy in the church in Grafton, Ebenezer Parkman, who
had been invited to preach, intended to deliver a severe sermon,
but changed his mind. After conversing with some of the townsmen
he says he perceived "that some of the people were so very wavering and not able to bear at present the least Severity," that he "drew
up a Conclusion to treat them with Gentleness," and changed his
sermon.[77] Increase Mather once decided to preach against suicide
because of an inclination that seemed to be from God. Afterward
one of his parishioners told him "that she was at that time about
to murder herselfe, only that sermon prevented her." Realizing the
importance of preaching timely sermons, Mather prayed "that the
Lord will direct me what texts and subjects to handle in my public
ministry."[78]

A sermon topic that was always pertinent in New England was
the relationship of God to each man's soul. These discourses in
which ministers sought to explain the divine scheme of redemption
were the staple of pulpit oratory. If a minister sought to carry out
a complete and systematic treatment of Puritan theology, he could
easily devote hundreds of sermons to this subject. Increase Mather
reported that he had taken eighteen years "to preach over the whole
body of divinity."[79] But it was also possible for a minister to review
principal doctrines of Puritanism in a much shorter time. Josiah
Flynt, for example, combined twenty-six sermons into a coherent
discourse on the basic Puritan views of sin and salvation.[80]

The Puritans believed that it was through hearing the word
preached that men were saved. If a man preached well, then it was
likely that God would accompany his sermons with divine grace
and that the members of the congregation would be converted.
Ministers should preach "awakening, warming, and enlivening
truths," said one clergyman, "and invite sinners to the acceptance
of eternal life."[81]

The need for ministers to lead sinners to salvation conditioned
another aspect of their preaching. As well as being polished, graceful, and orderly, good preaching was supposed to be "fervent."
"OUR Preaching should be *Earnest* and *Moving*," said Daniel
Lewes, "Our hearts should be visibly in our work, that so our Hearers may be convinced that we do indeed believe our selves what we
preach to them."[82]

Such statements did not contradict the basic Puritan belief in rational, orderly preaching. Just as ministers advocated a preaching style that was elegant but plain, they believed that the preacher could make a well-balanced appeal to both the emotions and the intellect. Ebenezer Gay argued that the minister "is to communicate not only *light* to the Understanding, but also *heat* to the Affections: to be a burning as well as a shining light." To maintain this balance, he said, the emotions must be held in check; the sermon must not fall into "wild disorder; like the Waves of the Sea."[83]

Thus the ideal sermon would appeal to both the heart and the intellect of the auditor. But the emotional part of preaching was to be kept tightly in control. The appeal to the affections as well as to the intellect was to be "deliberate." So Cotton Mather recommended that after a minister finished each section of his sermon, he should "make a Pause" and get his "own Heart suitably affected" with the material of the ensuing section.[84] This is emotional preaching, but of the most restrained sort, and hardly a protoype of the style of the great revivalist sermons of the 1740s.

In advocating a decorous and graceful style, the ministers were clearly adapting their sermons to eighteenth-century taste. The quest for elegance, which appears in these statements, was also apparent in the architecture of the new meeting houses, in the popularity of jewels, family crests, and other ornaments, and in the New England cemeteries. Even the fervency of the sermons was to be decorous.

In general, it is apparent that the ministers were concerned about the effect of their sermons upon their audiences. They sought to accommodate their preaching style to their people's aesthetic tastes. They suited their language to their congregations' intellectual capacities. They matched the content of their sermons to their audience's interests. And they advocated a form of preaching that would produce immediate, visible signs of joy or sorrow from their listeners.

But were eighteenth-century audiences being "enlivened" by the sermons they heard? The ministers themselves seem to have had frequent doubts about this point. Many appear to have delivered their sermons in a dull fashion, despite the many rules they developed for effective preaching. In the seventeenth century, most New England ministers preached without using notes,[85] but by the beginning of the eighteenth century almost all of the ministers used notes. Some ministers held "down their heads within an inch of the cushion to read what is hardly legible." Others popped "up and

down every moment from the paper to the audience."[86] Increase
Mather complained that the young ministers had "a lazy way of
reading all their sermons."[87] Sometimes a minister failed to complete his sermon in time to review it before preaching. John Hancock believed those ministers could not preach well who were "but
just finished when the second bell rings."[88]

Simply by observing their audiences, ministers were able to know
whether they were preaching effectively. When the congregation
"gave vast attention," or there were "many in tears," it was clear
that the sermon had been well received.[89] The conduct of the people between the two meetings on the Sabbath was another sign of
their response to the sermon. In periods of great religious awareness, people would quiz the minister and each other about the sermon or listen to readings from published religious tracts.[90] In other
periods, however, the minister might have to issue "a solemn warning against drunkenness and haunting the taverns between meetings."[91]

The clearest indication of the effect of sermons on laymen is in
the writings of laymen themselves. Many were very diligent in taking advantage of sermons. Some fathers urged their children to
take notes on sermons and then go over the sermon in "family repe-
tition."[92] Edward Goddard used his notes taken from a discourse
by Rev. Henry Gibbs in working out a definition of faith and examining his own soul. In his autobiography, Goddard praised Gibbs.
"Under his ministry," he wrote, "I sat many years with great delight and I hope with some spiritual profit. . . . Oh how sweet were
the returns of sabbath opportunities to my soul in those days."[93]
Edward Goddard and many other New Englanders would agree
with John Loring who "did delight to see and hear a good minister
in the pulpit."[94]

But often people did not feel themselves religiously affected by
the sermons. Captain Brown of Concord, for example, said that although he had lived under the preaching of Cotton Mather for
many years and admired Mather greatly, he "supposed he was not
converted by it."[95] In the period before the Great Awakening, the
most frequent complaint of the preachers against their auditors was
not that they actively resisted the Gospel, but that they seemed
apathetic. In 1723 William Waldron noted that it is "an uncommon
and rare thing for persons to write or talk about religious matters
that concern our souls' interest."[96]

At a ministerial meeting in Medfield, Massachusetts, a group of
clergymen found it necessary to confront the problem of "what are

the best remedies to prevent wanderings of the mind in attendance on divine worship?" Joseph Baxter described a number of signs of the congregation's inattentiveness. Many failed to sing the psalms or sang only half-heartedly. They did not listen to the sermons and failed to apply them to their own souls. And at the end of the service, "some run out of the house before the public blessing is given." Baxter blamed this situation on the worldliness of the times. He argued that men who spend the week "contriving how to get the world . . . , will find it an impossible thing to keep their hearts with God in those stated times wherein they are to be giving their attendance on divine worship."[97]

In the early eighteenth century, many ministers were worried about their audience. Some clergyman undoubtedly preached as movingly as the best pastors of the early seventeenth century. Many made pastoral visits and remained sensitive to the spiritual needs of their people. Almost all of the ministers sought to conduct their own lives in a Christian spirit. In their congregations there were many laymen who were probably as pious as their Puritan ancestors had been.[98]

Nonetheless, the clergymen of the early eighteenth century were concerned with the apparent failure of New England to live up to the ideal standards of a holy community. The "gross ignorance" of many adults, the bored faces in church, and the pressing worldliness of the times all suggested that the ministers were losing their audience. If, however, many men paid more attention to their worldly than to their spiritual lives, the ministers themselves were in part to blame. The decorous form of preaching that they advocated was hardly designed to shock men out of their lethargy.

Since the ministers' work involved them in a series of close relationships with their people, the tendencies toward religious indifference were difficult to ignore. The clergymen developed two strategies in the eighteenth century that served to reduce the sense of failure caused by popular indifference. The first emphasized the unique and holy character of the clerical community and suggested that the validity of a ministry did not depend on the religious condition of a parish. The second sought to renew popular piety through a series of religious revivals. These two movements would collide during the Great Awakening with profound effects on the nature of religious leadership in prerevolutionary New England.

CHAPTER IV

ℭONGREGATIONAL CLERICALISM

The typical minister in the early eighteenth century was uneasy about his professional role. A clergyman's training and ordination elevated him to membership in a highly selective, self-perpetuating provincial elite. But his domestic obligations required him to share in the prosaic daily exertions of his people, and his pastoral duties required him to study and minister to the needs of ordinary men and women. Was the minister then a sovereign religious leader or was he a humble pastoral guide?

Although the clergymen did not state the question so bluntly, they did wrestle with the problem of their identity, and in the early eighteenth century they developed a view of religious leadership that emphasized the elite quality of their profession. This self-image bears a striking resemblance to the "court persuasion" in civil affairs, a philosophy which held that the source of political legitimacy was the exalted station of the ruler, whose elevated position enabled him to rule wisely for the good of the common people. In a society where, as we have seen, there were many signs that self interest had broken free of ancient restraints, the courtly philosophy offered a solution to a serious problem. However, even in the early eighteenth century many colonists resisted this point of view and held that the commonwealth was best protected by the closest representatives of the common man, the colonial legislators. The so-called "country philosophy" of these people emphasized the consent of the governed and warned the people that the greatest danger to their liberty came from corrupt rulers who governed for their own good rather than for the good of the people.

The ministers thus had two models in civil government from which to choose in understanding the nature of their own authority. Significantly, in the early eighteenth century clergymen, with near unanimity, adopted a courtly image of themselves. This conception was reflected in the ceremony of initiation into the ministry, which, as we have seen, had become a stately procedure emphasizing the novitiate's elevation into an exalted profession. It is not surprising that the clerical sensibility that was revealed in the ordination ceremony should also find expression in other aspects of eighteenth-century ministerial life.

CLERICAL AUTHORITY. The courtly view of the minister's power is apparent in many pastors' pronouncements about their profession. In ordination sermons, funeral sermons, and other conventional forms of discourse the ministers reminded New England of the importance of the ministerial profession. Daniel Lewes expressed a common sentiment in 1720 when he argued that the ministry was "the most weighty, awful and important work that ever mortal man was employed in."[1] Even John Wise, who is reputed to be a kind of clerical populist, is said to have advised his people on his death bed to "pay a special veneration to your ministers."[2]

In justifying their claim to esteem the ministers frequently claimed a special proximity to God. So John Hancock compared clergymen favorably with angels: "One said, if he should meet a preacher and an angel together, he would salute the preacher and then the angel afterwards."[3] Because ministers cared for men's souls, while civil leaders cared only for their bodies, they existed in a special relationship to God that made their position more honorable even than that of the civil leader. "There is no order of men in the world," Joseph Baxter said, "that do stand so near unto the great and holy God as ministers by their office do. They are God's mouth unto his people, and his people's mouth unto him."[4]

The ministers' sense of their official importance is apparent also in statements about their relationship to their people. They were superior in dignity, they held, and should therefore be aloof from their congregations. Joseph Baxter argued: "Ministers may expose themselves to scorn, and contempt by those actions and practices whereby they discover too great a freedom with their people." John Prentice agreed that clergymen should not indulge in "too great familiarity with their people." And Grindall Rawson said that ministers can demean themselves "by neglecting to keep up a due distance between themselves and their people."[5] The ministers sought to give visible expression to their preeminence by demanding salaries that would allow them to live in a fashion befitting their exalted station. So Ebenezer Gay declared: "If a Preacher's *Condition* . . . be not, as well as his Pulpit, somewhat *elevated* above the lowest Station, few will mind his words or obey him."[6]

In short, the minister, a man whose exalted position was sanctioned by God, should be visibly superior to the men and women of his parish.

This sense of clerical preeminence displays a different ministerial sensibility than that of the early Puritans. They, too, believed that the minister was an important man who stood in a special relation to God. But they were less inclined to insist that he must be regarded as uniquely holy and admirable. The emphasis in eighteenth-century sermons on the "preeminence," "distance," and "elevation" of the ministers reflects an important new emphasis.

The new sensibility may conveniently be styled "congregational clericalism." In this philosophy the minister is not viewed primarily as the servant of a congregation. Instead his office appears independent and superior. This perception influenced the ecclesiastical history of this period.

As we have seen, the ordination had moved gradually from a primarily congregational to a primarily clerical function. In several other ways as well, functions that in the seventeenth century had involved a close cooperation of ministers and laymen in the eighteenth century were increasingly dominated by the clergy.[7] This tendency is apparent in their new ideas about a pastor's relationship to his congregation and in the formation of ministerial associations and consociations by which the pastors attempted to govern the church.

In the early years of New England's settlement the clergyman was considered to have ministerial power only within his own parish. He could preach to other congregations, but he could not administer the sacraments of communion and baptism outside of his parish. On his way to the New World, John Cotton followed this practice by refusing to baptize his own son, who was born at sea, until he became pastor of a church in New England. On shipboard there had been many Christians, but these were not associated as a congregation. Since Cotton was not their pastor, he could not administer the sacraments among them. But in the late seventeenth century some clergymen began to suggest that their ministerial authority was not limited to the communities where they lived. In 1693 a group of ministers published a tract entitled *A Pastor's Power*, which argued that the minister's religious character extended beyond his own parish. The authors asserted: "The ministerial power, which a pastor has received from the Lord Christ, is not so confined to his particular flock, as that he shall cease to be a minister when he does act in the name of the Lord elsewhere." They argued that if a church had no clergyman of its own, it could ask a neighboring pastor to administer communion and baptism until it settled a new minister.[8]

In the eighteenth century, ministers began to baptize children outside of their parishes in regions where there were no settled pastors. This practice signified an important shift in ecclesiastical sensibilities from seventeenth-century beliefs. In both ages it was the church that babtised, but in the seventeenth century the church consisted of the whole body of Christian believers. It was the Christian community, through its ministers, that baptised the child. In the eighteenth century, however, the clerical profession took it upon itself to exercise this churchly power.

The belief that a man's ministerial character transcended his ties to a particular congregation is also apparent in other contemporary developments. In the dismissal of ministers it became common practice for councils to decide that a man was unfit for a particular congregation, but at the same time to recommend him for the ministry in general. John Hancock justified this practice by saying, although "ministers are married to the ministry, yet I see no reason or scripture ground to think they are married to ye people." He argued that the minister is bound first to the universal church, then to a particular congregation. "To engage absolutely to a particular church," he said, "may be to engage against God."[9] If, as Hancock argued, men were "married to the ministry" rather than to a particular parish, they could easily serve one congregation rather than another. By implication the clergy was a separate order, independent of the congregation.

This separation of the clergy from the community also produced changes in the Boston Thursday lecture. Originally, the Boston lecture was designed for the whole Christian community. It was so popular in the early years of settlement that men and women came from outlying towns to attend, and the authorities feared that the practice would disturb the people's work patterns. But by the end of the century attendance had fallen off. In 1697 Cotton Mather even suggested that the lecture would have to be discontinued if more people did not attend.[10] Increasingly, in the eighteenth century the lectures were delivered to audiences consisting mainly of clergymen, and the topics began to focus on ministerial subjects. "The lecture," according to Perry Miller, "became increasingly a professional exhibition."[11]

In keeping with the dignified and separate character of the ministry, it was natural that the ministers should become uncomfortable with a system of church government in which they shared power with common men who lacked their special training and station. In the early Congregational churches, laymen had been fully involved in church government. Many important decisions had been made in church meetings where the minister's vote counted no more than that of any other church member. In addition, the executive leadership of the church was shared with one or more "ruling elders," an office occupied by laymen.

The ministers did not totally abolish this sytem in the eighteenth century, but in many cases they attempted to do so. The office of ruling elder was abandoned soon after the first settlements in many churches, although the office still existed in the eighteenth century, and often ministers and congregations battled over whether it would be filled. Sometimes ministers were required to accept a ruling elder as a condition of settlement.

In addition, there were many local struggles over the respective powers of the ministers and the congregations in church meetings. It became common for ministers to declare that they could exercise a negative voice in church meetings, and in many parishes there were struggles between ministers and laymen over the issue.

The desire for increased ministerial power was reflected also in the tendency of the ministers to adopt an informal hierarchy of clerical leaders. Here, again, as in their ordination practices, they gravitated toward a high-church conception of proper practice. Although the Congregationalists had no bishops and archbishops whose judgments were authoritative, an informal hierarchy did develop within the church. The oldest ministers were usually the religious leaders of their area. When, for example, a senior pastor in Hampshire County died, Stephen Williams felt the increased responsibility of being "left the eldest minister of the country."[12] Clergymen also had a sense of the ranking of the chief ministers in their province. In New England in 1700, Increase Mather was the leading clergyman. In 1725 Cotton Mather had inherited his position. And by 1740 the influence of the Mathers had passed to Benjamin Colman. The pervasiveness of the idea of clerical rank is apparent in a letter from Colman to George Curwin after the death of Joseph Green. "Our opinion of him was such here in Boston," Colman said, "that when we were last year thinking of sending two of our order to appear for us at court and in the king's presence, I remember that Mr. Pemberton and I in a private nomination of persons gave Mr. Green about the fourth place."[13] In recognition of their importance some clergymen received informal titles. Several ministers became known as "bishop,"[14] and in the Connecticut valley, Solomon Stoddard was known as "Pope Stoddard."

As important as these innovations were, the most significant institutional manifestation of the clergy's growing sense of separate ecclesiastical identity was the formation of ministerial associations. In Connecticut these were given legal status by the Saybrook Platform. In Rhode Island, Massachusetts, and New Hampshire, their influence was informal. But in all four colonies the formation of these organizations reflects the clerical aspiration for authority and independence.

MINISTERIAL ASSOCIATIONS. The significance of the association movement has generally been overlooked by historians who contend that the failure of the Massachusetts Proposals of 1705 to gain provincial support effectively ended the movement toward the creation of authoritative ministerial associations in New England's foremost colony. The conventional view underestimates the actual strength of the association movement. In fact, given the extensiveness of the movement, it is difficult to name an element of early American ecclesiastical history that is so little understood. The extent of the misunderstanding is suggested by the fact that most accounts place Increase Mather, the leading New England minister of this time and a staunch opponent of the Proposals, among the chief supporters of the movement.[15] More significantly, historians have greatly exaggerated the impact of the "defeat" of the Proposals of 1705. Until the present writing the last thorough examination of the association movement was completed eighty years ago.

The beginnings of clerical association in New England can be traced to the earliest years of settlement. In the 1630s the ministers of Massachusetts Bay were accustomed to meeting privately at John Wilson's house after John Cotton's weekly lectures. There is evidence that at least 160 deliberative meetings of ministers were held between 1630 and 1672. But these were ad hoc affairs, and no regular ministerial associations appeared until the late seventeenth century. The first of these whose records survive was the Cambridge–Boston Association, which was formed in 1690 and met on Monday mornings once every six weeks at Harvard. In their regular meetings, the members of the Cambridge–Boston Association discussed a number of religious questions, such as whether ministers should visit their sick parishioners, whether scripture could be read in church without exposition, and "whether to drink healths be a thing fit to be practiced by the professors of the Christian religion."

The ministers also passed judgment on pressing social and political questions. It was their association that met on August 1, 1692, to warn the judges at the Salem witchcraft trials that "devils may sometimes have a permission to represent an innocent person."[16]

Several other associations were established in the late seventeenth and early eighteenth centuries. At the first meeting of the Mendon Association, Joseph Baxter offered a rationale for organization that must have appealed to many of his colleagues. By frequent meetings, he said, the ministers' "hearts may be more engaged and knit to one another and their love and affection to each other may be augmented."[17] It was natural that the ministers should consider regularizing such meetings, and before the end of the seventeenth century, Benjamin Colman drafted a set of "Proposals for promoting and settling an universal correspondence among Protestant Dissenters." Colman suggested that "fixed and stated meetings" of clergymen should be formed in every part of New England. They should meet regularly and debate "things of weight, moment, and concern." These meetings should correspond with each other and should "endeavour to spread and propagate religion . . . to all desolate places and people around about them."[18]

Drawing on their experience in informal ministerial associations, the clergy who met at the Massachusetts Ministers Convention in 1704 passed a resolution in favor of strengthening the associations. In November of that year, the Cambridge–Boston Association sent a circular letter to the churches describing the action of the ministerial convention and adding its own arguments in favor of the proposal on ministerial associations. The letter suggested that such meetings should be "lively maintained" where they already existed and that where they were not yet formed the ministers should establish them "that they may not incur the inconveniences of him that is alone." The letter also recommended that all such associations communicate with each other.[19]

At a meeting the following year of the Cambridge–Boston Association, Benjamin Colman presented a further proposal, calling for "standing councils" to be established throughout New England. He suggested that these councils should consist of representatives of from ten to twelve churches in a region. Each delegation should consist of one layman and one minister, so that the ministers could have an "equal vote." Colman stressed the importance of the clergy, arguing that "the government is confessedly first lodged in them [the ministers] and they may be modestly supposed to be the superiors in knowledge and grace."[20]

The idea of standing councils was a significant innovation. Traditionally, New England church councils had been ad hoc bodies that were called into being by a particular church when that church was unable to resolve a dispute. They regulated the ordination and dismissal of ministers and they passed judgment on many types of problems within churches. Their authority extended far beyond the advisory power of the ministerial associations. The councils generally consisted of a minister and one or more laymen from each of several invited churches. Laymen could exercise considerable influence in these councils, since their votes often outnumbered those of the ministers. The formation of Colman's standing councils would change this.

A month after Colman set forth his ideas, representatives from ministerial associations in Boston, Weymouth, Salem, Sherborne, and Bristol met at Boston and drafted the Proposals of 1705. These consist of two sets of suggestions, one dealing with ministerial associations, the other with church councils. On the subject of associations, the clergymen proposed that ministerial gatherings be organized where they did not yet exist. These associations should debate questions of importance and give advice to individual ministers on matters of difficulty. The associations should also make recommendations concerning the qualifications of ministerial candidates and suggest suitable ministers for vacant pulpits. And they should correspond with each other and "Prevail with such Ministers as unreasonably neglect such Meetings" to encourage them to attend.

The second section of the proposals suggested that standing councils be formed alongside the ministerial associations. These bodies should have all the usual powers of ecclesiastical councils.[21] Each participating church should choose one or more delegates to attend with their pastor. The councils should meet at least once a year to "Inquire into the Conditions of the Churches, and advise such things as may be for the advantage of our holy religion." In addition, the councils should meet in special sessions, at the direction of the local association, to deal with emergencies. The association should determine whether the whole council or only part should meet on such occasions. Within these councils the ministers would have the decisive voice, for no act of a council was to be considered decisive "for which there had not been the Concurrence of the Major part of the Pastors therein concerned." A right of appeal was allowed to a larger council, chosen by the pastors of a neighboring ministerial association, but again the participating clergymen would have a veto. Thus, the ministers would be responsible for calling the councils into session and would dominate their proceedings.

The delegates from the five associations signed these proposals on September 13, 1705, and the general convention of ministers approved them on May 30, 1706, but they were never enacted into law. The governor of Massachusetts at this time was Joseph Dudley, an Anglican, who had no interest in seeing the ecclesiastical power of Congregationalism increased.[22] It is also apparent that some of the clergy disliked the proposals. John Wise did not publish *Churches Quarrel Espoused,* his famous attack on the proposals, until 1713; so that tract was not decisive in the opposition. But the sentiments he published in 1713 were probably views that he and others held as early as 1705. Another minister who was hostile to the proposals was Increase Mather, who, contrary to the assumption of most historians, did not favor the proposals.[23] Many years later Benjamin Colman reported that the pro-council party "prevailed so far that the whole body of ministers through the province, five or six excepted, of whom Dr. Increase Mather was the chief, passed it into a vote, first in every Association, and then by delegates from each association meeting in Boston." Colman believed that Increase Mather's opposition was crucial in the defeat of the motion for standing councils. "Under the Doctor's frowns," he said, "and the stiffness of some churches it came to nothing."[24]

Increase Mather's reasons for criticizing the proposals are significant, for they reveal his perception that ministers were adopting a courtly view of their powers. In a short treatise published in 1716, he argued that ministers have no more authority than laymen in ecclesiastical councils.[25] This position is reflected in an earlier manuscript entitled "Answer to the Proposals," which is among Increase Mather's papers and was probably drafted shortly after the Boston meeting of September 1705.[26] The "Answers" was critical of the supporters of the proposals for attempting to deprive laymen of their traditional ecclesiastical roles. Mather said the proposals take "the very same path the church of Rome walked in . . . their beginning was a taking the power of privilege from the brethren."[27] He suggested that if standing councils were ever adopted, the ministers would then "consult, contrive and determine how to make themselves such lords in their churches that no brother should dare to wag his tongue against anything."[28]

Mather and, later, Wise touched a vital nerve when they suggested that acceptance of the proposals was tantamount to Romanizing the church. The movement toward greater clerical authority was only possible as long as the ministers were united in support of the changes and could claim that they were only making reasonable adjustments of traditional polity to New England experience. Increase Mather's "frowns" made such a course impossible in 1705.

But the "defeat" of 1705 was something other than it seemed. Although it allowed the opponents of clericalism to win a symbolic victory, the movement for clerical association continued, even without the formal acquiescence of the state.[29] As the proposals recommended, more associations were formed.[30] These groups did correspond with one another; they passed judgment on the qualifications of ministerial candidates; and informally they began to perform some of the functions of councils.

Before the Great Awakening, associations were formed in most parts of Massachusetts. In southern Massachusetts there was an association in Bristol County.[31] On Cape Cod the ministers of Eastham, Truro, and Provincetown formed an association.[32] To the north the ministers joined in the Plymouth Association.[33] On the southern shores of Boston Harbor there was the Hull Association.[34] On the outskirts of Boston there was one association that included the ministers of Milton and Dedham and another that included Concord, Billerica, and Wayland.[35] At some time in the early eighteenth century, the Cambridge–Boston Association divided into two associations, one centered in each of the two towns.[36] To the west of Boston was the Sherborn Association, which subscribed to the Proposals of 1705. As more towns were settled in this region, this association was divided into the Mendon Association and the Marlborough Association.[37] Further to the west was the Hampshire County Association.[38] In the north there was an association in the Salem region, which subscribed to the Proposals of 1705.[39] On the Massachusetts–New Hampshire border there was the Bradford Association. In 1740 it divided into two groups, which were reunited in 1745.[40] There was another association near the coast on the Massachusetts–New Hampshire boundary.[41] Further north there was an "Eastern Association" in York, Maine, that probably included some of the ministers from the adjacent part of New Hampshire.[42] And in Rhode Island there was also an association.[43]

Although never formally recognized by the provincial government, these groups soon exercised many of the functions proposed for associations and even for standing councils under the Proposals of 1705. As anticipated in the proposals, the associations supervised the process of settling ministers in vacant parishes. The ministers of the Plymouth Association, for example, agreed to take turns preaching at Providence when a new Congregational society was forming in that town.[44] When the Congregationalists attempted to begin a church in Nantucket, the Bradford Association subscribed for "the support and encouragement of the Reverend Mr. White" on the island.[45] The association also encouraged or discouraged young men from accepting the call of particular parishes.[46]

More importantly the ministerial associations began to judge the qualifications of pastoral candidates. In 1700 Cotton Mather published A Warning to Flocks, urging the people of New England not to be fooled by "imposter ministers." He described several such men who were welcomed by particular congregations only later to prove themselves frauds. (One, according to Mather, used his popularity in Boston to try to seduce some of his female followers.) Mather suggested that the "several Associations and Vicinities throughout the Country" should test the qualifications of ministers.[47] Two years later he and other ministers published Proposals for a Trial of Candidates to the Ministry. The authors recommended a seven-part test for candidates. The young man should belong to a particular church. He should give "An Account of the Principles, that act him, in his desire to preach the Gospel." He should be tested on his knowledge of the "Three Learned Languages" and the "Sciences." He should preach a "Probational Sermon" on a text that his examiners assigned. He should be examined on his theology and should "make it evident, that he has considerably read, Ames' Medulla Theologiae." Finally, he should prove his ability to refute errors and should declare his adherence to the Westminster Confession of Faith.[48]

The elaborate series of tests proposed by Cotton Mather and others was never universally adopted. But it did become customary for a ministerial candidate to present himself to a local association for approval.[49] Samuel Osborne's trial before the Barnstable ministers on May 8, 1718, was probably typical of these tests. First he preached. Then he was called upon to answer ten questions, each of which touched upon a fundamental point of Calvinistic doctrine. For example, he was asked: "What influence has faith to our justification?" and "If we are justified by Christ's Righteousness, what need of our obedience to the Law?"[50] Through examinations such as these the ministers increased their power over ministerial settlements.

The associations also came to assume important advisory functions and thereby to reinforce the power of individual clergymen. When, for example, one minister called for fasting in his town, his voice might not be heeded, but when the association called for a fast, and eight ministers assembled, their combined presence was more impressive. Joseph Baxter stated the point concisely: If one dog barks, "the deer is not alarmed, but the full cry rouses him."[51]

As time passed the associations began increasingly to offer advice and even to make authoritative decisions about ecclesiastical matters. In so doing they began to function as councils and to make important practical decisions, even though they met without laymen.[52] The following examples are worth noting as illustrations of the range of ecclesiastical and theological matters that fell within the competence of the associations. When Moses Hale of Byfield had "difficulties by reason of a new meeting house set up in his parish," he referred the problem to the other ministers of the Bradford Association for advice.[53] When a Boxford man named Peabody was displeased at being kept from the Lord's Supper he brought his complaint to the Bradford Association. There he was met by the minister and some of the brethren of his church. The ministers heard both sides of the case and drew up a document with their advice.[54] The ministers often used their combined influence to try to bring religious quarrels to an end. James Cushing, minister of Haverhill, reported to one meeting that his town was divided because of a woman who wanted to enter the church. Some people objected because she had recently borne a child that was probably conceived before she was married. The ministers agreed that for the sake of peace the matter was best forgotten and "advised that in such dubious cases the interests of religion would not be served by being over inquisitive [and] that therefore it would be better to wave so difficult and uncertain an inquiry and hope the best."[55] An association might even seek to bring about peace in purely secular matters. A ministerial meeting in Marlborough considered the problem of two men in the parish of Rev. William Cooke in Sutton, "who were uneasy with one another in a Bargain they had made about some land."[56]

Occasionally, ministerial associations were called upon to pass judgment on points of doctrine. At its meeting on April 12, 1726, the Marlborough Association considered the argument that Rev. John McKinstry of Sutton was preaching unorthodox doctrine when he maintained that "we ought to give Thanks to God not only for Prosperous but even Adverse Dispensations." The ministers considered the question, then drafted a document in which they assured McKinstry's parishioners that the doctrine was "agreeable to the Sacred Scriptures and Sentiments of the most Judicious Expositions of Orthodox Divines."[57]

By making decisions about such important questions as the validity of John McKinstry's theological ideas, the association often handled problems that might otherwise have necessitated the calling of ecclesiastical councils. In determining proper policy, as in licensing ministerial candidates, the associations greatly expanded traditional clerical power. Thus the Proposals of 1705, far from marking the height of association efforts in Massachusetts, was but an aspect of a movement toward greater clerical cooperation and control that continued despite the "defeat" of 1705. Cotton Mather's discussion of the Proposals in *Ratio Disciplinae* in 1725 indicates that he was satisfied that many of the original goals had been achieved. "These *Proposals* have not yet been in all regards *universally* complied withal," he wrote, "Nevertheless, the Country is full of *Associations,* formed by the *Pastors* in their Vicinities, for the Prosecution of *Evangelical Purposes.*"[58]

In Connecticut the extension of clerical power in areas that had traditionally involved cooperation between ministers and laymen together is even more striking, although again the full extent of the change has hitherto been neglected. Here the call for a stronger ecclesiastical system in the early eighteenth century came from the civil government. Gurdon Saltonstall, the governor of Connecticut at the time, had been minister of New London and had himself experienced the problems of a church controversy.[59] On May 24, 1708, the legislature called for a synod to "draw a form of ecclesiastical discipline."[60] The synod gathered at Saybrook, Connecticut, on September 9, 1708, and considered various proposals prepared by county councils. Eventually, they adopted fifteen Articles for the Administration of Church Discipline. These are almost identical to the Massachusetts Proposals of 1705. The articles recommended that the churches in each Connecticut county form one or more "consociations," or standing councils. No decision should come from these councils that lacked approval by a majority of the pastors. If an erring church refused to reform after being condemned, the consociation could sentence that church to noncommunion. The articles recommended further that the ministers of the various counties form themselves into associations that would assemble at least twice a year to "consider and resolve Questions and Cases of Importance" and to "have power of examining and Recommending the Candidates of the Ministry to the work thereof." They would also recommend candidates for vacant pulpits. The last article suggested that all of the ministers of the colony meet annually for a general association.[61]

The Saybrook Platform was immediately approved by the general court in its October session. In 1709 five consociations were founded. Two in Hartford County and one in New London County adopted the Platform almost without change. Fairfield County regarded the Platform as too liberal and adopted a stricter version providing for the excommunication of recalcitrant churches. New Haven County adopted a somewhat more lenient version. And a few churches, such as East Windsor, refused to accept the Platform. But for the most part, the new order won easy approval.[62]

Thereafter, in Connecticut, the consociations performed many of the functions that had traditionally been carried on by church councils. The ministers maintained tight control over these bodies. In Fairfield County, for example, the consociation met once a year, but could also be called into special session by the moderator and one other minister. To assure that the clergy would control these meetings, the consociation ruled that no business could be transacted if the ministers did not form a majority of those in attendance.[63]

Although historians have generally recognized the power of the consociations, they have overlooked the fact that in spite of their preponderant influence in consociations, the Connecticut ministers preferred to settle many ecclesiastical problems in their associations, where no laymen at all were present. The attendance rules for these meetings were stricter than for the Massachusetts associations. Members of the Windham Association, for example, were required to send an excuse if they failed to attend a meeting, and if they did not provide a satisfactory excuse, an admonition could be recorded in the association records.[64] The associations often handled problems that might otherwise have been referred to church councils or consociations. Thus, when Windham Village became embroiled in a doctrinal controversy, the county association recommended that the disputants choose ministers from the association to try to resolve the conflict so that they would not need to call a "council of the consociation." Potentially devisive problems, such as whether a child could be baptized who had been conceived out of wedlock, were also to be settled by the associations. Moreover, the Connecticut ministers, like their colleagues in Massachusetts, examined candidates for the ministry.[65]

In addition to meeting together in associations and consociations, the New England ministers gathered annually in their provinces for ministerial conventions. In Massachusetts these meetings took place at the time of the election of the provincial council. Even though the convention included an election sermon, which one minister preached to the General Court, the gathering was preeminently a meeting about the ministry, and the business transacted usually concerned the welfare of the clergy.[66] The ministers took collections for their poorest colleagues and discussed such pastoral problems as the Anglican threat to Joseph Torrey's ministerial lands in Rhode Island. In 1737 the ministers voted that in addition to the election sermons there should be an annual sermon preached for the convention.[67] It is probable that many of these sermons were about the ministry. In 1749, for example, John Barnard preached on the subject, "seeing we have this ministry, as we have received mercy we faint not."[68] The following year William Williams repeated a sermon which he had preached at the ordination of Ebenezer Bridge.[69]

The General Convention in Connecticut was organized differently than the Massachusetts Convention, but it performed essentially the same function. It was not a gathering of all of the ministers of the province who wished to attend; instead it consisted of two or three representatives from each association. Between 1725 and 1735 the meetings were held alternatively in Hartford and New Haven.[70] In 1735 the convention voted to meet successively in each county.[71] Many of the problems the delegates considered were proposed by the associations. These included such general questions as "What are the provoking evils in the Land?" and more concrete issues, such as the proper rules for examining ministerial candidates.[72] At the 1738 meeting, held in Stratford, the delegates summarized the purpose of their meetings "according to our Ancient Constitution and Practice" as follows: "To take care of and Inspect the General State of Religion, to Promote Unity and Order in our Ecclesiastical Affairs, and to Recommend to the Consideration of the Particular Associations such matters and things as they shall Apprehend to be for the General Good."[73]

It would be an exaggeration to claim that the association movement fulfilled Increase Mather's bleak prophecy that such developments would make ministers "lords in their churches." But clearly the associations, consociations, and annual meetings were, to an extent hitherto unrecognized, a significant embodiment of the aspiration toward clerical unity and preeminence.

RELIGIOUS LIBERALISM.   In addition to manifesting itself in the idea of clerical preeminence and in the movement toward greater ministerial authority, Congregational clericalism involved a distinct attitude toward important ecclesiastical and doctrinal questions. In sanctifying the position of men whose real qualification for the ministry was educational preparation, it was natural for the ministers to believe that God's movement in the world was rational and predictable. The pastors generally believed in the Calvinistic scheme of redemption, which emphasized a man's inability to bring about his own salvation. They sought signs within themselves of the working of God's grace, and they attempted to see the hand of an almighty Lord in their daily experiences. But when they considered their own professional status, they emphasized man's role in human affairs. It was assumed that the man who had prepared himself properly would be a good minister and that by the nature of his office an able pastor would be especially holy. This means that in discussing their own profession, the pastors came to identify preparation with sanctification. In addition, out of an acute consciousness of their own professional position, the ministers tended to discourage firm and potentially devisive defenses of traditional beliefs. Thus, both their emphasis on clerical training and their aspiration for ministerial unity inclined the minister to a bland form of religious liberalism.

This is not to say that the ministers consciously rejected the Calvinistic ideas of their forefathers. Most of them continued to believe that man was innately depraved and could not be saved without God's grace. But they often tended to mute the more mysterious aspects of their God and to emphasize the reasonableness of Christianity. The affirmation of both reason and Calvinism was, in fact, the *via media* of the early eighteenth century in New England. In part, the assumption that reason would support religion was a product of contemporary English religious thought. From the middle of the seventeenth century "latitudinarian" Church of England theologians had asserted that the fundamentals of religion were few and that on most issues a variety of opinions were acceptable. Contemporary English theological treatises were readily available in New England. William Wollaston's *Religion of Nature Delineated,* for example, found its way to the country town of Westborough within two years of its publication in London.[74]

One of the foremost colonial advocates of reasonable religion was Benjamin Colman, who had spent four years in England before he settled as minister of the Brattle Street Church in 1699. In the winter of 1698-99 Colman preached a series of sermons at Bath that show the influence of Locke's *Reasonableness of Christianity.*[75] When Colman answered the call of the Brattle Street Church in 1699, he carried his love of reason back to New England with him. He continued to believe that rational proof of the existence of God could be found in the visible world. In his best known work, *A Humble Discourse of the Incomprehensibleness of God* (1715), he repeated the idea, which he first expressed in his Bath sermons, that the design of the universe proved the existence of God: "How Great is that *Providence* which keeps these *vast Bodies* in their Places, and makes 'em so kindly minister to one another thro' every Generation? So that *Day* and *Night, Summer* and *Winter; Tydes, Dews* and *Rains* do not fail us; but *Vital Heat and Moisture and Respiration is* provided for and preserved unto us and all the Living Creatures!"[76] Colman's confident assumption that God is clearly revealed in nature was accompanied by a belief that men should tolerate each other's ideas. Although his settlement in the new church was marked by a bitter controversy with the Mathers, Colman came to stand for the "catholic" ideal of reason and toleration in religious matters. He urged his fellow New Englanders to be understanding of each other's opinions; he said: "It is indeed best to err on the charitable Side, and no Temper is more hateful than a censurious, jealous, judging one, suspecting every Body of Evil but our selves."[77]

The toleration of new ideas is apparent in some of the topics discussed by members of the religious society that met at Harvard in 1722 and 1723. For example, Nathaniel Rogers reflected the ethical thought of the Earl of Shaftesbury and Francis Hutcheson when he read a lecture on "Virtue naturally leading to our happiness." The students questioned the authoritarianism of a more dogmatic age by asking "Whether there be any Infallible Judge of Controversies" and "Whether there be any Standard of Truth."[78]

In considering ideas such as these, eighteenth-century New Englanders generally agreed that questions of importance should be settled by reason. Samuel Willard believed that "None of the articles of the Christian Faith are to be rejected because there are difficulties in them which cannot be solved by reason." But he believed that in most cases faith and reason were compatible. He concluded: "I think faith to be so far from being an enemy to reason, that I apprehend reason to be the basis and foundation of all faith. So that that opinion which involves least of difficulty in it, is rather to be embraced than a contrary one which is more dark and doubtful."[79]

The ministers were agreed on the value of discussing and debating religious questions, but they felt that men should not become deeply divided on doctrinal issues. The object of debate was "to improve us in those rude and obscure notions of things which ought to be perfected." In the midst of an argument with Josiah Cotton on the nature of faith, Samuel Willard said that even when men disagree "We should not set the world in a blaze as some men have done about things as trivial as these."[80] The ministers generally believed that factional quarrels brought out the worst in men. Benjamin Colman cited Archbishop Tillotson to the effect that "zealots of all parties . . . have got a scurvy trick of lying for the truth."[81] The New England clergymen felt that except on most issues, a wide variety of opinions should be accepted.[82]

Although the spirit of toleration did not result in a movement to abandon all Calvinistic ideas, it did mean, in practice, that many ministers regarded Calvinism itself as a doctrine that should not be advocated too zealously. In this spirit one eighteenth-century minister once complimented a colleague by noting that although he was "as orthodox a Calvinist as any man," he was "too much of a gentleman, and of too catholic a temper, to cram his principles down another man's throat."[83]

The clergy's tendency toward a diluted version of Calvinism and their desire to avoid fundamental doctrinal controversy is apparent in the history of the two most important theological issues of the early eighteenth century: the conflict between liberalism and conservatism and the rise of Arminianism. In confronting each of these issues the ministers sought to work out compromise positions. As a result they muted controversy, but they also avoided a rigorous application of Calvinistic ideas.

The first important division in our period was already in existence by 1700. In the early eighteenth century, some men thought of themselves as belonging either to a "conservative" or a "liberal" wing of the clergy. A liberal identified himself by his position on a number of ecclesiastical and social questions. He generally opposed making a formal relation of religious experience the criterion for full church membership. If the church demanded such a relation, he usually preferred that it be made in private rather than before the whole church. He probably supported John Leverett for the presidency of Harvard in 1708. He was lenient in administering church discipline and preferred to guide his church without ruling elders. If he had a hand in writing his church's creed, he opposed rigid, dogmatic statements. He approved of reading the scriptures in church without discoursing on their meaning. He might also approve of the Lord's prayer and attend a Church of England service on Christmas Day. He enjoyed a good meal, sometimes he played cards, and he might even indulge in what some conservatives considered the depths of depravity and wear a wig.

Although this set of attitudes describes a consistent liberal position, it is doubtful that there was a consistent liberal among the
ministers. Solomon Stoddard was a liberal on church membership,
but he despised wigs. Benjamin Colman occasionally wore a wig,
but he preached against health drinking. The idiosyncracies of a
particular minister and the circumstances of his parish probably
had more to do with determining his point of view on each of these
questions than his conscious adherence to a consistent set of principles.

The most important point of issue between the two groups was
the question of proper admission standards for full church members. The conservatives held to the traditional New England custom
of requiring men and women to describe the work of God's grace
on their souls before they could take communion. They believed
that this provision would result in the formation of churches of
communicants who had actually been converted by God.

But in the late seventeenth century a number of churches, particularly in the Connecticut valley, had abandoned this rigorous test
in favor of a simpler requirement that the prospective communicant
be familiar with Christian principles and lead an outwardly moral
life.[84] This movement found supporters in Boston, who in 1699 established the Brattle Street Church. The controversy over this
church helped define the liberal and conservative factions in the
early eighteenth century.

The Brattle Street Church was founded by a group of Boston
merchants with the support of several important ministers of the
colony. Early in 1699 these men wrote Benjamin Colman, a young
Harvard graduate, urging him to return to New England and become the pastor of the new church. They told him that "this affair
is neither begun nor carried on by strife or faction, the government
both civil and ecclesiastical having been consulted and consenting
to it."[85] Ebenezer Pemberton, a Harvard tutor, who soon became
minister of Boston's Old South Church, assured Colman: "The gentlemen that solicit your return are mostly known to you men of
repute and figure; from whom you may expect generous treatment."[86] John Leverett, later the president of Harvard, told Colman
that "The men engaged in the affair are able, vigorous, and sincere."[87]

The organizers of the new church alleged that the main reason
for their project was "the want of convenient seats in other meeting
houses," but they also indicated their dissatisfaction with certain

contemporary practices in the New England churches. They disliked the requirement that men must relate their conversion experience in order to join many churches, and they favored the reading of holy scriptures in worship. Moreover, they were willing to break with Congregational ordination practice and urged Colman to obtain his ordination in England "from the most eminent ministers there." One of the organizers wrote Colman that he "could wish it were obtained from the Bishop."[88]

Although the founders claimed that the new church had not been planned by a "faction," the manifesto of the Brattle Street Church was greeted with alarm by the more conservative pastors of the colony. John Higginson and Nicholas Noyes, ministers of Salem, asked Colman's supporters: "Sirs, how could you forsake the dear churches some of you belong to, whose breasts you had sucked, and on whose knees you had been dandled, without dropping one tear for them in your declaration?"[89] Nathaniel Saltonstall, a Harvard tutor, reported that Colman spoke "treason against our great men." He forecast the downfall of New England. "Great things are threatened," he said, "the mountains are shaking and some think ere long will fall."[90] Samuel Sewall, fearing the Anglican tendency of the new church, "expostulated" with Colman for not showing more respect for traditional New England practices.[91]

The memory of the Brattle Street controversy divided men for at least fifteen years. According to John Barnard's account of the formation of the New North Church in 1713, Barnard himself would have been settled as pastor of the New North had it not been for one of the congregation who opposed him as a "manifesto man," because of his friendship with Benjamin Colman.[92] But although Colman favored the new standard for church admission, he did not publish a defense of the innovation. In fact, the controversy did not find its way into print until 1708, when Solomon Stoddard published *The Inexcusableness of Neglecting the Worship of God.* In this tract Stoddard argued that New Englanders were offending the Lord by strict admission standards that permitted only one in four to take communion. He denied that one had to be assured of salvation before he could attend the Lord's Supper, and claimed that the sacrament could itself be a converting ordinance. The only admissions requirements that he recommended were moral behavior and a knowledge of the creed. In response, Increase Mather published *The Strange Doctrine Confuted* (1708). Mather upheld the traditional New England Congregational view that only those should be admitted to communion who appeared to have undergone a conversion experience.[93] Stoddard replied in the following year with a second defense of his position, *An Appeal to the Learned.*

Considering the divisiveness of the Brattle Street Church controversy and the Stoddard–Mather debate, it might seem that the church membership issue had produced a deep and permanent rift in the ranks of the New England clergy, but this was not the case. In retrospect, what is most remarkable about the issue is that the clergy were able to preserve an outward show of unity in spite of their disagreement. After settling as minister of the Brattle Street Church, Benjamin Colman soon united with his fellow clergymen on the important issues of the day. As we have seen, he was one of the chief advocates of the Proposals of 1705, which were aimed at strengthening clerical unity.

It is even more remarkable that the Stoddard–Mather controversy did not generate a permanent division in the ranks of the clergy. We might expect that after the initial exchange of pamphlets between the two ministers, dozens of other clergymen would have added their thoughts to the controversy, but this did not occur. Instead the membership problem simply became a local issue. Different churches adopted different practices, but no effort was made to impose a single standard throughout New England. Moreover, it is also apparent that in actual practice Stoddard and Mather admitted approximately the same types of men and women to communion in their respective churches. Mather accepted men and women into communion who showed the slightest trace of a regenerative experience, even if they still had doubts. Thus, he, like Stoddard, admitted that there was no way of being certain whether a man had been converted. Because the conservatives on the question of church membership did not insist upon holding all of the churches of New England to strict standards of communion membership, they were able to preserve clerical unity.

But by preserving unity they made it possible for men who were not deeply pious to feel comfortable in the church. Thomas Brattle, a merchant who was one of the founders of the Brattle Street Church, had failed to gain communion membership in another Boston church. Of the twenty-one original founders of the church, many were merchants. Their alienation from the Standing Order is indicated by the fact that almost one-third had contributed earlier toward the founding of King's Chapel, the first Anglican church in Massachusetts. Colman's biographer, Clayton Hardin Chapman, describes them as men who lacked the piety of the first Puritans:

"With increasing stakes in the material welfare of the country, they were helping to develop it through their monied and intellectual culture. . . . Their theology had not changed, but their sense of sin had died out, and the unregenerate, being of good character, were demanding respectability."[94] Thus, the men who sought to avoid dogmatism in determining who were church members, allowed men who were uncomfortable with traditional Calvinistic ideas to enter the church.

A similar aspiration for unity and distilling of Calvinism is apparent in the development of Arminianism in New England. In 1715 Cotton Mather was confident enough of the doctrinal uniformity of New England to write: "I would with all possible modesty observe, that for ought I can tell, we have in our New England near 200 churches, wherein the faith and order of the gospel is maintianed, with as little a measure of the epidemical corruption as any part of the Christian world can pretend unto."[95] But as the century progressed it became less easy to characterize New England as theologically placid. The most fundamental divergence from Puritan orthodoxy in the early eighteenth century was in the direction of Arminianism. In New England, "Arminian" was a term used to describe anyone who believed that man's own efforts had an important role in winning his salvation. The idea was anathema to the strict Calvinist, who emphasized man's complete inability to achieve his own salvation and his absolute dependence on Christ's justifying grace.

In 1732 John White, the pastor of the first church in Gloucester, published a tract entitled *New England's Lamentations,* in which he described the decline of religion in New England and warned of the danger of Arminian principles. "It is a matter of lamentation," he said, "that some of Our *Young men,* and such as are devoted to and educated for the *Ministry* of the Gospel, are under *Prejudices* against, and fall off from, important Articles of the *Faith* of these *Churches,* and cast a favourable Eye upon, embrace, and as far as they dare, *argue for, propogate,* and *preach* the *Arminian Scheme.*"[96] Jonathan Edwards also noted the trend when he wrote that in 1734 Arminianism "seemed to appear with a very threatening aspect upon the interest of religion here."[97] The first Arminian theologian to have an important influence in New England was the Anglican, Archbishop Tillotson. In the eighteenth century he was read avidly by New England college students and ministerial candidates, who admired his brilliant style and his clear thought. But Tillotson's God was hardly the all powerful deity of the early Puritans. He was a God in whom it was *reasonable* to believe. John Hancock made a note of Tillotson's argument that it was safer to believe in God than to doubt his existence, because the danger of unbelief in a real God was infinite and "he that is a thoroughly prudent man will be provided for all events."[98] This God, whom one followed from "prudence," was very different from the early Puritan God whom men worshiped in awe.

Despite their respect for Tillotson, few New England ministers in the early eighteenth century became outspoken Arminians. Of the three important disputes in this period over ministers' beliefs, only one produced clear evidence that the accused clergyman was an Arminian. This was Samuel Osborne, minister of Eastham, Massachusetts. According to members of Osborne's church, he had adopted several Arminian views: (1) that Christ's death did nothing to diminish man's obligation to the law; (2) that men's sins were not pardoned unconditionally; (3) that men can do that which will result in their salvation; and (4) that man's obedience is a cause of his justification. He was dismissed in 1738.[99]

Although one could not hold explicit Arminian views in the early eighteenth century and remain a minister, there was a tendency by many pastors to reject strict Calvinism, and there were some individuals who privately espoused Arminian ideas. A few men tacitly acknowledged their toleration of the Arminian viewpoint by claiming to believe in the Bible, rather than in either Arminius or Calvin. When, for example, Benjamin Doolittle, pastor of Northfield, Massachusetts, was accused of espousing "Arminian principles both in pulpit and private conversation," he replied: "The word of God must and shall be the only rule by which this matter shall be decided. . . . For I am no papist to make either Calvin or Arminius my pope to determine my articles of faith for me."[100] Some ministers advocated Arminian views in private conversation. In 1740 Nicholas Gilman "Had a considerable private conversation with a clergyman about the Arminian tenets—he much opposed the doctrine of imputed righteousness and the doctrine of native corruption and vanity."[101]

The ministers of New England were willing to tolerate mild Arminian viewpoints, because they believed that the outward unity of the clergy was too valuable to be impaired by purges of doctrinal deviants. The ministers agreed that it was better to accept some diversity than to quarrel among themselves in a search for a single truth in doctrine and practice. This concern for unity is particularly apparent in the Robert Breck case. The problem was ostensibly doctrinal in origin, but soon the matter of clerical relations became the chief issue. In a previous post Breck had privately espoused Arminian principles—perhaps, in part, to shock a neighboring pastor, Thomas Clap. When Breck was called to Springfield, Clap charged him with Arminianism, and a contest developed which soon involved most of the important ministers of New England. Breck was unable to win sufficient approval among the ministers of Hampshire County to achieve his ordination; so he went to Boston to gain allies. There John Webb, William Cooper, and several other Boston ministers were willing to support him. They were thwarted in their first attempt to ordain Breck, and a second council had to be called before the ordination could finally be carried out in 1736. The Breck case divided the ministers of Boston as well as those of Hampshire County. Benjamin Colman, Cooper's colleague and senior pastor, was one of the chief opponents to the ordination.

Although Colman did not approve of Breck's alleged Arminian statements, he was more concerned about Breck's actions in Springfield. William Cooper, who was, if anything, a stricter Calvinist than Colman, was actually a supporter of Breck.[102] Colman's main reason for opposing Breck was on the issue of church government. He believed that no man should be settled in the ministry without the approval of nearby pastors.[103] He said: "I wish with all my heart his usefulness and peace, but can have no heart or hand in bringing on his settlement in opposition to the minds of the neighboring churches and pastors." He criticized Breck's supporters for sending to Boston for support "When they have so many churches nigh to them."[104] He was particularly annoyed that when Breck was in Boston gaining support, he had not admitted the difficulties that he was having with the Hampshire Association.[105] It is significant that Colman's main objection to Breck's supporters was that they caused a division among the clergy by traveling half way across Massachusetts to support a man whose neighboring clergy opposed his ordination.[106] Colman probably would have approved of Breck's ordination, forgetting his Arminian statements, if the local ministers in Hampshire County had approved.

In the Breck case, as in the Brattle Street Church controversy, the issue of clerical unity soon outweighed all other considerations. Immediately after his installation in the Brattle Street Church, Benjamin Colman had sought to make peace with his fellow Boston pastors. Similarly, in 1736 Breck began a successful campaign within the Hampshire Association and among his neighboring pastors to heal the wounds of his settlement controversy. In these cases, as in others, the desire for cooperation enabled the ministers to avoid or stifle divisive controversies, but the effort to maintain clerical unity in the early eighteenth century undermined Puritan orthodoxy. In refusing to adopt rigid, dogmatic positions, the ministers tended to avoid preaching rigorous Calvinistic sermons about God's awesomeness and man's humility. By shunning doctrinal controversy, they allowed men to develop Arminian viewpoints.

In permitting new standards of church membership and in avoiding rigorous Calvinistic orthodoxy, the ministers acted in a fashion compatible with their professional experience. They believed that God's approval of humane standards of merit was apparent in their own elevation to the ministry and that unity was essential to the influence and dignity of the clergy. But even these developments did not complete the process that defined New England's religious norms in terms of the professional life of the clergy. The movement that expanded the minister's authority, led to the formation of ministerial associations, and influenced religious liberalism, found its quintessential expression in the pastors' new perception of their relationship to God.

PREACHING THEMSELVES.   In his writings on early New England Puritanism, Perry Miller has shown that the colonists' early concern with leading a reformation of Europe disappeared after the English Civil Wars, and the colonists' sense of history was then concentrated on the peculiar destiny of New England. In a similar fashion, in the beginning of the eighteenth century many early Puritan ideas were focused even more narrowly upon the destiny of a particular group within New England. With increasing frequency the ministers preached sermons about themselves. Their desire for higher salaries, a phenomenon that is discussed more fully in the next chapter, was the immediate occasion for many sermons on the ministers' importance. Others were preached at clerical funerals and ordinations. In these discourses, ideas that had once been applied to the whole body of Christians in New England were identified exclusively with the ministers. In effect, the preachers tended to equate the religious life of New England with the life of the clergy.

The pattern was apparent in the ministers' use of religious authority to support their demand for higher salaries. Nowhere is this change more striking than in the new use of the jeremiad; there the people's failure to support their ministers became one of the chief sins of the land: "I cannot help observing," said Eliphalet Adams,

(however Invidious it may seem and some may think that it looks too much like pleading our own Cause, which will scarce be allowed us to do) that it is Probable, that a great part of that Displeasure, which God in his Providence hath Manifested against the Country, is owing to that Disingenious Treatment which they who serve them in the Concerns of their Souls, have met with, and that People would thrive a great deal more, both in their Temporal & Spiritual Interests, if they mended their hand in this point.[107]

Congregations were warned that if they failed to pay the ministers properly they were not merely inconveniencing a few clergymen; Cotton Mather described low salaries succinctly as "the robbing of God."[108]

The full weight of the federal covenant, an agreement between God and man which guaranteed that men would be outwardly rewarded for their good deeds, was also brought to bear on the salary problem. Jabez Fitch, for example, declared: "those who in Obedience to God are conscientious in discharging their Duty to their Ministers, shall fare the better for it on Temporal Accounts."[109] Along with the jeremiad and the covenant, one other old idea, that of New England's peculiar historical destiny, was now applied to the question of the ministers' income. John Tufts argued that "RELIGION was our Fore Fathers' Errand in . . . this Country"; and concluded that ministers should therefore received "their Just Dues from the People."[110]

The result of applying the jeremiad, the covenant, and the idea of New England's historical mission to themselves was that the ministers began to equate the life of their professional class with the religious life of the whole community. In a typical statement, Solomon Williams argued that not only a people's temporal benefits, but their chances for salvation as well, are dependent upon the well being of their pastor. If you treat your minister kindly, said Williams, you will "secure your share in a Prophet's Reward, when He shall shine as the brightness of the Firmament, and as the stars for ever and ever."[111]

There was undoubtedly a degree of truth in these statements, and in some cases the minister's life could be said to embody the religious life of the whole community. Some ministers were truly charismatic leaders and were able to give voice to the spiritual aspirations of their people. Cotton Mather was one such clergyman. A country minister who rode to Boston to attend his funeral reported that the whole town was in mourning: "It looked very sad—almost as if it were the funeral of the country."[112]

But in "Preaching themselves" the ministers came to emphasize their own importance above that of other Christians. Solomon Williams argued that a minister's heavenly reward would be greater than that of other Christians: "The Ministers of Christ who have had greater Advantages by their Gifts and Station in the Church than other Men, if they have faithfully Improved those Advantages . . . will have a distinguishing and eminent Reward above other men."[113] William Shurtleff declared that a minister's life should be more noble than that of his fellows: "Let us labour that our Lives and Actions may be at an equal Distance with our Rank from the common Level. Since we move in such advanc'd Orbs and are plac'd so much nearer to God than others, let us endeavour to be further remov'd from every Thing that is sinful and impure, and from whatever may justly be accounted mean and low."[114] Benjamin Colman asserted that the minister's office distinguished him from other men, and as "it is the chief End of a *Christian* to glorify God, so it is of a Minister to magnify his Office."[115]

It is evident in all these arguments that the early Protestant ideal, present in the founding of the Dedham Church, of a "priesthood of all believers" had all but vanished from the New England of 1740.[116] The change was probably more subtle than some of these statements about the ministry would suggest. The ministers did not withdraw into monasteries and many were good friends and spiritual counselors of the people. However, many clergymen in this period did show a heightened consciousness of their professional, social, and religious status as ministers. Increasingly, they preached about themselves, and in doing so, they tended to apply ideals to their own class that had once been directed to New England society as a whole. No example of this change is more dramatic than an assertion that appeared in two ordination sermons in 1726. On January 19, 1725/26, at the ordination of John Lowell in Newburyport, Massachusetts, Thomas Foxcroft declared: "Ministers are (as Parents in the Family) in a somewhat elevated and conspicuous Station; they are as a City set on a Hill, which can't be hid."[117] Eight months later, on September 14 at the ordination of Nathanial Morrill in Rye, New Hampshire, William Shurtleff echoed Foxcroft's words: "The Ministers of Christ should remember that they are in a peculiar manner the Lights of the World; that they are as a City set upon a Hill, which cannot be hid."[118]

When John Winthrop had uttered his famous words about the "City set upon a Hill" almost a century before, he had intended to describe all of the residents of New England. But now an image that had once evoked the coherent destiny of a whole community was limited to the description of a single profession. In such passages the eighteenth-century ministers symbolized their peculiar tendency to identify the church with themselves. They also revealed, however, the fundamental weakness of congregational clericalism, for a concept of leadership which concentrated so narrowly on the status of the leaders was, by implication, irrelevant to the ordinary people in the church.

CHAPTER V

ℭHE FAILURE OF CLERICALISM

In the early eighteenth century, Congregational clericalism, in its various manifestations, provided ministers with a sense of professional importance. The new ordinations were impressive ceremonies of initiation into the clergy; ministerial associations increased the authority and unity of the pastors; and rational religion provided a theoloigcal endorsement of the intellect, education, and training that were the hallmarks of the clergy. The ministers enjoyed the illusion of courtly authority—of prestige that accrued automatically to them as members of a sacred caste.

But without the support of laymen, the ministers' exalted status was simply an illusion. And such support could not be taken for granted, for even in the midst of the secular tendencies of the early eighteenth century, many laymen were deeply pious and were highly interested in religious matters. They objected to the dimunition of lay authority in the churches; they criticized ministers who apparently confused their own self-interest with the welfare of the congregation; and through their control of ministers' salaries, laymen reminded the ministers of their literal dependence on the people.

LAY PIETY. The role of laymen in New England's religious affairs is more difficult to chronicle than that of ministers. Most of the surviving manuscripts and books that discuss religious matters were written by clergymen, giving the impression that lay people were not deeply involved in such affairs. But this was not the case.

Lay participation in religion took many forms. Laymen often were deeply concerned about the state of their souls and were well versed in Christian doctrine. They took part in Christian fellowship by giving religious counsel to their families and friends, and, as church members, they participated in ecclesiastical government and served as deacons, ruling elders, and members of councils. Laymen were, of course, dependent upon their ministers in a variety of ways. They received most of their religious training from their pastors, and frequently they attributed their conversions to the preaching or writing of particular clergymen. Edward Goddard, for example, believed that as a young man he had grown to religious maturity through the guidance of Rev. Henry Gibbs. In later years he still recalled his "delight" in attending church under Gibbs's ministry.[1]

But although laymen received much of their religious guidance from ministers, their piety was not simply a passive reflection of clerical pronouncements. They frequently considered religious issues without the direct guidance of a particular pastor. Their writings frequently contain religious meditations. "For his own quickening," Solomon Hancock, brother of Rev. John Hancock, wrote this note: "Oh the thoughts of death are enough to rend a heart of stone, the thoughts of going out of this world, and to behold man's face no more are dismal indeed . . . yet these things are but a mean shadow, to what shall be when God shall say, depart from me ye cursed into everlasting fire, prepared for the devil and his angels."[2] Harvard tutor Henry Flynt often reminded himself of the transitory nature of earthly pleasures. "The present life," he wrote, "is very empty of true satisfaction and happiness. The best estate of it can afford little more comfort than arrives from meat, drink, sleep and clothing necessary for the body. . . . Nothing remains but the sting of conscience. The strengthening of this even is the sting of death."[3]

One of the best surviving examples of lay piety is the "Meditations and Self Examinations" of John Barnard. For many years this spiritual autobiography was attributed to Rev. John Barnard of Marblehead. The manuscript was in the Barnard papers, and it was natural to assume that these religious meditations were from the pen of a clergyman. But a careful reading of the manuscript indicates that it was actually written by another John Barnard, the father of the Marblehead minister. The elder Barnard was a carpenter, who lived in Boston and attended the Mather church. According to his son, he and his wife Esther were "remarkable for their piety and benevolence."[4] As a carpenter, Barnard made an irregular living. During periods when trade was slow, he consoled himself with the thought that God was just and that worldly treasures were unimportant in comparison to spiritual rewards. For example, he once wrote:

For about a month past I have had very little to do at my trade, and it is still a dead time; I have no prospect of a full employment, only some small jobs to do. I acknowledge the justice and righteousness of God in it; I desire nothing, but I hope to see the goodness of God in it too, in helping me not only the more to live to God, but also more to depend on him for my daily bread. . . . I remember that word, he that gathered much had nothing ever, and he that gathered little had no lack. Lord all is well because of thy ordering. Only give me a heart to conform to thy will.[5]

John Barnard believed that man's only true comfort was in heaven. "At best this world is full of briars and thorns," he said, "as the most desirable things in it can't satisfy the cravings of an immortal soul; but the world to come, though the ungodly shall be in blackness and darkness forever, yet there the righteous shall shine as the son in the kingdom of their father."[6]

It was as important for a layman as for a minister to know whether he was one of God's saints. Barnard admitted that he sometimes had doubts about his own salvation. "In respect of . . . effectual calling," he said, "Alas my cloudy, dark, sinful soul, is often ready to question it." But he realized that he must strive after salvation in order to be one of the elect. "Eternal happiness," he wrote, "is not to be expected without labor, for we are commanded to work out our own salvation . . . we must run, wrestle, fight if we would win the prize."[7] Barnard sought to make his whole life worthy of his relation to an eternal God, and he was at least as interested in his spiritual as in his material life. In his meditations Barnard speaks directly to God and to his Saviour. He is the true Protestant, who admits no intermediary between his own immortal soul and an almighty Lord.[8]

Pious laymen like Barnard often tried to communicate their religious ideas to their friends. The ministers, of course, were the foremost religious "teachers" in New England. Their sermons, printed works, pastoral visits, and catechism classes were all intended to convey religious precepts to laymen. But common men and women were also involved in the process of giving religious instruction. Pious laymen exhorted, advised, and encouraged each other on the subject of their spiritual lives. For example, John Loring of Hull gave spiritual advice to his relatives. Loring was a farmer and a ruling elder in his church. He was a deeply religious man who once remarked: "My God and I (when all alone) I thought good company." To Caleb Loring, he wrote, "Dear Brother, be persuaded to make religion the main business of your life and resolve to spend the strength and flower of your days in his service." He told his brother Rev. Israel Loring of Sudbury, we should all "be preparing for death, for we know not when our Lord will come whether at midnight or at cock crowing in the morning." He also gave religious encouragement to men in the parish who sometimes came to him with their spiritual doubts.[9]

A family tragedy was often the occasion for relatives to give spiritual advice to one another. When John Parkman was robbed by pirates in a ship bound for Jamaica, his brother William wrote, urging him to get some spiritual advantage from the incident. He said, I "desire God would give you his grace to make a wise and good improvement thereof, and when you see the uncertainty of these things, let it quicken you to make sure of a part in Christ who is the pearl of great and price and will stand us in stead when all other things fail."[10]

On some occasions laymen even gave religious council to ministers. During a salary controversy in Westborough, a man once counseled Ebenezer Parkman to follow a particular Biblical precept and "Speak kindly to this people." After John Cotton, Jr., was dismissed as minister of Plymouth, Samuel Sewall warned him not to become obsessed with his earthly troubles in Plymouth and thereby "neglect the cords thrown out to him by Christ and so be drowned."[11]

The laymen's ability to develop religious ideas and give counsel to their fellow Christians points to a common religious life that was shared by the ministers and their congregations. This involvement also extended into ecclesiastical affairs. Sometimes lay influence in church government was informal. In many instances important laymen exercised considerable control over their ministers. Benjamin Colman indicated that such men were common in churches. He said that many congregations have "a kind of church within a church, leading men whom we privately consult before we offer anything to a public debate and vote."[12] In extraordinary cases, a powerful man might have influence over laymen and ministers in parishes far beyond his own. In the months before his dismissal by Northampton, Jonathan Edwards attributed the weakening of his position to the influence of Colonel Williams of Hatfield. He wrote to Thomas Foxcroft that Williams "has great influence on many of the neighboring ministers; and his thus appearing [in opposition to Edwards] will doubtless greatly embolden many people."[13]

In addition to exercising informal influence in ecclesiastical affairs, many laymen filled posts in the churches. The most common lay office in the Congregational Church was that of deacon.[14] The deacon was chiefly responsible for minor administrative chores, such as distributing funds to the poor or supplying communion wine. For example, when an English benefactor gave the Chelmsford Church a set of Baxter's *Works,* Deacon Ephriam Spaulding was appointed a "trustee" of the books, which were to be read in the meeting house in the intermission between the two Sunday services. In Westborough a deacon received and counted the votes in a church meeting, when Ebenezer Parkman was forced to leave early. The deacon's most important role in the church was often informal. As a layman holding an office, he could function as an intermediary between the minister and the congregation. If there were complaints about the minister's conduct, the deacon might tell him. Sometimes the deacons helped the ministers to decide whether to hold church meetings.

Another lay office in the church was that of ruling elder. In theory the office was second only to the minister's in importance. The Cambridge Platform defined it as follows: "The *Ruling Elder's* work is to joyn with the *Pastor* and *Teacher* in those acts of spiritual *Rule* which are distinct from the ministery of the word and Sacraments." The Platform goes on to say that the ruling elders should participate in ordaining church officers, appointing church meetings, and administering discipline.[15] But in these, as in other, particulars the Cambridge Platform was not strictly observed. Williston Walker maintains: "Of no office was the theoretic necessity more stoutly maintained, and yet none was so speedily abandoned in practice." Walker argues that the office was neglected because the ruling elder's position, half way between the minister and the brethren, was ineffective. Some of his functions, particularly those regarding discipline, led to ill feelings. Although the minister ran the same hazard, his risk was counterbalanced by "the more pleasing duties of preaching the word."[16]

Walker's argument may explain why some laymen were reluctant to become ruling elders in the seventeenth century, but it fails to take into account the fact that in the eighteenth century the office was still alive, and it was the ministers rather than the laymen who sought to abolish it. In order to assure that their churches had ruling elders, many congregations had to force the ministerial candidates to allow the office to exist as a condition of their settlement. Ministers, on the other hand, increasingly disparaged the office. In 1718, for example, the Sherborne Association discussed the question: "Whether there be such an office as a ruling elder distinct

from a teaching elder by a divine right?" In responding, Robert
Breck, minister of Marlborough, argued that the post was not scriptural. He admitted that the Cambridge Platform approved of the
office, but pointed out that the apostles do not mention it.[17]

In the early eighteenth century, few ministers approved of the
office of ruling elder. Highly conscious of the professional character of their work, they were reluctant to share their responsibilities
with laymen. (The deacon's office, which was secretarial in character, was continued because it did not interfere in the same way
with the ministers' work.) A number of parishes waged bitter feuds
with their ministers over the question of ruling elders. But the ministers were generally agreed that the office should be abandoned
and had little patience with those whom they called "rigid sticklers
for the Church discipline of Lay Elders."[18]

Another area where this controversy of prerogatives was fought
was in the debate over the proper character of church meetings.
Many clergymen argued that the minister should have a negative
vote in church meetings and that no meeting could be conducted
in the minister's absence.[19] The same ministers usually refused to
have ruling elders appointed in their churches. In this way they
sought to assure that the final determination of all religious matters
would rest in their own hands.[20]

It was natural that eighteenth-century laymen would resist these
innovations. As Christian saints and as church members, pious laymen were deeply involved in the spiritual life of the community.
The piety of a carpenter like John Barnard was surely as genuine as
that of many ministers. Religious counseling by lay people was
probably as important as that given by ministers. And the congregation's role in ecclesiastical government was jealously maintained
in many churches. It was inevitable then that New Englanders
would oppose a movement that tended to elevate ministers to a
position of sacred authority.

ANTICLERICALISM.   In the eighteenth century, ministers were frequently subjected to public criticism. So extensive was this hostility
at times that in 1722 Cotton Mather declared to the Massachusetts
ministers convention that a clergyman must expect to endure "the
vilest *Ingratitude*," "the basest *Misconstruction*," and "heaps of In-
dignities." No doubt Mather was responding to the exceptional circumstances of his recent involvement in the Boston smallpox controversy. But his sense of the hostility ministers encountered is
reflected in statements by many other clergymen. John Hancock

declared that ministers' "messages are sometimes entertained with resentment and rage."[21] Azariah Mather asserted that "the very Heathen Pay a greater Honour and Deference to the Idol Priests of their Dunghill Deities, than some that would be accounted Christians."[22] And a layman, Samuel Sewall, lamented "the present contempt of our ministry."[23]

Historians have frequently noted the existence of this criticism, but have generally overlooked the peculiar thrust of opposition to the clergy in this period. The term "anticlericalism" is frequently associated with hostility to ministers and to religion in general. But in New England it was commonly a movement based on piety rather than apathy, and it did not oppose ministers, per se, but rather clericalism, the concentration of undue authority in the pastors' hands.

Since laymen did participate fully in the religious life of New England, they reacted unfavorably to the extension of clerical authority. When the pastors "preached themselves" and sought to expand their power in ecclesiastical affairs, they were implicitly belittling the piety and judgment of laymen. Many people were reluctant to relinquish their own role in church government. In 1739, for example, Edward Goddard gathered his thoughts on church government "for the use of my posterity." He reported: "I have heard a great deal of talk about the power of the ministers and the duty of the people to obey them. Some of the talk seemed to me to have a tendency to ecclesiastical tyranny and slavery, and some of it to introduce anarchy or popularity." Goddard distinguished spiritual and ecclesiastical rule in the church. The spiritual rule, he said, consists of preaching the gospel and administering the sacraments, and it rests in the hands of the minister. "To these rulers, in the exercise of this spiritual rule we are to submit ourselves and obey them in the lord." But of ecclesiastical rule, disciplinary proceedings, and other matters of church government, Goddard said: I cannot "concur in that which seems to be the general opinion of the ministers and churches in this part of the country, viz, that the ecclesiastical rule or government of each particular church belongs only to the minister." He argued that important decisions in the church should not be made by one man alone. Should that one man err, he said, "the remedy will be out of reach of the poor of the flock." Goddard preferred that the minister share the church government with lay elders.[24]

Criticism of the ministers was not limited to the defense of traditional lay offices. Pious New Englanders were disturbed whenever

the ministers' actions seemed contrary to the best interests of religion. In a time when the clergymen were generally willing to tolerate a variety of religious opinions, the laymen were often the strongest advocates of doctrinal orthodoxy. For example, Edward Goddard worried that he was witnessing the growth of divers opinions, subversive not only of that good order and discipline that the
word of God prescribes, but also of the most important and fundamental truths of the gospel." In order to help his grandchildren
avoid these subversive views, he left them a list of "hints whereby
they may know how I have been taught." Here he described the
doctrines of original sin and salvation through Christ, and he
warned his progeny to "avoid as far as may be thin and empty discourses advancing philosophy or mere morality as the path to heav-
en and happiness and pressing good works antecedent to faith as
conditions of a sinner's acceptation with God."[25] Laymen were often
more conservative than their ministers in religious matters. Several
clergymen, for example, ran into difficulties with their congregations
when their ideas of Sabbath-keeping proved less strict than those of
the congregation. Ebenezer Parkman, for example, once reported
with chagrin that "a considerable number" of people in Westborough refused to attend a precinct meeting because he had called
it by a notice posted on the meeting house door on the Sabbath.[26]

Pious laymen were particularly suspicious of ministerial associations. The ministers tried to show that religion would benefit from
the strengthening of their profession. But they were forced to admit
that "some do imagine and pretend [that associations meet] to be-
tray the liberties of the churches, and wrest that out of their hands
which the Lord Jesus Christ hath given to them." There is evidence
that some laymen were suspicious of the ministers' motives in holding private gatherings. In the Marlborough Association the ministers
did not "read letters or transact association business while any
stranger was present." On one occasion the ministers stopped their
proceedings because a layman had entered the room. Feeling offended, the stranger "insulted the whole association at a very intol-
erable rate."[27]

One of the most extensive criticisms by a lay person of the increase in clerical authority was drafted in the 1730s and circulated
in manuscript. The essay, titled "A Narrative of the Troubles in the
Second Church in Windsor," was written by Roger Wolcott, a Connecticut layman who became a Supreme Court justice, a major general, and governor of Connecticut. A dispute in the Second Church
over a matter of discipline led Wolcott to attack innovations that

reduced the role of the congregation in church government. In particular, he objected to the notion that if the minister was not given a veto in church meetings, "a mere democracy" would result. Wolcott cited other administrative bodies in which no veto power existed, and in a well-chosen phrase he noted that the existence of the veto created a "mere monarchy." Wolcott believed that by separating themselves from the congregations in matters of church government, the pastors damaged their relationship with the people. He noted that in the early years of the church there had been no such division between ministers and people and that traditional congregational government had yielded "much cordial love between ministers and people." His appeal to the traditional Congregational ideal of the priesthood of all believers must have embarrassed many ministers who preferred not to be reminded of the more "democratic" aspects of the seventeenth-century church.[28]

It is significant that in arguments such as Wolcott's, lay criticism of the ministers was often set forth in the name of religious principles. There was nothing irreverent in the people's opposition to innovations in church government. The ministers may have wished to monopolize religious power and even to claim a major share of New England's store of piety and religious knowledge, but pious laymen refused to equate the ministry with religion. In the eighteenth century, anticlericalism was often based upon religious scruples rather than upon religious indifference. The ability of laymen to criticize ministers in the name of religion was particularly apparent during the Boston smallpox controversy of 1721 and 1722. At this time almost 10 percent of the people of Boston died in a period of a few months. Late in 1721 James Franklin began printing the *New England Courant* and launched the first published attack on the clergy in New England's history. This was an unusual episode, restricted mainly to Boston, but it reveals tensions that existed between ministers and laymen throughout New England.

Although the *Courant* was often critical of the New England clergy, many of the authors who wrote for the paper were men of deep religious piety. This is apparent throughout the journal. On August 28, 1721, as the smallpox epidemic was just beginning in Boston, the *Courant* announced that *"Epidemical Distempers . . . proceed from a Divine-Stretched Out Arm, and are sent as Judgments from an Angry and displeased God."* In facing such judgments there was only one proper response: "the greatest Humiliation, the strictest Observation of the Duties of Repentance."[29] The religious concern of the editors of the *Courant* is apparent in dozens of articles in the paper aimed at the "incouraging of Piety and Virtue" and the "detecting of Vice and Prophaneness." The *Courant* urged its readers to attend Thursday lectures and chastised those who "stand in the Street with a Pinch of Snuff between their Fingers, making Remarks on, and ridiculing those that frequent that sacred Place."[30] It approved of the current trend toward singing in church by rule, but criticized the women who sat during prayer and "smile and play with their fans, an Indication of criminal Carelessness, and Unthoughtfulness of the awful Presence they are in."[31] The *Courant* argued that men who professed to be Christians should practice their beliefs and not "condemn that by our Lives, which we justify by our words."[32]

Thus, the *Courant* urged its readers to lead religious lives, but at the same time it often condemned the people's religious leaders. It urged its readers not to follow their ministers slavishly and condemned that man who would "give up his right and Title to his Senses, and allow his whimsical Ministers (for some such there are in all Countries) to dispose of his Body and Soul."[33] The *Courant* said that the ministers were unable to understand the sufferings of the poor, because "they are honourable supported (as they ought to be) by their People, and see nor feel nothing of the Oppression which is obvious and burdensome to every one else."[34] The *Courant* even suggested that the clergy's sympathy for the rich blinded them to the sins of their wealthy parishioners. One such sin of the well-to-do was their driving coaches on the Sabbath. One author wrote: "I am of the Opinion that if the Common People had followed this Practice, the Pulpits had rung with it long ago."[35]

There are really two aspects to the *Courant's* criticism of the ministers. The first is the argument that the ministers were interfering in matters that had nothing to do with their profession. At the beginning of the smallpox epidemic, a group of ministers led by Cotton Mather had begun to advocate inoculation as a means of warding off the dread disease. Although history has vindicated the ministers who favored inoculation, they seemed to the authors of the *New England Courant* to be ignoring their religious duty to call upon men to humble themselves and repent. The *Courant* asserted that ministers should preach the gospel and not "foist their own *Whims* and *Notions* into the Pulpit; much less may they Vent their own Spleen, and Revenge their private Quarrels there."[36] The paper was particularly critical of those ministers who, it said, demanded that men support inoculation simply because the ministers did: "Twas hop'd, that those Gentlemen of Piety and Learning who pleaded for the Practice, would have brought some other arguments upon the stage than the *naked Merits* of their Character."[37]

A second and even more dangerous practice of the ministers, according to the *Courant,* was their identification of the interests of their profession with the interest of knowledge and religion in general. In a satirical poem the paper accused the ministers of trying to hold a monopoly on knowledge. It read:

> And truly 'tis a fatal Omen,
> When Knowledge, which belongs to no Men
> But to the Clergy and the Judges,
> Gets in the Heads of common Drudges.[38]

The *Courant* asserted that by claiming to be infallible the ministers were actually undermining religion. " 'Tis the Misfortune of many a good Man," the paper argued, "to construe all that is said against his Opinion (In Matters of Indifference) to be against *Religion,* which is in effect to derive it from the Power and Pleasure of Men; and tends (in its Consequences) To destroy *all* Religion." If men are condemned as antireligious for criticizing ministers when they are wrong, the paper said, then they will come to question religion itself. Thus, the fundamental charge that the *Courant* made against some members of the clergy was that they were seeking to found their doctrines and statements on their infallible ministerial character. Against this position James Franklin and his colleagues asserted that religious truths find their origin in a supernatural Being and not on any group of "sacred" men: "Religion derives its authority from GOD alone," Franklin said, "and will not be kept in the Consciences of Men by any Humane Power."[39]

In such statements New England laymen announced that they would not accept the ministers' pretense of ruling over the people by virtue of their sacred clerical status. It was to be hoped, certainly, that ministers were men of God. But so, too, were pious laymen. Roger Wolcott, James Franklin, and others like them refused to indulge the ministers by accepting the creation of religious affairs of a "mere monarchy."

CLERICAL SALARIES. Although the ministers attempted to acquire unaccustomed powers and prestige in the eighteenth century, their ambitions were checked by the refusal of laymen to support an authoritative and wealthy class of religious leaders. Although most pastors remained associated with their original congregations throughout their life, few, if any, were able to command the unquestioning respect of their people. Pious lay people tended to respect the effective clergyman, but they resisted the clerical tendency to identify the voice of the ministers with the voice of God. For example, when Sarah Gill, the daughter of Rev. Thomas Prince, heard that Rev. William Cooper was dangerously ill, she was "exceedingly distressed with the apprehension of losing him." But then, she says, "this thought came into my mind, 'will you have Christ or Mr. Cooper?' and my heart answered, I'll part with Mr. Cooper for Christ."[40]

The perspective that enabled Sarah Gill to "part with Mr. Cooper," allowed other lay people to regard individual ministers as human beings to be judged by their own merits rather than as indispensable clerical leaders. In a variety of ways New Englanders showed their opinions of their ministers, and through their distribution of clerical salaries they controlled their ministers' financial condition and refused to allow clergymen to assume an economic status consistent with their pretentions to a courtly position.

Sometimes the people's judgment of their ministers was affirmative. Laymen who respected their clergymen took notes on sermons and repeated them to their families. Many, like Edward Goddard, recalled the advice of their clergymen many years after hearing a particular sermon.[41] There were numerous ways in which an appreciative people could express their affection for their minister. In Boston, where laymen could attend one of a number of churches, a man might show his respect by attending a particular minister's service. On one occasion, for example, William Waldron was able to write his brother: "Yesterday was our holy communion and I tell you (without vanity) that Judge Sewall was with us all day for no other reason that I know of but to show his good affection to us."[42] Sometimes laymen showed their appreciation by giving the minister small gifts, such as fruit, fish, or candles, or by diligently performing tasks, such as gathering the minister's firewood or helping him in the fields. Timothy Edwards knew that his son Jonathan had won the affection of the people of Northampton when they "continued their usual kindness to him" and built him a barn.[43]

But just as there were many informal ways that laymen could show their approval of ministers, so too there were means by which they could show disapproval. One indication of the congregation's attitude to the minister was conveyed by the people's conduct in church. If the congregation was attentive to the pastor's words, its respect was evident. If, however, the people slept during the sermon, sang lethargically, and ran "out of the house before the

public blessing," their disapproval or apathy was equally apparent.[44] If the laymen of a parish were seriously dissatisfied with
their minister, then, as a last resort, they could dismiss him from his
charge. The dismissal could not be effected without the approval of
a church council, but even with this restriction, many ministers,
including such important clergymen as Samuel Mather and Jonathan Edwards, were dismissed in the eighteenth century. In these
proceedings the power of laymen to create or disavow ministers
was most apparent.

Dismissal was a serious blow to a minister's career. Some could
never attain another parish. Others, who did continue in the ministry, often served inferior parishes. Jonathan Edwards went from
Northampton, one of the chief towns in the Connecticut valley, to
frontier Stockbridge. John Cotton, dismissed from Plymouth, went
to South Carolina.[45] Those ministers who were fortunate enough
not to be in danger of dismissal looked with apprehension on the
fate of their unhappy colleagues. Ebenezer Parkman made a list of
"ministers dismissed from their people since my observation." In all,
he named fifty-five clergymen.[46] A relatively small proportion of
ministers in the early eighteenth century were dismissed from their
parishes, but the possibility of dismissal was a continual reminder
to them that in spite of their pretensions to an important professional status, their continuation as ministers was dependent upon
the approval of laymen.

The ministers' dependence upon their people was particularly apparent in the payment of their salaries, which were raised by a levy
that the people voted upon themselves. In the early eighteenth
century, the salaries generally tended to lag behind inflation. As a
result, many clergymen actually found their earnings declining.
Pastors frequently complained that they were underpaid. In accepting a call, a minister had to deal with men who believed in John
Tufts's phrase: "a Cheap Minister is the Best." Tufts charged that
congregations would often hire a young minister who was ignorant
of the cost of supporting a family, and the young man would accept
the offer thinking "he can live at a much Cheaper Rate, than he
can; and so, thro' his Ignorance in this point, the people impose
upon him, and take advantage to his Hurt, and force him to lie at
their mercy during Life."[47]

Even if a minister had a generous salary at the time of his settlement, he would soon find that his income was insufficient. The wife
and family that he usually acquired soon after accepting a call
would greatly increase his expenses. Furthermore, the clergy were

vulnerable to the inflationary trend in eighteenth-century New England. Josiah Cotton, a preacher to the Indians and a Plymouth justice of the peace, was one of many New Englanders who realized that because of inflation, "Men that have salaries and set fees have been very much wronged."[48]

The ministers, many of whose salaries were fixed at the time of their settlement, were especially "wronged." In 1724 Jabez Fitch asserted that merchants, farmers, tradesmen, and laborers had all raised their prices before accepting colonial bills of credit, with the result that the bills "will not serve for dealing with any sort of persons, upon the same terms as formerly." But while everyone else could raise his prices to keep pace with inflation, the clergymen were caught with fixed incomes. In 1725 Tufts calculated that a minister who had accepted a salary of one hundred pounds a few years before would find his income steadily declining: "For a Hundred of those Bills would then buy about as much as an Hundred and Fifty will now."[49]

Even the Boston ministers, who presided over the wealthiest congregations in New England, experienced financial difficulties. In 1720 Cotton Mather admitted to Thomas Hollis, the English philanthropist, that he would have been unable to send his son to college without help. Cotton said: "You may wonder perhaps, that one in my station here, and not altogether unknown in the world should need the help of any charity on such an occasion." He explained that small ministerial salaries, inflation, and the high cost of living in Boston had impoverished him. "I have several years," he said, "very much subsisted on my revenues of my personal estate, which is now so wasted that I can do no more as formerly."[50] By 1724 the problem of clerical salaries was so general that the Bradford Ministerial Association "spent the day in fasting and prayer in private, principally to implore the compassion and aids and direction of heaven, for ourselves and other ministers in the country under their difficult and distressing circumstances, by reason of a short and scanty maintenance."[51]

The ministers had little power to increase or even to maintain their salaries. When a salary agreement was worked out each member of the parish was assessed a certain portion. Often these dues came to the minister in the form of "country pay." A farmer might pay in wheat, a blacksmith by shoeing the minister's horse, and a tailor by making clothes for the minister's family. If a parishioner's account fell into "arrears" it was extremely difficult for the minister to collect, since going to court was generally discouraged. Cotton

Mather, for example, warned that if the ministers should "take the Remedy which the Law gives them for the recovery of their Arrearages, they would find the Remedy worse than the Disease."[52] John Tufts advised that ministers should "chuse to *Prophecy in Sackcloth* all their Days or betake themselves to the Field . . . rather than Sue their People at the Common Law."[53]

The need to set a good example and to be charitable made it difficult for the minister to take any effective action to raise his income. David Hall, for example, was caught between his desire to treat others kindly and the necessity to pay his debts. The difficulty of his situation is apparent in his effort to "be just and pacifick to my creditors and not cruel by my debtors."[54] When he felt that he was not adequately paid, he advised himself to be patient. During one squabble over his salary, he reflected, "a dog will make a sad noise when hurt; so have I. A sheep will be patient and not open its mouth and so I should have been."[55]

The ministers made a number of proposals to improve their incomes. One of the most elaborate of these plans was John Tufts's suggestion for a graduated income tax. Given a congregation with a hundred families, he said, let the poorest go untaxed; the next poorest twenty should pay the minister with "one day's labour out of Thirty Days"; the other three groups of twenty should pay the minister with one day in twenty-four, eighteen, and twelve respectively. Tufts concluded, "allow Three Shillings for each day, and this will amount to about Two Hundred a Year."[56] This would be considerably more than the average country minister received at that time. Cotton Mather's calculations, set forth in 1700, were more succinct. He declared: "That man does not enough own the Lord for his God, who is not willing to give so much as the Tenth unto Him."[57] Increase Mather also argued that one-tenth of a man's income should be set aside for God, but explained that not all of this need go to the minister. Some could be used to buy Bibles and other religious books, to build churches, help the "Lord's Poor," and support "Colleges, or Schools of Learning."[58]

None of these plans was adopted, and in spite of the number and urgency of the pleas for higher salaries, the financial condition of ministers did not improve. Under these circumstances, numerous clergymen found it difficult to provide well for their families. John Tufts asked: "Must their Prosperity be singled out for Poverty and Misery without having so much as an Hovel, Stable, or Cave for their Shelter; without any thing to feed & cloath them, when their Head is taken from them?"[59]

If a minister's salary was small, and he was forced to spend much of his time doing secular work to supplement his income, all aspects of his ministerial work could suffer. Azariah Mather offered a concise statement about the relationship between a minister's salary and his preaching: "mean Maintenance, what can be the effect but mean Sermons."[60] There was also the danger that these difficulties could discourage able young men from entering the profession. John Tufts warned that a "Scanty Pinching allowance made to the ministers of the Gospel tends to hurt Religion exceedingly in after Ages, by discouraging abundance of our Young Scholars from the study of Divinity."[61]

Salary problems also undermined the relations between many ministers and their people. Clifford K. Shipton has found that between the years 1680 and 1740, 12 percent of New England's ministers were "seriously involved" in financial disputes with their people and 5 percent left their parishes because of such controversies.[62] The salary problem created an atmosphere of clerical anxiety that extended even to those ministers who were not personally troubled by low salaries. Ebenezer Parkman reports that his experience in raking hay one day made him consider "the unhappy times we are fallen into in the Ingratitude of most of the people of the Country to their Ministers, very few besides the Boston ministers being able to Support themselves with what they Receive from their People." Parkman was concerned about the impact of low salaries on the relationship of ministers and people. The people's respect, he wrote, "is much proportion'd to our Externall appearance; when therefore it becomes mean thro their neglect it will be in Danger of becoming worse thro their Contempt."[63]

In this statement Parkman raised the matter that was most troubling in the salary issue: the nature of the ministers' "Externall appearance." Despite their complaints, the ministers still received better incomes than most New Englanders. In the early eighteenth century, for example, ministers earned twice as much as school teachers, and they derived additional income from their farms.[64] Although many were required in John Tufts's phrase to "betake themselves to the Field" for support, none were required to "Prophecy in Sackcloth." The ministers' sense of being underpaid was as much a cultural as an economic phenomenon. The pastors, believing themselves members of the provincial elite, wanted to be able to live like the wealthiest members of the community. But in the matter of clerical salaries, as in disputes over church government and writings about the clergy, the people of New England refused to support the minister's pretentions to an exalted status.

Thus, pious men and women, holding a common interest with

their ministers in religious affairs, refused to accept a concept of leadership that made clergymen uniquely holy and authoritative. Their reluctance prevented Congregational clericalism from providing a satisfactory definition of the minister's role in provincial society.

CHAPTER VI

R EVIVALISM

Clericalism did not work. Far from solving the underlying problems of secularism and fragmentation that troubled eighteenth-century religious leaders, it contributed to those forces by encouraging ministers to become another faction simply contending for its own interests. Moreover, since laymen were unwilling to support in principle or with money the new pretentions of their religious leaders, clericalism did not serve as an effective philosophy around which to organize New England's religious life. It failed to reunite or spiritualize the community, and it failed to win respect for the ministers. The failure of clericalism contributed, however, to the strength of another movement that would have an important bearing on the ministers' position. This was revivalism, the effort to bring about the spiritual regeneration of the whole community. In the eighteenth century, increasing numbers of ministers sought to effect an awakening of piety. Their longing for a revival derived its strength both from the clergymen's self-interest as religious leaders and from their calling as pastoral guides. A religious awakening would deliver the clergy from the tensions and frustations they had experienced and would produce a godly society where pastors and people could dwell together in "mutual love."

COMMUNAL REGENERATION. New England Puritans believed that societies as well as individuals could be either sinful or regenerate. In the seventeenth century, many Puritans had come to America because they believed that England, as a society, was entering a period of religious decline. In the eighteenth century, many people believed that the whole of New England had become degenerate. The essence of the problem was that most men's hearts seemed set upon the selfish quest for worldly gain rather than upon the religious search for Christian grace. The ministers believed that the people's greed made them unattentive during Sunday services; it

109

made them quarrel with each other; it even made them hostile to their pastors. They frequently identified religious decline with divisions in the community. Samuel Dexter, for example, complained that "contention eats out the very vitals of religion."[1] Pastors frequently preached about the need for harmony. They argued that men should concern themselves less with their own personal prosperity and more with the good of the whole community. Joseph Baxter identified salvation with brotherhood. "We know that we have passed from death to life," he said, "because we love the brethren."[2]

The Congregational ministers had little difficulty in listing New England's deficiencies. But it was one thing to describe the problem, another to produce a solution. One means they had used since the seventeenth century was to describe natural disasters, such as epidemics, droughts, storms, or earthquakes, as chastisements from God. If men could be made to feel that their earthly well-being was dependent upon the favor of the Lord, they might be less obsessed with worldly goods and more with divine favor. Thus, the most obscure personal tragedy could be viewed as a warning from an angry God. When a well caved in and killed a man in Framingham, Samuel Sewall concluded his description of this "lamentable accident" by saying: "The Lord help us and his New England people to repent that we may not likewise perish."[3] Tragedies such as the Indian raid on Deerfield in 1704 were treated as loud calls for reformation. Samuel Sewall interpreted this episode as a skirmish "before the slaughter of the witnesses." He asked that "the Lord fit us for the coming of the main battle."[4] When the colonists had difficulties in an Indian war on the Nothern Frontier in 1724, William Waldron wrote his brother: " 'Tis strange to me that the Indians should so escape us seeing we have so many men out after them. . . . Heaven frowns and we may expect nothing of success while Heaven is angry with us."[5]

But although these events could be regarded as judgments from God, their impact was limited. Most of New England's afflictions either affected only individuals or small groups of people or else they were so general as to appear to be ordinary events. A well's caving in or an Indian raid were remarkable and unusual events, but they touched only a few people. However, in the early eighteenth century one remarkable event did affect large numbers of New Englanders. This was the great earthquake of 1727, which shook much of eastern New England. In response there was a religious revival in many towns, which encouraged the ministers to believe that the regeneration and reunification of communities would lead also to renewed respect for their ministers.

Christopher Sergeant, minister of Methuen, Massachusetts, described the earthquake as follows:

It began on Sabbath Day Night between ten & eleven of the clock which put people into the utmost consternation and fright. Many [had] fears that it was the Great Day of the Son of man's appearing in the clouds of heaven. People in general were in expectations of sudden destruction. It began like a most violent clap of Thunder. . . . It was accompanied with most dreadful shocks of the Earth. It continued a minute and a half at least, falling and then returning with violence three times in said Term. It returned very often all night and between five and six a clock in the morning it returned very violent but not so bad as the first. It came with a sudden and sharp crack like firing a gun.[6]

Although the earthquake probably did not take any lives, its destruction was extensive. One man, William Bradbury, reported that in his house, "The windows and doors flew open, the pewter fell off the shelves; glasses, mugs, cups, fell off the mantle tree shelf, [the] chimney broke and shattered."[7] The earthquake was immediately interpreted as an act of God. As Christopher Sergeant reported, many men believed that the end of the world was actually upon them, that it was "the Great Day of the Son of man's appearing."

The earthquake was followed by a period of heightened religious awareness. In Boston after the violent night, "Doctor Mather had a full meeting at his church next morning and Mr. Sewall and Mr. Foxcroft at their churches next night by candle light."[8] In Dedham, Samuel Dexter's people were unusually interested in his sermon. He writes: "I entertained my people on the Sabbath following with discourses suited to the awful occasion and I felt much enlargement in prayer and my affections warm in all the services of the day—the people seemed very attentive."[9] In all, some thirty sermons dealing with the earthquake were published. In some areas in the months following October 29, many new communicants joined the church.

The period of religious regeneration occasioned by the earthquake was associated with a cessation of party strife in many towns. But the impact of the event was usually shortlived, and contentions were soon revived. Samuel Dexter noted that shortly after the earthquake the people of his parish were squabbling about the general court election. Dexter recorded his disappointment in these words: "Lord, what is man that though thy providence may make him tremble, yet [he] stands so little in fear of thee."[10] Ebenezer Parkman began the year 1728 with the hope that the sins that had caused the earthquake would be reformed. But the next month he saw the need to pray to God "graciously to interpose for his people of this town and restore peace and unanimity to us."[11]

It is significant that the ministers associated the religious revival occasioned by the earthquake with social harmony and an increased interest in the word. For a short time whole communities seemed to have been regenerated. The people had been united to one another, and they had expressed an increased interest in their pastors' religious leadership. Although the earthquake revival lasted only a few months, it provided a model for the expectations of further religious awakenings.

The earthquake was followed by other signs of God's disfavor—storms, drought, and disease. But earthquakes and Indian raids could produce only local, temporary religious reformations. What was needed was a more direct outpouring of God's spirit upon the people of New England. The ministers began to hope that God's influence would succeed where earthquakes and Indian raids had failed. So Samuel Dexter prayed: "where people seem to be too much settled upon the lees of carnal security, oh that the still small voice of God's holy spirit might speak with light and efficacy to their hearts in these awakening providences." In Longmeadow, Stephen Williams wrote: "Oh, Lord, thou knowest how to compose our spirits; do it humbly intreat thee by uniting us to Christ and so to one another."[12] In 1737 Jonathan Edwards expressed the general sense of expectation. He wrote: "A dark cloud seems to hang over the land . . . and particularly a spirit of contention, disorder, and tumult, in our capital town and many other places. What seems to be for us to do, is to wait upon God in our straits and difficulties."[13] With the outpouring of God's spirit, the ministers hoped contentions would end and ministers would finally command the respect of their people.

THE MINISTERS FOSTER A REVIVAL.   In 1740 a great revival did occur in New England. Few events have had a greater impact upon American culture than this religious awakening. It affected almost every church in New England, led to thousands of conversions, and resulted in important changes in the ecclesiastical structure of the Puritan colonies. Historians have pondered the causes of the revival for over two centuries. Most modern scholars agree that the revival was related somehow to social tensions in New England, but none has developed a definitive explanation for this unprecedented manifestation of religious emotion.[14] What is apparent, however, when we look at the events culminating in the revival through the ministers' eyes is that the Awakening was sought after, fostered, and nourished by the Congregational ministers. The revival was not, as many authors have suggested, the work of itinerant ministers. It was rather the product of scores of local pastors throughout New England. Moreover, the ministers had a clear conception of what to expect from the revival—attentive congregations, an unusual concern for religious matters, respect for the minister.

These expectations were based upon their experience with episodes such as the earthquake of 1727. They were reinforced by their experience with revivals that preceded the Great Awakening. These revivals were usually local and had affected only one or two communities at a time, but they were remarkable for having occurred without the encouragement of natural causes. In Northampton Solomon Stoddard's "harvests" had regularly brought large numbers of people into the church. Further south on the Connecticut River, Timothy Edwards led an impressive revival among his people in 1716. Stephen Williams described this awakening as "an extraordinary stir among the people at East Windsor."15 Revivals of this sort, where large groups of people became intensely interested in the state of their souls, were interpreted as direct outpourings of God's spirit.

The most extensive revival experienced in New England prior to 1740 was the awakening of 1735 that swept the Connecticut valley. This movement began in Northampton, when large groups of people suddenly showed increased religious concern. Soon the same phenomenon occurred in other valley towns. Like the revivals occasioned by storms and earthquakes, the 1735 awakening was accompanied by a temporary cessation of parish quarrels. In a letter to Benjamin Colman, Jonathan Edwards regretted that with the end of the revival strife had returned: "Contention and party spirit has been the old iniquity of this town," he wrote, "and as God's spirit has been more and more wtihdrawn, so this spirit has of late manifestly revived."16 The awakening of 1735 was short-lived, but its influence was great. For it showed that large groups of people could become involved simultaneously in a religious revival. Edwards's account of this awakening, the *Narrative of Surprising Conversions,* enjoyed wide circulation and helped people prepare for a more general revival.

Five years later the Great Awakening began. Its origins in New England are usually traced to the preaching journey of George Whitefield in the fall of 1740. But before Whitefield even arrived in New England many ministers had anticipated and were preparing for a religious revival. Early in 1740 there was news of an awakening in Southold, Long Island, under the direction of James Davenport. Eleazar Wheelock, minister of Lebanon, Connecticut, visited Southold and found Davenport "full of life and zeal." In a letter to Rev. Stephen Williams he described Davenport's success and wished that he and Williams could be as effective in their own parishes.[17] The news of George Whitefield's triumphs in the middle colonies, like the local achievements of Davenport, led ministers to hope for awakenings in their own parishes. Whitefield's sermons were published in Boston in 1739 and 1740, and Benjamin Colman gathered news of Whitefield's successes and sent reports throughout New England. Hearing of the evangelist's success, William Williams, minister of Hatfield, wrote Colman that he hoped that "Mr. Whitefield's labors might provoke to emulation the ministry everywhere."[18]

On September 14, 1740, Whitefield arrived in Rhode Island. He preached in Newport on the 15th and 16th and in Bristol on the 17th. On Thursday evening, September 18, he came to Boston. There the Congregational ministers encouraged him in his work. On Friday Whitefield went to the home of William Cooper, Benjamin Colman's college at the Brattle Street Church. There "most of the ministers of the town met him and gave him a hearty welcome." They told him that they had already let "the world know in print our esteem of him" and that they would welcome him into their pulpits. That afternoon he preached in the Brattle Street Church to a congregation that included between twenty and thirty ministers. Colman reports that Whitefield's "holy fervour of devotion in prayer and of address to the souls of his hearers in preaching were such as we had never before seen or heard." The next morning he preached "a more excellent discourse yet" at the Old South Church. Colman was careful to point out to Whitefield that many ministers were in his audience and were deeply affected by his words. He says: "After the sermon I observed to him the pews of the room full of ministers wherein he might read their hearts, their visible pleasure and joy at his arrival, and satisfaction in the taste they had had of his ministry."[19]

Colman wished to make it plain that in Boston the ministers supported Whitefield and were among those most moved by his preaching. He hoped that all people would benefit from Whitefield's preaching, but he was particularly pleased that Whitefield's presence seemed to encourage men to support their ministers. He asserted that if the ministers could emulate Whitefield, then "the love of our people to us, their pastors, and ours to them will be increased and confirmed greatly to our mutual edification and growth in grace." Colman noted further that the people were already drawn more closely to their ministers when they saw the clergy's "pleasure in their satisfaction" with Whitefield's preaching.[20]

After Whitefield's initial success in Boston, he visited other parts of New England, where he was continually encouraged by the settled ministers. In Cambridge he entertained a number of clergymen at the home of Rev. Nathaniel Appleton with an account of "the Time and Manner of the powerful working of the Spirit of God upon him." Later he preached in the Harvard Yard "to incredible multitudes, and with wondrous power."[21] In Hampton, New Hampshire, on October 1, Nicholas Gilman reported that he heard "an excellent sermon from the Reverend Mr. Whitefield on the green." He and a number of other ministers dined that evening with Whitefield. He concluded: "O my God, I pray for him, that he may have larger proportions of thy spirit. Let his heart be confirmed, his reason continued, and his labors prospered for the good of souls."[22]

At the news of Whitefield's success, ministers throughout New England sent him invitations to preach in their churches. From the frontier in Longmeadow, Massachusetts, for example, Stephen Williams watched Whitefield's progress with increasing interest. On September 23, four days after Whitefield's first sermons in New England's metropolis, Williams recorded: "this day I heard the Rev. Mr. Whitefield is come to Boston and his preaching is well approved of—Oh, Lord, grant good may come by this, his visit to our country." On October 11, Williams said: "I hear of the extraordinary labors and services of the Reverend Mr. George Whitefield in one place and another." A few days later he wrote Whitefield asking him to preach in Longmeadow and noted: "If he does come, I desire it may be to our edification and real benefit and advantage." Whitefield was unable to come ot Longmeadow, but he did preach in nearby Westfield and Suffield. Williams attended him in both places. In each town, Williams says: "I heard him preach to a great auditory. He is a warm fervent preacher; he has an inimitable faculty of touching the affections and passions." Two days later he prayed for a still greater revival: "Oh that God would appear, and advance his own kingdom amongst his people in this land."[23]

George Whitefield spent only a few weeks in New England, but in the two years following his triumphant journey the revival affected almost all of the towns and villages of the region. After Whitefield's departure another itinerant, a Presbyterian revivalist from New Jersey, Gilbert Tennent, arrived in Boston and made a more lengthy trip through New England, preaching in many places that his English predecessor had missed. Tennent was, in turn, followed by dozens of other preachers, who carried the gospel to all areas of New England with the encouragement of local pastors.[24]

Itinerant ministers like Whitefield and Tennent were important catalysts to revivalism in New England, but their dramatic successes should not be allowed to obscure the far greater contribution to the Awakening which came from local pastors. For many years they had tried to foster religious revivals. Now many of them sought the help of itinerants to produce revivals in their parishes, but they alone nourished the revival from week to week after the itinerants left. In its early stages, the Congregational ministers were the strongest supporters of the Awakening, for, seemingly, they had everything to gain from the new enthusiasm for religion. The awakened people attended church in large numbers, listened attentively to the preacher's words, and respected the minister's religious leadership.

In parish after parish the revival was fostered by the settled pastor. After a town was visited by an itinerant, the regular minister was left to preside over the awakened community. For example, when Gilbert Tennent visited Westborough, Ebenezer Parkman reported that the people became increasingly interested in religion and formed six religious socities. Quite possibly the visit by an important itinerant had initially helped produce the Westborough revival. But the problems guiding the movement rested entirely in Parkman's hands. He told Jonathan Edwards that he hoped to give careful direction to his people. "I wish," he wrote, "I might be able suitably to preside over them and teach them the good knowledge and right way of the Lord, that I might with skill and success, conduct and promote and ripen their convictions, that they may be truly converted and their sanctification carried on."[25]

Throughout New England local ministers carried on the revival after the itinerants had helped to generate initial religious enthusiasm. In Cambridge, for example, Henry Flynt reported that "many scholars appeared to be in great concern as to their souls and eternal state." They were "first moved by Mr. Whitefield's and after by Mr. Tennent's preaching." But after the departure of these itinerants the regular minister, Nathaniel Appleton, was "more close and affecting in preaching," and led other students to a state of religious concern.[26]

Even villages that were not visited by evangelists had revivals in the early 1740s. The news of a revival in a nearby town always encouraged hopes of a similar awakening in a community. Early in 1741 Stephen Williams reported with enthusiasm that the revival was making progress in the towns north of Longmeadow. He wrote: "I hear there is a hopeful revival of religion at Deerfield and at Northampton especially among young ones. I rejoice to hear of this and I pray God this may be the case in all our towns and parishes."[27] The story of the revival in Boston particularly impressed people in outlying areas. In New Hampshire, Nicholas Gilman responded enthusiastically to the news from the metropolis. On May 5, 1741, he wrote: "Hear that at Boston and other places particularly Cambridge Newton people continue to be more and more awakened. Oh Lord may they all be converted. Oh that the glorious work may be carried on thro the land."[28]

Many pastors actually generated their own awakenings; so the movement actually had focal points in hundreds of communities throughout New England. For example, in June of 1741 Marston Cabot of Thompson, Connecticut, reported that there were signs of a revival in his town. "There seems to be a shaking of late among the dry bones. God increase it and let those that have life already have it more abundantly." In August three candidates whom he examined for communion told him "they had been much enlightened and quickened by my late preaching."[29] In Sutton, Massachusetts, David Hall reported that on April 26, 1741, at his sermon he "observed many in tears" and on the previous Sabbath he had "observed almost the whole assembly in tears at the same time, so mighty came the word of the Lord upon them." Private religious meetings were established where Hall's preaching was occasionally "attended with Great Awakenings."[30]

Local ministers frequently helped one another produce revivals in their parishes. Eleazar Wheelock, who had preached successfully in his own Lebanon parish, was invited by other ministers in his region, including Jonathan Edwards, to assist them.[31] The story of the events surrounding the most famous discourse of the revival provides a valuable example of the way that local pastors cooperated in fostering the Awakening. On July 7, 1741, Stephen Williams, Eleazar Williams, and a third minister conducted a religious service at the meeting house in Suffield, Connecticut. Stephen Williams reports that "the congregation [was] remarkably attentive and grave." That evening at a second service in Suffield "there was considerable crying among the people, in one part of the house or another, yea, and a screeching in the streets." The following morning the congregation was again "considerably affected and many cried out." At noon the three ministers dined with Rev. Peter Reynolds "and then went over to Enfield where we met dear Mr. Edwards of Northampton."

The distance from Suffield to Enfield was only three miles. So it is quite possible that many of the Enfield people had attended the recent Suffield meetings, and that the Suffield people, already wrought up to a high pitch of emotional intensity, accompanied the ministers to Enfield. That afternoon Edwards preached what Williams called "a most awakening sermon." Williams reported the consternation caused by Edward's preaching. "Before the sermon was done there was a great moaning and crying out throughout the whole house—'What shall I do to be saved. Oh, I am going to hell. Oh, what shall I do for a Christ.'" Edwards was "obliged" to stop preaching because of the "amazing" shrieks and cries. When the congregation finally became still, the ministers met separately with the people. Williams reports: "The power of God was seen and several souls were hopefully wrought upon that night and Oh the cheerfulness and pleasantness of their countenances. . . . We sung a hymn, and prayed, and dispersed the assembly." From Williams's account it is not clear whether Jonathan Edwards even completed his "Enfield Sermon." It is clear, however, that before Edwards even arrived in Enfield, the people of the region had been brought to a high pitch of religious excitement by the local ministers.

After the Enfield sermon there were revivals in other parishes in the region. Stephen Williams reports that on July 9 "in the morning when I awoke I had a great desire in my soul to see at Longmeadow what I had seen at Enfield." He rode home, accompanied by his brother Eleazar. Longmeadow was only seven miles from Enfield, so some of its citizens may have attended the recent services in Suffield and Enfield. At any rate they would have heard stories of the great outpouring of God's spirit in those towns. In Longmeadow, Williams then conducted a religious service where many people were affected, including one girl who had "such a discovery of Christ that was almost too much for the human frame to bear."

Each of these revivals was directed by local ministers who assisted each other in conducting services. Similarly, the early revival in Boston and other towns was led by local pastors, who were assisted occasionally by itinerants who were invited to preach. These were the halcyon days of the religious movement that came to be known as the Great Awakening. The community seemed reunited in piety and holiness. Men treated each other with charity. The ministers were able to offer dramatic religious leadership to their people, and the people, in turn, held their ministers in high esteem. But the clerical euphoria of the early months of the Awakening was short-lived. An episode in Springfield after the Enfield sermon, and many other similar incidents throughout the colonies, indicated the course that the movement would soon take. After Stephen Williams had conducted his first revival meeting in Longmeadow, he went to an evening service in Springfield. At the end of the meeting, he left the church and found his son, John, in the churchyard, "speaking freely boldly and earnestly to the people and warning of them against damnation and inviting them to Christ." Williams tried to interrupt his son, but the youth "seemed beyond himself and had great discoveries of the love of Christ and had a great concern for souls."[32] Overwhelmed by the spirit within, the youth was determined to preach to others.

This was Williams's first encounter with an aspect of the revival that was soon to challenge all the settled pastors of New England. It had been assumed that an awakened laity would honor the religious leadership of the regular clergy. But what would happen if excited laymen, who believed they were guided by the spirit of the Lord, decided that they should not only receive, but also give, religious instruction? When this did occur, it became apparent that revivalism could undermine as well as enhance the religious authority of established ministers.

CHAPTER VII

⚌OWARD A NEW IDENTITY

The early months of the Great Awakening were undoubtedly among the most satisfying times in the lives of many Congregational ministers. They often gained a new confidence in their preaching and were able to deliver long sermons without notes. Their audiences listened closely to their words and responded with obvious emotion. During the week many people sought their pastors' counsel in spiritual matters. Obscure country parsons suddenly became charismatic leaders. But the ministers' satisfaction was often short-lived, for the course of religious enthusiasm proved fickle and could not be contained within the traditional ecclesiastical structure of New England. Awakened laymen were as ready to denounce as to follow their pastors. Many deserted their former ministers for new pastors or new churches. In the religious turmoil that followed the radical revival, the ministers found that neither clericalism nor revivalism provided a stable description of their professional role. Bereft of both of these identities they began to redefine the basis of ministerial leadership and arrived at a distinctive American conception of the status of the religious guide.

RELIGIOUS ENTHUSIASM. In the early stages of the Great Awakening, roughly from 1740 to 1742, the ministers believed that the revival would revitalize the ecclesiastical order of New England. At first most New England ministers ardently supported the Great Awakening, for it seemed to be the advent of a new era of religious sincerity, brotherly love, and respect for the ministers. Rev. William Shurtleff's report on the revival in Portsmouth expresses the optimism that many ministers felt. He wrote: "Families are in general stirred up to perform family duties which have been shamefully neglected; praying and singing of psalms and discoursing of the things of God is become common." He was particularly pleased with the cessation of bickering and rivalry in the town. "We seem united together to praise and serve God in one mind and heart loving one another with brotherly love and dear affection."[1]

But, unfortunately, the early harmony of the revival lasted for only a short time. The ministers had hoped to channel the revival spirit through their own religious leadership. During the Awakening, however, men began increasingly to challenge religious institutions in the name of religious spirit. As we have seen, New England laymen had occasionally criticized the ministers for failing to live up to their own religious ideals even before the Great Awakening. Now those isolated and infrequent criticisms reached a crescendo of vituperation.

At first the ministers themselves had led the Awakening by preaching moving sermons to their people. Then the people began to participate more actively in religious services by crying out, exhorting, and having visions. Next the radicals of the revival, laymen and clergymen who believed they were directly inspired by God, began to disregard traditional religious practices. Uneducated laymen preached without formal preparation. Itinerants "invaded" parishes and delivered sermons without the approval of regular pastors, and enthusiasts claimed that many clergymen were unconverted and hence unfit to lead their people. Thus, instead of fulfilling the purpose of the ministerial profession, the Great Awakening actually undemined the position of the clergy. Ironically, the nourishing of the Great Awakening was the greatest achievement of the ministers in the eighteenth century, but at the same time, the fruition of the Awakening posed the century's greatest challenge to their ideal of professional religious leadership.

The transformation of the Awakening from a religious revival to a social crisis was subtle and gradual. From the start, the movement was accompanied by a sense of God's immediate presence in the world. In the early stages the new spirituality was controlled by the regular ministers. This is most evident in their revivalistic preaching. After 1740 many ministers actually felt that God spoke directly through their preaching. Believing that he would direct their words, they rejected the use of notes and preached extemporaneously. After a revivalist had delivered a sermon he would often claim that he had been graciously assisted."[2] On one notable occasion, after Nicholas Gilman had preached an eight-hour sermon, he reported: "I found myself grow lively in sermon, and I trust the spirit of the Lord came powerfully on me and the assembly." He believed that he had been divinely assisted in understanding the scriptures before him. "Jesus (I am persuaded) opened my understanding to understand the scriptures. . . . The nature of the present work much unfolded. . . . Many portions of scripture opened."[3]

The new conception of God's immediate influence in religious affairs soon manifested itself in other ways. Earlier New Englanders, who believed that God seldom made his presence known to men, were restrained and orderly in their worship. But in the period of the revival it was not unusual to hear that a congregation had been "drowned in tears" or that a dozen people had fainted.[4] Ministers justified such disorders by claiming that they were manifestations of God's spirit.[5] The idea of God's immediate presence made a difference in the way that the word was preached. It also made a difference in the conduct of laymen. In episodes such as the series of awakenings in Enfield and Longmeadow, it is sometimes difficult to know who was actually leading the revival movement. The ministers appear to have initiated the awakening in these towns, but it is quite possible that the crying out of the congregations was equally important in keeping people's emotions inflamed. Sometimes the revival appears to have come simultaneously upon the minister and his congregation.

Such a revival occurred in Durham, New Hampshire, under the leadership of Rev. Nicholas Gilman. In November 1741, the townsmen showed signs of heightened religious interest. On the seventeenth day of that month Gilman reports that in the evening thirty or forty people came "from all quarters on the rumor that there was to be a meeting at my house." He prayed with them, read from a religious tract and "added a word of exhortation." Three days later he held another meeting in the evening at his home. Though the night was "dark and dirty" a large crowd gathered. Significantly, the work that Gilman chose to read them was Jonathan Edwards's *Narrative of Surprising Conversions.* Gilman says he "read part of it and made some remarks to the people." Quite possibly the news from other parishes where the revival was already in progress and the information from Edwards's *Narrative* prepared the people of Durham for the events that followed. At any rate, the town was soon to experience one of the most intense awakenings of the period.

On January 29, 1742, Gilman reports that he "had more joy than usual through the day." In the evening, when at the end of the service the people seemed in a great haste to leave the meeting house, Gilman says: "I was moved to tell them that if I could see them flocking to heaven as they were from meeting it would make my heart leap within me." On hearing this admonition the parishioners "drew into the house again and were attentive." Gilman resumed his discourse, and he and his people "continued in religious exercises all night." He says that it seemed the Lord did "anoint me with that holy anointing . . . and as it were touched my eyes as with a coal from his altar." Gilman was not the only person affected that night. He says the whole congregation "had the presence of the Lord with us in a very wonderful manner." The people "held on through the night, blessing and praising, admiring and adoring God and the redeemer, sometimes praying, then singing, exhorting, advising and directing and rejoicing together in the Lord." Some members of the congregation even had visions. One "saw a white dove come down into the meeting house." Another "declared he saw two angels." A third "saw a bright light like an exceeding bright star about as big as a man's fist," come into the building. Later, Gilman recalled, "it seemed the shortest, and was, I think, the sweetest night that I have seen."

The religious intensity continued in Durham for the next few months. Gilman was passionately involved in the revival and his preaching seems to have inspired the town's awakening. But his ministerial voice was soon joined by the voices of laymen who believed that the spirit moved them to participate in the revival. On March 4, Gilman encouraged a girl named Mary Reed to describe a vision she had had to the whole church. After she had spoken, Gilman added a "word of exhortation" and then he says: "It appeared to me that the Holy Ghost came down with power upon the people so that there was almost an universal outcry, some rejoicing and others lamenting, but few I believed were unmoved."

As time passed the laymen of the parish were increasingly involved in the movement. A meeting on March 14 seems to have been built largely around their religious utterances. First Gilman preached a sermon; then he read "Mary Reed's last vision," which he had transcribed from her words the previous day. Then for a time the congregation appears to have led the service: "Two youths under good influences and of regular life, fell into visions and spake out, so that they were heard all over the congregation. . . . People attended, some spake and exhorted, presently an outcry began which lasted til within night." Gilman concluded the service by reporting on one of his parishioner's religious experiences—"I read over two visions or trances of Stephen Bruse."[6]

Although Nicholas Gilman maintained a semblance of control over his parish, it is clear that the spiritual powers that had enabled him to initiate the revival were soon shared with many other Christians. Apparently, God did not simply speak through the religious leader to his followers. Instead he chose to speak through many plain men and women in Gilman's parish. Thus, the Awakening began to undermine the unique position of the minister relative to his congregation.

The pastor's distinctive position was also challenged in many cases by ministers from other parishes. Just as many revivalists believed that God should guide them in their actual preaching, some also believed that he should direct them in deciding when and where to preach. In following their inclinations they disregarded traditional New England ideas about preaching in other ministers' parishes. Since the early days of the Puritan colonies, ministers had exchanged pulpits and combined their efforts in leading religious services, but they had only preached in other men's pulpits by invitation. Even the first itinerant preaching during the Awakening had worked within this traditional pattern. Ministers such as George Whitefield and Gilbert Tennent were invited to preach in Boston and in other New England towns by the settled pastors. Typically, when Chester Williams wanted to encourage a revival in Hadley, Massachusetts, he wrote to Jonathan Edwards entreating him to "come over and assist us in seeking God by prayer [and] fasting for the outpouring of his holy spirit upon this place."[7]

A new pattern developed, however, when revivalistic fervor was at a peak. Increasingly, men who believed they were directed by God's spirit began to preach without the invation of settled pastors. David Hall, an enthusiastic preacher and minister of Sutton, Massachusetts, once believed he had a call to preach in Hopkinton and was enraged when Rev. Samuel Barrett refused to allow him to preach in his meeting house. Hall had gone there "at the request of the people" and believed he should have been allowed to preach. Later he reports that he was in "great concern" because Rev. Isaac Burr of Worcester refused "the urgent request of some people of Worcester to hear me preach again with them." In his diary, Hall commented disparagingly on the condition of Burr's soul. Rev. Burr, he said, "is, I fear, a stranger too much himself to the power of Godliness; otherwise surely he would rejoice in having his people in concern about their souls and in the help of such ministers as wish them salvation."[8] Like David Hall, Nicholas Gilman believed that an invitation from a congregation to preach should outweigh the opposition of the minister. Gilman was contemptuous of ministers who opposed his preaching in their parishes. On one occasion he reports that Rev. Christopher Toppan of Newbury "was fierce in his opposition to any strangers speaking among his people." In his diary Gilman reflected: "May he be brought to a better mind." When he was denied the pulpit in a town, Gilman would often preach in a private house.[9]

In addition to the regular ministers who traveled from parish to parish, there were other men who became itinerants even without formal training or a regular call to the ministry. Many itinerants preached a few times and then returned to their ordinary tasks. Others became Baptist or Separatist ministers. One of the most persistent of these lay preachers was Joseph Prince. In 1743 he appeared at the home of Nicholas Gilman in Durham, New Hampshire.[10] He preached in Durham on July 25 and 29. Three years later John Cleaveland heard Prince in Brookline,[11] and in 1748 he was in Sudbury and Exeter.[12]

Inevitably, the enthusiasts of the Awakening began to criticize the more moderate members of the clergy. The radicals felt that the immediate presence of God had established a new standard of legitimacy for preaching and preachers. Enthusiasts believed that it was the spirit of God that led men to deliver passionate sermons and to preach in parishes other than their own. They were critical of ministers who seemed to them to lack a call from God. One such enthusiast was Richard Woodbury, who considered himself an ambassador of God and warned the ministers to beware of their unholiness. For example, he wrote William Parsons, minister of South Hampton, New Hampshire, that a great battle was coming. "We hear the sound of the trumpet and the alarm of war," he said. "Prepare to give account of your stewardship since you have had the care and charge of precious souls committed to you." He warned Parsons against being on the wrong side when the end came and identified opposition to the Awakening with opposition to Christ. "If you have not experienced the love of Christ . . . (and I fear you have not, if you oppose the reformation of the present day), humble yourself before the Lord and seek the Lord before it is too late."[13]

Implicit in Woodbury's warnings to Parsons is the idea that a man must be converted in order to be a successful minister. New England's pastors had always agreed that clergymen should be converted, but they were reluctant to make conversion a prerequisite for ordination and generally agreed that God's grace could be conveyed by the preaching of any minister, good or bad. Men like Woodbury, however, often made spirituality the sole test of a minister's qualifications and made harsh judgments concerning the religious estate of ministers. George Whitefield had said after his first visit to New England that "the generality of preachers talk of an unknown, unfelt Christ." Subsequently, other revivalists condemned particular clergymen for a lack of piety. Itinerants like James Davenport preached against local ministers who denied them their pulpits. According to tutor Henry Flynt, Andrew Croswell had "publickly in great assemblies declared that half the ministry in Connecticut and this province [Massachusetts] are unconverted." He said Croswell had incited the populace to disregard their settled ministers. "These things people love to hear and follow his preaching from tavern to tavern, many having puffed up in themselves and livened with ill disposition against the college ministers."[14] This form of criticism was practiced even in the halls of Harvard and Yale. John Cleaveland, for example, sympathized with a classmate who, he said, was fined five shillings "for speaking the truth in the hall, and the truth was that he stayed home [from worship] because of the coldness of the air and of the preacher."[15]

The enthusiasts believed they had the spirit of God on their side and that therefore there was no need to observe the old restraints that had prevented ministers from judging each other's spiritual condition. The case was stated succinctly by Jonathan Parsons in a letter to Ebenezer Turrell. He declared that truth was more vital than peace. "I pray God," he wrote, "that I may never have my eyes so blinded as to imagine that quietness in the churches with a corrupt ministry, is better than the boldest meet endeavors to alarm mankind of the danger of the same though it stir up strife."[16]

The enthusiasts' assumption that the spirit of God accompanied them was reflected in their ordinations, when they began to establish their own clergy. As we have seen, the conventional New England ordination had become a formal ceremony accompanied by a hearty feast. In contrast, the enthusiasts believed that in their ordinations the spirit of God was actually present. The sanctification of the new minister was carried on by God rather than by man. In a letter to her son John, Abigail Cleaveland sought to explain the differences between the old and the new ordinations. She wrote: "I have been at several ordinations before this day and I used to think it too solemn a transaction to be frolicken days, but I never saw such ordinations before as I see now. The God of heaven comes down. I cannot tell you, it is so wonderful."[17] John's father, Joseph Cleaveland, told him about a recent New Light ordination. "Jedediah Hyde was ordained over the church of Christ in Norwich," he wrote, "and it was such a day as Norwich never knew before. It was even like unto the day of Pentecost. The spirit of God descended like a mighty rushing wine upon the saints of God."[18] When John Cleaveland was himself ordained the next year in Essex, Massachusetts, his brother Ebenezer inquired about the ordination and spoke of the wonders of ordinations he had seen. "I want to know," he wrote, "whether you was anointed over that glorious flock with the unction of the holy ghost in such a glorious manner as I have seen some since I came home. I have seen the descent of the holy dove upon several persons when they were ordained in such a manner as the oil ran upon every saint so that every one was a witness that God did the work and that he separated them for that holy work."[19]

The enthusiasts were not all as radical as the Cleavelands. But these extreme views show their tendency to believe in the immediate presence of God in their souls, in their churches, and in their ministry. Against this confidence neither a college education, nor Congregational ordination, nor ministerial associations could persuade an awakened people to remain loyal to their traditional religious leaders.

THE MINISTER AS PASTORAL GUIDE. The enthusiasts' threat to the traditional pattern of religious leadership in New England was profound. The Congregational ministers believed that one became a clergyman by being well educated, by serving a term of ministerial apprenticeship, and by receiving a dignified ordination. The enthusiasts argued that one became a minister by being converted by God, by receiving a direct call from the Lord to preach, and by being ordained by the Holy Spirit. The established ministers believed that a clergyman composed effective sermons by spending long hours in the study and that he should preach in another congregation than his own only by invitation of the settled pastor. The enthusiasts often entered the pulpit without formal preparation and relied upon God's spirit to direct their words; they preached whenever and wherever they believed the Lord called them; and they delivered their sermons with or without the permission of settled ministers. When the established pastors expressed their hostility to these innovations, the enthusiasts claimed that their opponents were unconverted and that hence their ministry was illegitimate. Thus, the enthusiasts sought to replace the traditional conception of religious leadership in New England with a new scheme that emphasized God's immediate presence in the world.[20]

The Congregational ministers had difficulty in answering the charge that they were not called to their work by God. They had traditionally claimed that proper training qualified them to become ministers, and yet they believed that a prospective clergyman should feel that God had chosen him to enter the ministry. They had come to regard this divine sanction simply as the Lord's approval of the institutions they used to educate and ordain their ministers. But at the beginning of the Great Awakening they were attracted to individuals who appeared to have received a more direct call from God. The most striking example of this attraction appears in a letter Benjamin Colman wrote to George Whitefield, urging him to visit New England. He admitted that he and his fellow clergymen, well trained as they were, had begun as ministers without Whitefield's spiritual gifts. "It is we," he said, "that are lying at your feet to receive justification, reproof and correction in righteousness, because we did not begin our ministry with that life and spirit with which God has inspired the late happy methodists from Oxford to begin theirs."[21] This was a remarkable statement from the man who was the most prestigious New England minister at the time of the Awakening. It indicates the depth of the clergy's yearning for a new "life and spirit" to enhance their own ministries.

This clerical longing for a deeper sense of God's presence in the world was apparent wherever Whitefield preached. For example, after hearing him, Samuel Dexter, minister at Dedham, wrote: "Ten thousand worlds would I give, . . . to feel and experience what I believe that man does." He called himself "a poor, dull ignorant creature" and admitted that he needed "enlightening and quickening continually."[22] In such statements the pastors' interest in developing a more vital and emotional relationship to God and to their people is apparent. At the same time, however, they were cautious about what they perceived as extremes of religious emotion. Even before Whitefield arrived in New England, some ministers were concerned that Davenport's Southold revival was out of control. In a letter to Eleazar Wheelock, Stephen Williams asked "Whether when the affections of Christians or ministers are lively and vigorous they are not in some special danger."[23]

As we have seen, the Congregational clergy generally approved of the revival in its early stages. But when enthusiastic supporters of the Awakening began to challenge the professional position of the ministers, themselves, most clergymen were dismayed. Early in January 1741, Stephen Williams, who had ardently admired Whitefield's recent preaching, noted cryptically: "I am concerned because of the conduct of some preachers and candidates." On June 12, 1741, he reported: "I hear of strange things—ecstasies that

persons fall into. I am full of fears." When he learned of the increasingly frenetic activities of the radical New Light, James Davenport, he prayed: "Oh, Lord graciously preserve from extrava-
gances."[24]

The regular ministers were generally hostile to lay preachers.[25]
In 1748 Israel Loring included in a "catalogue of mercies" his
thanks that "no encouragement was given to [a] wandering blind
exhorter, who came among us, by people's going to hear him."[26]
Ebenezer Parkman was usually glad to welcome regular ministers
to his Westborough pulpit, but he had no patience for "rambling
Fellows that go about preaching" and would not open his pulpit to
them.[27] Even Nicholas Gilman, who was himself one of the Awakening's great itinerants, was unwilling to accept every self-styled
preacher who came to Durham.[28]

As time passed, divisions of opinion concerning the revival developed among the ministers themselves. Some, who were called "New
Lights," generally approved of emotional preaching and of the
Great Awakening. Others, who styled themselves "Old Lights,"
believed that intellect should play a predominant role in religion
and felt that much of the revival was a fraud. But in spite ot their
dis agreement on these points, both factions were in agreement that
they, the well-educated Congregational ministers, were the legitimate religious leaders of New England. When their own position of
leadership was threatened by enthusiasts, the differences among
them quickly vanished. On the question of the ministry, the real
division created by the Great Awakening was between the vast
majority of the regular clergymen, New Light and Old Light alike,
and the enthusiastic pastors and laymen who challenged their authority. For example, when the Boston Association of ministers
announced on June 30, 1742, that they would not invite the itinerant
James Davenport to preach in their pulpits, the members were careful to distinguish their disapproval of him from their approval of
the Awakening. The ministers particularly warned against "the im-
prudence of its friends" and "the virulent opposition of its ene-
mies."[29]

Often men who were supporters of the revival were critical of
enthusiast itinerants who sought to preach in their parishes. David
Hall, for example, described one meeting in which he was overwhelmed by exhorters. First, he said, a "mulatto fellow fell to exhorting." Hall "strove to check him but could not stop him." Then
another man "fell to shouting Hosanna or Hallelujah and got up on
a chair and uttered some wild rapture." Then, Hall reports, a third

man "thrust his fist out near my face and perfectly railed at me uttering such words as these, that the devil was in my heart."[30]

Increasingly, the established ministers of New England looked upon the Great Awakening as a period of disorder. Ebenezer Parkman, whose own parish was not deeply troubled with religious divisions, regarded the turmoil of other towns with great apprehension. Some of the entries in his diary for 1744 convey his sense of the chaos of the times. On February 1, 1744, he reported: "Disturbances in Hopkintown are risen to great Heights and Richard and Nathaniel Smith are sent to Jayl for breaking up the worship last Sabbath. Great Troubles also in Leicester. Reverend Mr. Goddard in such Darkness about his own State that the last Sabbath, though Communion Day, he went not out to preach."[31] A few months later he reported that "Great Disorder" had been caused in Ipswich by Richard Woodbury's letters in the name of "the King of Kings and Lord of Lords."[32]

The New England clergy had hoped that a great religious revival would heal the divisions that had developed in the early eighteenth century between the ministers and their people. The revival that did occur in the early 1740s was probably more intense than any had ever hoped for. But instead of reuniting men, it seemed to divide them further. Instead of enhancing the ministers' position, it exposed the clergy to new challenges. These challenges forced the ministers to shore up and redefine their positions of clerical leadership, a process that is most apparent in the ordination sermons of the 1740s.

In part, the ministers' response consisted in a reiteration of traditional arguments about their own importance. As in the past, the clergymen portrayed themselves as a group of men who were elevated by education and office above their fellow Christians. Stephen Chase argued that "the Ministers of Christ, and the Holy Angels, who inhabit the celestial Regions, resemble each other in the glorious Work they are severally employed in."[33] Jonathan Edwards elaborated on this image. "The ministry in general," he said,

or the whole Number of faithful Ministers, being all united in the same Work as Fellow-Labourers, and conspiring to the same Design as Fellow-helpers to the Grace of God, may be considered as one mystical Person, that espouses the Church as a young Man espouses a Virgin . . . the faithful Ministers of Christ in general, all over the World, seem to be represented as one mystical Person called an Angel.[34]

In another sermon Edwards argued: "The Honour that is put upon faithful Ministers is in some respects greater than that of the Angels."[35] Although this kind of self-praise may have provided a degree of comfort to the clergy, it is doubtful that in itself the ministers' sense of professional importance could have enabled them to maintain their position of religious leadership in New England. In many of the ordination sermons in the first decade after George Whitefield's initial visit to New England, the ministers admitted the radicals posed a serious threat to the standing order. William Rand argued that they wished to take the place of the established ministers of New England. "They set themselves up for teachers and exhorters," he said, "while they decry the generality of the Ministers, as unworthy of their Office; as if they meant to exclude the standing Ministry to make way for themselves."[36] The ministers conceded that such preachers often had a great influence on the laymen. Charles Chauncy complained: "The People in this Land have a more than ordinary Itch to run after Strangers." Other ministers agreed that the critics of the standing order usually had a sympatheitc audience.[37]

In order to withstand the challenge of such "usurpers," the clergymen had to prove that they, rather than their opponents, were the legitimate preachers of God's Word.[38] Thus, they needed continually to emphasize what they considered the proper qualifications of the clergy, and they had to reconsider an old problem—must a minister be converted? In the early eighteenth century, the clergy had agreed that the ministers should have grace, but they often said that God could convert men by unconverted as well as by converted ministers. Believing it was impossible to judge whether a man was, in fact, one of the saints, they had emphasized the external qualifications of the minister—his education, his apprenticeship, and his regular call from a congregation. But in the period of the Awakening the ministers had to answer the criticism of men who claimed that many of the regular clergy were without grace. Such accusers, lay exhorters and itinerant ministers, claimed that they did have grace and that their spirituality gave them a greater claim to ministerial status than the regular clergy.

In answer to these claims, the ministers could hardly deny the importance of salvation. In one ordination sermon after another they agreed that clergymen should be converted. The Congregational pastors, like their radical critics, condemned the unconverted ministers. Joseph Fish said that if a minister lacks grace, then all of his learning and ability "will but serve to carry him with the greater Pomp and Soleminty to Hell."[39] John Graham argued that a minister is not fit to call sinners to salvation "when he himself is not in

Christ by faith."⁴⁰ Often the established ministers were as forceful as their critics in condemning clergymen who lacked grace. Samuel Willard compared them to traitors "that wear the King's Livery."⁴¹ Nathaniel Appleton said grace and knowledge were as different as "the finest Gold and a shining Piece of Sand upon the Floor."⁴²

The ministers had always agreed that grace was an important quality, but now, in order not to seem less loyal to the idea of salvation than their critics, they argued that grace was the preeminent virtue of a well-qualified minister. The title of Nathaniel Appleton's ordination sermon for Matthew Bridge is characteristic of the new emphasis. Appleton called the sermon *The Usefulness and Necessity of Gifts: But the Transcendent Excellency of Grace*. Samuel Porter compared the converted minister to the branch of a living tree. "As the Branch, which is united to the Stock, derives Sap and Nourishment from it and affords Shade and Fruit to those that sit under it; so the Minister being lively and fruitful thro' Grace and Strength deriv'd from CHRIST, the People of GOD may sit under his Shadow with Delight, and his Fruit be both pleasant and profitable to the Taste."⁴³

Jonathan Edwards compared piety to "an heavenly Fire enkindled in the Soul." In converted ministers, Edwards argued, "there should as it were be a Light about them wherever they go, exhibiting to all that behold them, the amiable delightful Image of the Beauty and Brightness of their glorious Master."⁴⁴

However, even though the ministers agreed that grace was important to a clergyman, none said that grace alone was sufficient to qualify men to preach. And only two of the forty-four ordination sermons published from 1741 to 1750 suggest that the spiritual estate of ministers should be examined before they are ordained. One minister, John Porter of Brocton, made a strong appeal for such examinations. On December 2, 1747, he preached an ordination sermon for Silas Brett at Freetown, Massachusetts, which he entitled *Superlative Love to CHRIST a necessary Qualification of a Gospel Minister*. He regretted that many youths "undertake to preach who have no *Grace;* or at least give no *sufficient Evidence* that they have any." Porter said that many such men, though lacking in grace, become ministers in the belief that with "the Lawrels of a first and second Degree conferred on them at the College . . . [they are] sufficiently qualified to preach the everlasting Gospel." Porter believed that education was important to ministers, but that learning alone, without a saving knowledge of Christ, did not qualify a man to be a clergyman. He argued that "these *light, airy, fashionable* young Men, who ridicule experimental Religion as Enthusiasm" did not deserve to be ministers.[45] John Graham, minister of Southbury, Connecticut, shared Porter's point of view. In an ordination sermon entitled *Such as have Grace fittest to teach the Doctrines of Grace*, he argued that the examination of potential ministers should include a statement by the candidate that he had experienced a work of faith. He said that ministers are "obliged in Faithfulness to their glorious LORD, and the Souls of Men" to make such enquiries.[46]

If the view that ministers should give testimonies of their conversion experience had been accepted by all New Englanders, the nature of the clerical office might have changed radically. The old foundation, the candidate's education and knowledge, might have been replaced by a new qualification, piety. But this change did not occur. The ministers refused to consider grace the sole prerequisite of the pastoral office. Even John Graham, who believed that a ministerial candidate's faith should be tested, insisted that one cannot always be sure whether ministers have grace and argued that education, along with grace, was necessary. He said that even clergymen who appear to be spiritually dead may have "a sweet sensible communion with GOD," and, he argued, the ministry should not be "opened to all Pretenders to Grace."[47] Moreover, he asserted that settled ministers rather than laymen should determine who could be a clergyman. God, he said, "has by the Holy Ghost appointed that Men shall have this sacred office committed to them by Men already in Office."[48]

Frequently, men who believed that ministers should be converted argued that there was no way of judging whether they were, in fact, in a state of grace. Charles Chauncy said that ministers should be "inwardly" men of religion, but asserted that neither ministers nor congregations can look into a candidate's heart.[49] The reluctance of most ministers to advocate examinations of candidates' religious experiences is apparent in the suggestion, made by many clergymen, that if a minister led an outwardly sober and religious life, he shuld in "charity" be considered converted. Samuel Willard said that if a minister was diligent in all his duties and was "to Appearance and in a Judgment of Christian Charity" a man of God, he should be honored.[50] Ellis Gray said that congregations should choose ministers whom "they have Reason in a Judgment of Charity to think, are no Strangers to the Grace of God." But he argued that no man has a right "to come when, or go where he will, and so enquire of whom he pleases, what Experience they have had of a Work of Grace on their Souls."[51] Most ministers doubted that there were ways of actually determining whether or not a candidate was converted. But if he was otherwise qualified to become a minister, they generally assumed he had grace. Solomon William's remarks at the ordination of Hobart Estabrook in East Haddam, Connecticut, typify this attitude. "We trust," he said, "thro' the infinite grace iof GOD, you have not only a Doctrinal, but some experimental Acquaintance with these things."[52] If a candidate was well educated and outwardly moral, the clergymen were, with few exceptions, willing to "trust" that he was converted.

Although ministers refused to establish any regular procedures for judging whether candidates were converted, they continued to insist that the candidates' knowledge could and should be judged. Most would agree that faith was more valuable than speculative knowledge, but they did not believe that faith alone qualified a man to be a minister. John Hancock made this point the central theme of a sermon entitled *The Danger of an Unqualified Ministry*. He predicted dire results to the church "if the hedge of a learned, able and faithful Ministry, which Christ hath set about it, were once taken down."[53] This theme was repeated constantly in the ordination sermons of the 1740s. Ward Cotton insisted that "an ignorant or unlearned Ministry, is certainly like to be an unserviceable one."[54] Even John Porter, whose sermon *Superlative Love* was a strong plea for a converted ministry, counseled his audience, "let none despise humane learning."[55]

In general, the ministers' statements about the proper qualifications for their profession simply reemphasize ideas that they had developed long before the Great Awakening. Although they joined with the revival's enthusiasts in celebrating the ideal of a converted ministry, they agreed among themselves that conversion was not in itself a sufficient qualification for the ministry and that a man needed a knowledge of languages and divinity in addition to grace if he intended to become a clergyman. Since a man's education could be measured and his spiritual condition could not be, it was education rather than grace that remained the primary qualification for the ministry.

But although the Congregational ministers were united in believing that their conception of the ministry was valid, they were forced to recognize that many New Englanders were no longer willing to accept them as religious leaders simply because they had a college education and filled an important office. In some of their sermons they even seemed to despair of ever winning the esteem of the people. In an ordination sermon for William Phipps, for example, Samuel Porter told the new minister to look for his reward from Christ, "as there is little Prospect that Ministers, in our Day, should attain to great Things in this World."[56]

If the ministers' status in the 1740s had depended only upon their formal training, it is likely that many pastors would have lost their congregations to enthusiasts who considered themselves "licensed" by the spirit of the Lord. But despite the great turmoil of the Awakening, surprisingly few ministers lost their posts. In fact, the average ministerial tenure in a parish during the 1740s did not vary significantly from tenure during other decades.[57] It is true that new churches were founded under Separatist ministers, and that Presbyterians, Anglicans, and Baptists gained new adherents, but a great majority of New Englanders were content to remain loyal to their Congregational pastors.

Thus, the stability of the clergy during the Great Awakening, which is generally overlooked in traditional accounts, requires explanation. Ironically, this stability derived from a characteristic seldom mentioned in clerical discourses before the Awakening. This was the close pastoral relationship between ministers and people. It enabled many ministers to withstand the challenge of enthusiasts, and it formed the basis of a new theory of clerical legitimacy.

We have seen that there was an important movement among the ministers in the early eighteenth century to set themselves off from their people by magnifying the importance of their office and by increasing their ecclesiastical power. But we have also seen that this movement was limited by lay refusal to accept an elevated authoritarian clergy. Because of its limited impact on religious life in New England, the dreams of clerical magistracy were simply illusions. Even ministerial associations, the chief institutional manifestation of Congregational clericalism, failed to command the ministers' full attention: when important matters were not being discussed, pastors frequently neglected Association meetings on such weak pretexts as misty weather or poor memories.[58]

Ministers enjoyed meeting with their colleagues at associations and conventions, but their primary clerical work took place in their own parishes, where they engaged in the day-to-day work of catechizing, giving counsel, and preaching "seasonable" sermons. In their frustration at inadequate salaries or inattentive audiences, the ministers may sometimes have longingly anticipated the next association meeting or ordination sermon, when they would assure one another that they were, indeed, important men. Nonetheless, the greater part of their ecclesiastical energies were consumed in advising and exhorting laymen—laymen whose spiritual hopes or fears could sometimes be nourished or assuaged by a compassionate pastor.

In the early eighteenth century, the ministers' status had been based in part upon their professional dignity and in part upon the effectiveness of their ministerial work. The Great Awakening forced the Congregational clergymen to place a new emphasis upon the more mundane, but more stable, source of their power, their ability to work with laymen. Although the activities of religious enthusiasts constitute the most dramatic events of the revival period, it was usually the settled pastors who guided the revival in their parishes and counseled the people who had experienced religious awakenings. When the violent passions of the Awakening subsided, the pastor remained with his people and continued the work of nourishing religious awareness in the midst of a secular world. In this regard, a sample passage from Ebenezer Parkman's diary describing a barn-raising in 1750 deserves our attention. "My neighbors raised my New Frame," he writes, "and we sung part of Psalm 127 . . . and Psalm 128. . . . Sundry Neighbors sent and brought Cheese, Cake, Wheat Bread, etc. which with Some Apple Pyes which my wife provided made up our Entertainment."[59] From such prosaic communal incidents the ministry of hundreds of Congregational ministers derived strength for many decades.

During the Great Awakening the ministers became increasingly aware of this unheralded source of clerical legitimacy, and during the 1740s they placed a new emphasis on the pastor's need to be close to his people. Joseph Parsons, for example, urged ministers to be familiar with their parishioners and to know "the character, were that possible, of every Soul committed to their Charge." Joseph Sewall counseled Samuel Cooper to "*Use your best Endeavours to know the State of the Flock,* that you may give to every one his Portion in due Season."[60] The ministers also advised one another not to think too highly of themselves. Jonathan Edwards asserted, "ministers are not Men's Mediators; for their is but one Mediator between God and Man, the Man Jesus Christ."[61] Thomas Barnard argued that although a ministers is entitled to respect, he should not be arrogant in dealing with his people. Barnard condemned, "The [minister's] maintaining himself much above them—The keeping at an awful Distance from them—The observing a great Reserve—The dealing in a haughty manner, especially with such as ask his Advices and Instructions, in a becoming modest Manner."[62] And John Graham counseled clergymen not to disparage their people. "Some," he said, "think they can never sufficiently maintain their Authority among their People, but by a supercilious, magisterial Air, whereas real Humility is the very best Preservative of ministerial Authority, and commands Respect and Reverence wherever it appears."[63]

The idea of clerical humility had not been a major theme in the ministers' thought about their profession in the decades preceding the Great Awakening. The changes they made in the ordination ceremony, the creation of ministerial associations, and the sermons that they preached about the clergy had all been designed to enhance the prestige of their office. But the theory and practice of clerical leadership were not the same. Although the ministers had preached many sermons in which they compared themselves to stars or angels, they had not, in practice, kept "an awful Distance" from their people. On the contrary, they shared many of the day-to-day experiences of their neighbors; they ministered privately to the spiritual needs of individual parishioners, and they carried the life of the community into the pulpit, where they preached "seasonable" sermons. While itinerants might come and go, the settled pastors stayed with their people, preached on the Sabbath, catechized, and gave counsel. The day-to-day work of the ministers was a subject that was often ignored in the loud debate over the qualifications of the clergy; but in actual practice it was the minister's pastoral work, his sensitivity to the needs of his people, which became the real foundation of his continuing status within the community.

EPILOGUE

By 1750 the structure of religious leadership in colonial New England had evolved through three stages since the first Puritan settlements. In the earliest period, the ministers were the admired religious leaders of a relatively harmonious society. In the second stage, the ministers sought to establish a quasi-aristocratic control over a society of contending factions. In the third stage, they based their leadership upon a principle of consent. The Great Awakening forced the ministers to acknowledge that their real power did not come exclusively from the importance of the ministerial office, but rather from the ability of individual pastors to work effectively and directly with their people. In a sense, the ministers came to engage in politics—to base their power on local support rather than upon prestige or association.

These stages were not, of course, completely separate and independent. The earliest New England clergymen were aware that their educations had qualified them to play a distinct occupational role as ministers. In this sense there was already a ministerial "profession" in 1630. In the second period, the ministers were still accorded a degree of traditional deference, albeit less than their predecessors. Finally, the ministers after 1745 continued to meet in associations, to license candidates, and to uphold their professional distinctiveness. The deferred-to-authority, the professional expert, and the pastoral shepherd were, in varying degrees, present among the clergy throughout the colonial period, but historical circumstances caused them to emphasize different parts of their work at different times. The first half of the eighteenth century was the preeminent period of the pastor as professional expert. Had not the Great Awakening undercut the tendencies that appeared among the clergy by 1740, it is possible that the Congregational clergy might have acquired the hierarchy, the ceremonies, and even the Arminian doctrine associated with the Anglican clergy.

138

But this did not occur. Instead the Great Awakening undercut the unique importance of the ministry by emphasizing the sanctity of all Christian believers. And, faced with new circumstances, the clerical community possessed the resiliency to adjust. The democratic leadership of the post revival Congregational ministers was, no doubt, made possible by many developments of the early eighteenth century. The ministers who had ju tified the plain style as a means of adjusting preaching to the intellectual capacity of an audience and who made pastoral visits in order to offer religious advice to their individual parishioners were already well aware of the need to apply religious principles to individual circumstances. What the Awakening did was simply to make this concern for the people the *essence* of clerical leadership.

What occurred then was not a complete transformation of the ministry, but rather a new emphasis upon an old aspect of the ministers' work. This shifting of emphasis was significant, however, for the future of American history, for this was the period in which American society was assuming the form it would carry into the American Revolution. The relationships between the Great Awakening and the American Revolution are as intriguing as they are elusive. Scholars have sought to discover connections in theological, social, and ecclesiastical history. The story of the clergy in the early eighteenth century furnishes one piece of the puzzle.[1]

In the past decade historians have become increasingly aware of the early sources of the American Revolution. The current view, best represented by the works of Jack P. Greene and Bernard Bailyn, stresses the ambiguity of the American identity in the pre-Revolutionary period. Americans were both attracted by Britain's apparent elegance and stability and repelled by her seeming corruption and tyranny. They were careful students of the English libertarian ideology, which stressed the duty of the ruler to the ruled, and at the same time they were followers of English standards of aristocratic leadership.[2]

As we have seen, the ministers, like other eighteenth-century Americans, were pulled in different directions by their society. On the one hand they sought to adopt a courtly conception of their position and authority. Their education, ordinations, and associations were calculated to confer upon them an elite status and exclusive authority in religious matters. Even revivalism, which ultimately worked against elitism, was originally expected to strengthen the authority of the minister by endowing him with a charismatic influence. But at the same time that the ministers were seeking to improve their status, they were drawn by their experience to a more democratic conception of leadership. The same men who received college educations, underwent dignified ordinations, and attended ministerial associations were also pastoral guides. In their parishes they shared the daily experiences of their people and ministered to their needs through sermons and pastoral visits. In practice, the effectiveness of their leadership in their own congregations depended on their ability to relate religious doctrine to the needs of their people.

Eventually, the idea of the leader who was close to his people would become an American norm. But despite the popularity of the country ideology of the early eighteenth century, most Americans were still attracted to an idea of political legitimacy based on the high status of the leader. Among the ministers, dependence on the people was still regarded as an unfortunate circumstance. The Great Awakening changed this situation by forcing the ministers to regard with favor a condition they had formerly regretted. To borrow from Bernard Bailyn's description of a later change in the American political consciousness, the Awakening resulted in a "lifting into consciousness and endowing with high moral purpose" what had hitherto been regarded as an aberration and an embarrassment.[3]

The revival, like the Revolution, caused Americans to reexamine their views of leadership. This is not to say that the new view of ministerial authority was a necessary precondition of the American Revolution. But the ministers' close relationship to the people did enable them to play an important role in that event. Many were among the foremost advocates of American liberties and were active participants in the Revolution as chaplains and as representatives to constitutional conventions.[4] Moreover, during the 1740s ministers had worked out problems in defining clerical legitimacy, which would be confronted in politics thirty years later. In the 1740s religious leadership based upon entrenched status proved too brittle to direct the energies of a religiously energized community. In 1776 the people of North America declared their independence from another power, a civil authority, that had proven too brittle to govern a politically awakened people. In each case the idea of government by virtual representation, by men whose power was based upon membership in an elite group, was rejected in favor of leaders who would associate with the people.[5] Finally, in each period the colonists were able to draw upon the past while entering the future. In 1776 the experience of self-government in town meetings and colonial legislatures furnished the foundations of a new political system. During the Great Awakening the ministers' experience in pastoral relations with their people furnished the basis of a new sense of religious community.

This brings us back to the point with which we began this exploration: the New England ministers were men of their own times. Although they sought, as God's messengers, to transcend their worldly society, their history is an integral part of the story of the larger community to which they belonged.

APPENDIX

LENGTH OF MINISTERIAL SETTLEMENT

	Number of settlements	Average tenure		Number of settlements	Average tenure
1620–24	1	9	1685–89	26	22
1625–29	3	4	1690–94	33	19
1630–34	17	10	1695–99	42	28
1635–39	54	15	1700–04	30	22
1640–44	27	17	1705–09	38	25
1645–49	15	15	1710–14	54	29
1650–54	17	21	1715–19	61	28
1655–59	17	31	1720–24	73	28
1660–64	33	18	1725–29	88	25
1665–69	31	23	1730–34	80	30
1670–74	26	25	1735–39	81	27
1675–79	17	18	1740–44	105	28
1680–84	37	22	1745–49	63	27

* This table is based upon information in Frederick Lewis Weis, *The Colonial Clergy and the Colonial Churches of New England.*

ABREVIATIONS

AAS American Antiquarian Society
Worcester, Massachusetts

ANTS Andover Newton Theological Seminary
Newton, Massachusetts

BLY Beinecke Library, Yale University
New Haven, Connecticut

BPL Boston Public Library
Boston, Massachusetts

CL Congregational Library
Boston, Massachusetts

CH Congregational House
Hartford, Connecticut

DCL Dartmouth College Library
Hanover, New Hampshire

DHS Dedham Historical Society
Dedham, Massachusetts

EDL Episcopal Diocesan Library
Boston, Massachusetts

EI Essex Institute
Salem, Massachusetts

FL Forbes Library
Northampton, Massachusetts

GLS Goodnow Library
Sudbury, Massachusetts

HLH Houghton Library, Harvard University
Cambridge, Massachusetts

LMPL Longmeadow Public Library
Longmeadow, Massachusetts

MHS Massachusetts Historical Society
Boston, Massachusetts

NEHGS New England Historic Genealogical Society
Boston, Massachusetts

NHHS New Hampshire Historical Society
Concord, New Hampshire

SL Stockbridge Library
Stockbridge, Massachusetts

NOTES

CHAPTER I

1. Benjamin Colman, *A Funeral Sermon on the Deaths of the Rev. Messrs. Brattle and Pemberton* (Boston, 1717), p. 44.

2. David D. Hall, "Understanding the Puritans," in Stanley N. Katz, editor, *Colonial America: Essays in Politics and Social Development* (Boston, 1971), p. 41. Hall's essay is an excellent survey and analysis of the secondary literature on sixteenth- and seventeenth-century Puritanism.

3. Norman Pettit, *The Heart Prepared: Grace and Conversion in Puritan Spiritual Life* (New Haven, 1966).

4. William Pauck, "The Ministry in the Time of the Continental Reformation," and Winthrop S. Hudson, "The Ministry in the Puritan Age," in H. Richard Neibuhr and Daniel D. Williams, editors, *The Ministry in Historical Perspectives* (New York, 1956); and David D. Hall, *The Faithful Shepard* (Chapel Hill, 1972), chapters 1 and 2.

5. Edmund S. Morgan, *The Puritan Dilemma: The Story of John Winthrop* (Boston, 1958).

6. In *Winthrop's Boston, A Portrait of a Puritan Town, 1630–1649* (Chapel Hill, 1965), Darrett B. Rutman claims that economic and political considerations were the primary forces in early New England. Perry Miller has argued that religion was the principal element in Puritan society—see his *Orthodoxy in Massachusetts* (Boston, 1959) and *The New England Mind: From Colony to Province* (Boston, 1961, first published 1953). In *Puritanism in America* (New York, 1973), Larzar Ziff is concerned with the relationship between social conditions and religious beliefs. Most historians today would agree with David D. Hall that "the history of the [Puritan] movement was somehow related to the contemporary culture and social structure." ("Understanding the Puritans," p. 33).

7. Kenneth A. Lockridge, *A New England Town: The First Hundred Years* (New York, 1970), p. 13.

8. Philip J. Greven, *Four Generations: Population, Land and Family in Colonial Andover Massachusetts* (Ithaca, 1970).

9. On the founding of Harvard College, see Samuel Eliot Morison, *Three Centuries of Harvard 1636–1936* (Cambridge, Massachusetts, 1936), and *Harvard College in the Seventeenth Century* (two volumes, Cambridge, Massachusetts, 1936); and Winthrop S. Hudson, "The Morison Myth Concerning the Founding of Harvard College," *Church History* 8 (June 1939): 148–59.

10. Bernard Bailyn, *The New England Merchants in the Seventeenth Century* (Cambridge, Massachusetts, 1955).

11. Sarah Kemble Knight, *The Journals of Madam Knight and Rev. Mr. Buckingham* (New York, 1825), p. 65.

12. *Historical Statistics of the United States* (Washington, D.C., 1961), p. 757.

13. Benjamin Colman to George Whitfield [no date, probably 1740], Colman Papers, MHS.

14. Benjamin Colman to "Mr. Holden," January 6, 1734/35, Colman Papers, MHS.

15. Samuel Sewall, *Diary of Samuel Sewall, 1674–1729*, Massachusetts Historical Society, *Collections*, 5th series, vols. V–VII (1878–82), V: 150–51.

16. Henry B. Parkes, "New England in the Seventeen-Thirties," *New England Quarterly* 3 (1930): 402.

17. John Hancock, Commonplace Book, HLH.

18. [Ebenezer Turrell], "An Account of a Society in Harvard College," Colonial Society of Massachusetts, *Publications* 12 (1909): 229.

19. Parkes, "New England," p. 207. In Andover, Massachusetts, 11.3 percent of the babies born between 1700 and 1729 arrived less than nine months after their parents were married. In Bristol, 10 percent of the babies born between 1720 and 1740 arrived less than eight months after their parents' marriage. (In the next two decades the proportion in Bristol increased dramatically to 49 percent.) Philip J. Greven, Jr., *Four Generations*, p. 113. John Demos, "Families in Colonial Bristol, Rhode Island," *William and Mary Quarterly* 25, no. 4 (October 1968): 56.

20. Stephen Williams, Diary, January 29, 1749/50, MHS.

21. Josiah Cotton, Memoirs, p. 167, MHS; Richard S. Dunn, *Puritans and Yankees: The Winthrop Dynasty of New England, 1630–1717* (Princeton, 1962), pp. vi, 191. Well-to-do New Englanders were highly conscious of their social standing in their communities. Some assumed the title, "gentleman," to distinguish themselves from their lesser neighbors. See Lockridge, *A New England Town*, pp. 152–53, 184–85.

22. Clifford K. Shipton, *Sibley's Harvard Graduates* IV: 76. Hereafter volumes I–III (1873–85) of this series of biographical sketches will be cited as Sibley, *Harvard Graduates;* subsequent volumes (1933–   ) will be cited as Shipton, *Harvard Graduates*.

23. These remarks on colonial gravestones are based in part on my own observation of some of these fascinating colonial artifacts. Two fine works on New England gravestones are: Harriette M. Forbes, *Gravestones of Early New England* (Boston, 1927); and Allan Ludwig, *Graven Images* (Middletown, Connecticut, 1966).

24. On the development of Arminianism, see Conrad Wright, *The Beginnings of Unitarianism in America* (Boston, 1955); Perry Miller, *The New England Mind: From Colony to Province* (Boston, 1961, first published 1953); Joseph G. Haroutunian, *Piety Versus Moralism: The Passing of the New England Theology* (New York, 1932); James W. Jones, *The Shattered Synthesis: New England Puritanism before the Great Awakening* (New Haven, 1973); and Norman Pettit, *The Heart Prepared* (New Haven, 1966).

25. T. H. Breen, *The Character of the Good Ruler: Puritan Political Ideas in New England, 1630–1730* (New Haven, 1970), p. 209.

26. Richard L. Bushman, *From Puritan to Yankee: Character and the Social Order in Connecticut, 1690–1750* (Cambridge, Massachusetts, 1967), pp. 72, 107.

27. Bushman, *Puritan to Yankee*, p. ix; Timothy H. Breen and Stephen Foster, "The Puritans' Greatest Achievement: A Study of Social Cohesion in Seventeenth-Century Massachusetts," *Journal of American History* 60 (1973): 20; H. Richard Niebuhr, *The Kingdom of God in America* (New York, 1959, first published 1937), p. 100. The fragmentation of New England society in the early eighteenth century is also described in Kenneth A. Lockridge, *A New*

England Town; Philip J. Greven, Jr., *Four Generations;* and Richard S. Dunn, *Puritans and Yankees.* In contrast to these works, Michael Zuckerman's *Peaceable Kingdoms, New England Towns in the Eighteenth Century* (New York, 1970) presents one argument that a strong communitarian ethos influenced town politics well into the eighteenth century.

28. Thomas Prince, Sea Journal, November 17, 1709, MHS.

29. Quoted in Josiah Cotton, Memoirs, pp. 108–09, MHS. In his *Jonathan Edwards* (New York, 1949), Perry Miller notes that the eighteenth-century ministers "regularly bewailed New England's declension, castigated tavern hunters and backbiters, and went home to solid dinners and a glass of Madeira" (p. 17).

30. Daniel Lewes, *Of Taking Heed to and Fulfilling the Ministry* (Boston, 1720), pp. 1–2.

CHAPTER II

1. See, for example, Nathaniel Appleton, *Isaiah's Mission* (Boston, 1728), p. 20.

2. Thomas Foxcroft, *A Practical Discourse* (Boston, 1718), p. 40.

3. These figures are based upon biographical information in Frederick Lewis Weis, *The Colonial Clergy and the Colonial Churches of New England* (Lancaster, Massachusetts, 1936).

4. For the social background of Yale graduates, see Richard Warch, *School of the Prophets: Yale College, 1701–1740* (New Haven, 1973), pp. 252, 269. My figures for Harvard are based on biographical data in Shipton, *Harvard Graduates.* In classifying well-to-do parents I have included men who were distinguished from the average New Englander by military or civic office, profession, and/or wealth. The ongoing investigations of the colonial social structure by demographers, such as P. M. G. Harris, will undoubtedly lead to a much more precise classification of social classes than is used here. Nonetheless, the general tendency of ministers to come from well-to-do backgrounds is evident in these figures. P. M. G. Harris has summarized his findings in "The Social Origins of American Leaders: The Demographic Foundations," in *Perspectives in American History* 3 (1969): 159–344. (His category "upper class families" is more restrictive than my "well-to-do parents," which leads to differences in our figures for prosperous Harvard parents.) Some of Harris's conclusions have been challenged by Daniel Scott Smith in "Cyclical, Secular, and Structural Change in American Elite Composition," *Perspectives in American History* 4 (1970): 349–74.

5. Nathaniel Eells, *Ministers of the Gospel* (1729), quoted by Shipton, *Harvard Graduates* VII: 474.

6. Nicholas Gilman, Spiritualia, Gilman Papers, MHS.

7. The standard accounts of schooling in colonial New England are found in Robert Middlekauff, *Ancients and Axioms* (New Haven, 1963); Bernard Bailyn, *Education in the Forming of American Society* (Chapel Hill, 1960); and James Axtell, *The School Upon a Hill* (New Haven, 1974).

8. For example, while teaching in Roxbury, Joseph Green, later minister of Salem Village, instructed his pupils in the principles of Christianity. Green, "Commonplace Book," pp. 236–37.

9. Joseph Baxter, Notes on Ministerial Meetings, p. 102, MHS. See also Cotton Mather, *Manuductio ad Ministerum* (Boston, 1726), p. 31.

10. Shipton, *Harvard Graduates* IV: 157.

11. Samuel Eliot Morison, *Three Centuries of Harvard*, p. 22. Hereafter cited as Morison, *Harvard.*

12. Morison, *Harvard*, p. 23. Much of this discussion of Harvard is based on "The School of the Prophets," chapter two of *Harvard.*

13. Franklin Bowditch Dexter, *Biographical Sketches of the Graduates of Yale College* (six volumes, 1885–1912), I: 773.

14. Benjamin Colman to White Kennett, November 1712, Colman Papers, MHS.

15. In 1723 Moses Noyes wrote to Samuel Sewall, "The first Movers for a College in Connecticut alledged this as a Reason, because the College at Cambridge was under the Tutorage of Latitudinarians, but how well they have mended, the Event sadly manifests." Dexter, *Yale Documents*, p. 242. See also Samuel Sewall and Isaac Addington to Thomas Buckingham, October 6, 1701, in Dexter, *Yale Documents*, p. 16, and especially Richard Warch, *School of the Prophets*, chapter 1.

16. Although the Dumner collection is most famous for its inclusion of latitudinarian works, Dumner defended himself from the charge that he had "fill'd the Library with every book for the Church & not one of the other side." He pointed out that "there never was an Eminent Dissenter & Author whose works are not in that Collection." Jeremiah Dumner to Timothy Woodbridge, June 3, 1723, in Dexter, *Yale Documents*, p. 24. See also Warch, *School of the Prophets*, chapters 8 and 9.

17. Proceedings of the Trustees, October 17, 1722, in Dexter, *Yale Documents*, p. 223. In accordance with these rules, Elisha Williams gave "Satisfaction of the Soundness of his Faith in Opposition to Armenian and prelatical Corruption" before being installed as rector in 1726. Proceedings of the Trustees, September 13, 1726, in Dexter, *Yale Documents*, p. 226.

18. Jonathan Edwards to Timothy Edwards, Yale, March 1, 1721, Edwards Mss., ANTS.

19. Morison, *Harvard*, p. 60.

20. Warch, *School of the Prophets*, p. 277.

21. [Benjamin Franklin], *New England Courant*, May 7–12, 1722.

22. John Cleaveland, College Diary, January 19, 25, 1741/42, EI.

23. Ebenezer Turrell, "An Account of a Society in Harvard College," in Colonial Society of Massachusetts, *Publications* 12 (1909): 227–31.

24. Philomusarian Club, Preamble and Rules, AAS. Statistics on Harvard graduates entering the ministry are based on Shipton, *Harvard Graduates*.

25. Mary Latimer Gambrell, *Ministerial Training in Eighteenth Century New England* (New York, 1937), passim.

26. Mather, *Manuductio ad Ministerum*, pp. 74–75.

27. Morison, *Harvard*, pp. 26, 35.

28. Samuel Willard, *Brief Direction to a Young Scholar Designing the Ministry* (Boston, 1735), p. 1.

29. Mather, *Manuductio ad Ministerum*, pp. 2, 5–20, passim.

30. Willard, *Brief Directions*, p. 3.

31. John Barnard, "Autobiography," Massachusetts Historical Society, *Collections*, 3rd Series, V (1836): 185–86.

32. On private meetings, see Cotton Mather, *Ratio Disciplinae* (Boston, 1726), pp. 91–94.

33. Barnard, "Autobiography," p. 186.

34. John Burt, Diary, February 27, 1737, AAS.

35. Ibid., October 2, 7, 11, 15, 1737.

36. Joseph Sewall, Diary, October 3, September 30, 1707, BPL.

37. Thomas Prince, Logs of Sea Voyages, passim, MHS.

38. In Shipton, *Harvard Graduates* VII: 304–05.

39. John Hancock, Commonplace Book, p. 70, HLH.

40. Nicholas Gilman, Diary, March 20, 1741, NHHS.

41. Samuel Dexter, Diary, December 5, 1723, DHS.

42. Joseph Green, "The Commonplace Book of Joseph Green (1675–1715),"

ed. Samuel Eliot Morison, Colonial Society of Massachusetts, *Publications* 34 (1943): 191–253.

43. Jonathan Pierpont, "Extracts from the Diary of Rev. Jonathan Pierpont," *New England Historical and Geneological Register* 13 (1859): 255.

44. John Barnard, "Autobiography," p. 185.

45. John Hancock, Commonplace Book, p. 75, HLH.

46. Sibley, *Harvard Graduates* III: 384.

47. Isaiah Dunster, Diary, May 26, 1746, EI.

48. Hull Abbot, Notes on Church Affairs, in Joseph Stevens, Commonplace Book, NEHGS.

49. William Williams, *A Painful Ministry* (Boston, 1717), p. 9.

50. See John Michael Bumsted, *The Pilgrims Progress: A Religious History of Southeastern Massachusetts* (Ph.D. dissertation, Brown, 1965), pp. 64–71. See also Richard L. Bushman, *From Puritan to Yankee* (Cambridge, Massachusetts, 1967), p. 153.

51. Bumsted, "Pilgrim's Progress," pp. 211–14.

52. William Waldron to Richard Waldron, November 11, 1723, MHS.

53. Ibid., October 14, November 18, 25, December 23, 1723, MHS.

54. Ibid., November 18, 1723, MHS.

55. Shipton, *Harvard Graduates* VII: 538.

56. Ibid., V: 634.

57. Green, "Commonplace Book," p. 248.

58. Stephen Williams, Diary, February 29, 1715/16, LMPL.

59. See appendix.

60. Shipton, *Harvard Graduates* VII: 15.

61. John Barnard, "Autobiography," p. 214.

62. Samuel Dexter, "Extracts from the Diary of the Rev. Samuel Dexter of Dedham," *New England Historical and Geneological Register* 13 (1859): 309.

63. Barnard, "Autobiography," p. 214.

64. William Waldron to Richard Waldron, November 18, 1723, MHS.

65. Josiah Cotton, Memoirs, p. 70, MHS.

66. See below, chapter IV.

67. *The Early Records of the Town of Dedham* 2 (Dedham, Mass., 1885): 9.

68. Ibid., p. 13.

69. Ibid., pp. 17–18.

70. Ibid., p. 18.

71. Ibid., p. 20.

72. Williston Walker, ed., *The Creeds and Platforms of Congregationalism* (New York, 1893), p. 216.

73. Samuel Sewall, *Diary* VI: 438. Cotton Mather explained that this practice was deemed suitable when the churches were in remote areas that were "destitute of *Ordainers*" (*Ratio Disciplinae*, p. 42). For examples of ordinations for remote plantations, see Shipton, *Harvard Graduates* IV: 183; VII: 570; VIII: 143–44.

74. Shipton, *Harvard Graduates* IV: 95.

75. Thomas Prince, *A Sermon Delivered by Thomas Prince . . . at his Ordination* (Boston, 1718), p. 17.

76. William Williams, *The Office and Work of Gospel Ministers* (Boston, 1729), p. 16.

77. Nathaniel Appleton, *Superior Skill and Wisdom Necessary for Winning Souls* (Boston, 1737), p. 50.

78. Ebenezer Parkman, Diary, American Antiquarian Society, *Proceedings*, series 2, vol. 71 (1961): 117.

79. Ibid., p. 117.

80. Eliphalet Adams, *The Work of Ministers* (Boston, 1725), pp. 1–2.

81. John Graham, *The Obligations Which the Profession of the Christian Religion, Lays Men under to Depart from Iniquity* (New London, 1725), p. 36.

82. Shipton, *Harvard Graduates* VI: 26.

83. Thomas Foxcroft, *Ministers, Spiritual Parents, or Fathers in the Church of God* (Boston, 1726), p. 2.

84. William Williams, *Gospel Ministers*, p. 2. See also Mather, *Ratio Disciplinae*, p. 25.

85. This figure is based on a count of the ordination sermons listed in Charles Evans, *American Bibliography* (reprint ed. New York, 1941 [orig. publ. Chicago, 1903–34]), and includes two sermons preached at the ordination of Baptist ministers and one sermon preached at an ordination on Long Island by Congregational ministers. The others were preached in New England for Congregationlist ministers and all were published in New England. There were only three other ordination sermons published in the colonies in this period, one in Pennsylvania and two in New York.

86. *Dedham Records*, II: 18.

87. Benjamin Colman, "Preface" to Thomas Symmes, *Ordination Sermon* (Boston, 1722).

88. See William Williams, *The Great Concern of Christians* (Boston, 1723), p. 1; Joseph Belcher, *God Giveth the Increase* (Boston, 1722), p. 24; Nathaniel Appleton, *Superior Skill and Wisdom*, p. 36; Nathaniel Henchman, *The Divine Pastor* (Boston, 1733), p. 20; and Ebenezer Pemberton, *A Plea for the Ministers of the Gospel* (Boston, 1706), p. 8.

89. These generalizations about the timing of ordination are based on Sibley–Shipton, *Harvard Graduates*, passim, and Mather, *Ratio Disciplinae*, p. 3.

90. William Waldron to Richard Waldron, October 9, 1723; March 9, 1723/24, MHS.

91. White Kennett to Benjamin Colman, Westminster, March 23, 1723/24 in Massachusetts Historical Society, *Proceedings* 63 (1919–20): 82.

92. Thomas Prince, *Ordination Sermon*, p. 19.

CHAPTER III

1. John Cleaveland to Mary Dodge, February 13, 1746/47, EI.

2. Shipton, *Harvard Graduates*, passim.

3. John Hancock, Commonplace Book, p. 254 (quoting Boyle, *Seraphic Love*), HLH.

4. David Hall, Diary, June 14, 1745, MHS.

5. Cotton Mather, *A Good Master Well Served* (Boston, 1696), p. 5.

6. William Waldron to Richard Waldron, February 24, 1723/24, MHS.

7. Marston Cabot, Diary, November 16, 23, 30, December 14, 1740, NEHGS.

8. David Hall, Diary, February 4, 1747/48, MHS.

9. Ebenezer Bridge, Diary, January 8, 1749/50, August 8, 1750, HLH.

10. Shipton, *Harvard Graduates* VII: 354; V: 46.

11. For example, Ebenezer Parkman reports that on May 30, 1726 he read "Bradley's General Treatise on Husbandry and Gardening" and the next day he read Cotton Mather's *Ratio Disciplinae*, "Diary" 71: 140.

12. Ezra Carpenter, Commonplace Book, HLH.

13. Ebenezer Parkman, "Diary" 73: 92.

14. Ibid., 71: 151–52.

15. Timothy Edwards, Account Book, June 3, 1718, BLY.

16. Stephen Williams, Diary, November 12, 1746, MHS.

17. Ibid., August 20, 1747.

18. Eliphalet Adams, *Eminently Good and Useful Men* (New London,

1720), p. 39.

19. Thomas Symmes, Diary, AAS; Isaiah Dunster, Diary, EI; Nicholas Gilman, Receipts, MHS.

20. Thomas Symmes, Diary, AAS; Ebenezer Parkman, Commonplace Book, MHS.

21. Ezra Carpenter, Commonplace Book, HLH; Nicholas Gilman, Receipts, MHS.

22. Shipton, *Harvard Graduates* V: 484; VII: 201; V: 539–41; Josiah Cotton, Memoirs, MHS.

23. John Burt, Diary, April 27, 1731, AAS; David Goddard, Diary, February 1741; Shipton, *Harvard Graduates* VIII: 26–28; V: 472; VII: 263; V: 303.

24. Hall, Diary, June 21, 1741, MHS. See also September 17, 1741 and July 31, 1742.

25. Parkman, "Diary" 72: 425–26.

26. Ebenezer Gay, *Ministers Are Men of Like Passions with Others* (Boston, 1725), pp. 5–6.

27. Solomon Stoddard, *The Duty of Gospel Ministers* (Boston, 1718), p. 13.

28. Joseph Baxter, Ministerial Meetings, p. 6, MHS.

29. Stoddard, *Duty of Gospel,Ministers*, p. 13.

30. Parkman, "Diary" 71: 131.

31. Clifford K. Shipton, "The New England Clergy of the Glacial Age," Colonial Society of Massachusetts, *Publications* 32 (1933–37): 51–52.

32. James T. Axtell, "The Ministers and Education in Colonial New England," *History and Education, A Report of the Fourteenth Yale Conference on the Teaching of Social Studies* (New Haven, 1969), p. 10.

33. Joseph Baxter, Ministerial Meetings, p. 5, MHS.

34. There is little information available about these meetings. Ministers who mention them in their diaries usually only note that they have occurred without giving any details. In this respect William Williams's diary entry for September 17, 1723 is typical: "Catechized the children. The frost killed the vines." (Diary, AAS). Perhaps the process was so simple—consisting merely of asking the children questions about Christian doctrine and helping them with answers—that most ministers felt no need to use notes or to comment on the procedure.

35. Marston Cabot, Diary, June 13, 1742, NEHGS; David Hall, Diary, September 26, 1741, MHS; Jonathan Townsend, Sr., Diary, April 4, 1737, DHS.

36. *Plymouth Church Records, 1620–1859*, Colonial Society of Massachusetts, *Publications* 22 (1920): 145–54.

37. Jonathan Townsned, Sr., Diary, April 4, 1737, DHS.

38. Samuel Sewall attended such meetings; so it is apparent that they were not held solely for the "ignorant." Sewall, "Diary" V: 467.

39. Israel Loring, "Directions for Private Instruction and Catechizing," Loring Papers, GLS.

40. Michael Zuckerman, *Peaceable Kingdoms, New England Towns in the Eighteenth Century* (New York, 1970), pp. 75, 77.

41. Shipton, *Harvard Graduates* VII: 30, 551.

42. Jonathan Edwards to Mary Edwards, Windsor, May 10, 1716, Edwards Papers, ANTS.

43. Parkman, "Diary" 71: 136–37, 159.

44. Israel Loring, Diary, April 16, 1750, MHS.

45. Cotton Mather, *A Brief Memorial for Pastoral Visits* (Boston, 1723), pp. 1–3.

46. See, for example, Ebenezer Bridge, Diary, August 9, 1749, HLH.

47. Thomas Clap, *The Greatness and Difficulty of the Work of the Ministry* (Boston, 1732), p. 14.

48. Joseph Baxter, Ministerial Meetings, p. 4, MHS.

152 NOTES TO PAGES 53–60

49. Parkman, "Diary" 71: 186–91.
50. See, for example, his diary, vol. 71, p. 425; vol. 72, pp. 202, 380.
51. Stephen Williams, Diary, September 24, 1716, LMPL.
52. Joseph Baxter, Ministerial Meetings, March 26, 1706, MHS. On discipline in the Congregational churches in Massachusetts, see Emil Oberholzer, Jr., *Delinquent Saints* (New York, 1956). Because Oberholzer only investigated cases of discipline that came before the church, his study does not take into account the less formal practice of ministerial admonishment. Many cases of misconduct were handled with clerical reprimands rather than with discipline before the whole congregation.
53. Joseph Baxter, Ministerial Meetings, April 1705, MHS.
54. Ebenezer Bridge, Diary, July 17, 1749; February 20, 1749/50, HLH.
55. Josiah Cotton, Memoirs, pp. 47–48, MHS.
56. Joseph Baxter, Ministerial Meetings, p. 177, MHS.
57. Solomon Stoddard, *The Duty of Gospel-Ministers to Preserve a People from Corruption* (Boston, 1718), p. 6.
58. Parkman, "Diary" 72: 182.
59. Increase Mather, *A Sermon . . . Preached at Roxbury* (Boston, 1718), p. 20.
60. Josiah Cotton, Memoirs, p. 48, MHS. Joseph Gerrish, Minister of Wenham, noted on July 28, 1718, "I began the Bible the 35th time." Joseph Gerrish, Diary, July 28, 1718, MHS.
61. Joseph Baxter, Ministerial Meetings, p. 102, MHS.
62. Matthew Adams to Josiah Cotton, January 31, 1739/40, Curwin Papers, AAS.
63. Samuel Dexter, Diary, September 28, 1723, DHS; David Hall, Diary, August 7, 1741, MHS.
64. John Hancock, Commonplace Book, p. 298, HLH.
65. Thomas Paine, *Pastoral Charge* (Boston, 1720), p. 20. See also Nathaniel Henchman, *The Divine Pastor* (Boston, 1733), p. 11; Azariah Mather, *Gospel Minister Described* (Boston, 1725); Nathaniel Eells, *Ministers of God's Word* (Boston, 1725); Daniel Lewes, *Fulfilling the Ministry* (Boston, 1720); Isaac Chauncy, *Faithful Evangelist* (Boston, 1725).
66. Joseph Baxter, Ministerial Meetings, p. 98, MHS; John Hancock, Commonplace Book, p. 93, HLH.
67. Ebenezer Turrell, *Ministers Should Avoid Giving Offense* (Boston, 1740), p. 15.
68. Paine, *Pastoral Charge*, p. 25.
69. Thomas Foxcroft, *Practical Discourse* (Boston, 1718), pp. 20, 30.
70. Isaac Chauncy, *Faithful Evangelist*, pp. 26, 27.
71. Benjamin Wadsworth, *Gospel Ministry*, pp. 13–14.
72. Cotton Mather, *Ratio Disciplinae*, p. 56; Robert Middlekauff, *The Mathers* (New York, 1971), p. 267.
73. Stephen Williams, Diary, February 16, 1746, MHS. Prayers also were expected to take contemporary events into account. Isaac Chauncy praised John Williams of Deerfield because he sought "to inform himself of the Transactions and Affairs of Europe, and to understand the State and Circumstances of this Province [Massachusetts], that he might Calculate his Prayers accordingly." Chauncy, *A Blessed Manumission*, p. 21.
74. William Cooper, *A Winter Sermon* (Boston, 1727), pp. 1–2.
75. Israel Loring, *Two Sermons* (Boston, 1724), pp. 2, 4.
76. Parkman, "Diary" 71: 445. See also 72: 219–20, 332, 399.
77. Ibid., 73: 89.
78. Mather, "Autobiography," pp. 306–07; Diary, January 27, 1693/94, AAS.

79. Mather, "Autobiography," p. 319.
80. Josiah Flynt, Sermon Book, passim, HLH.
81. Joseph Baxter, Ministerial Meetings, p. 66, MHS.
82. Daniel Lewes, *Fulfilling the Ministry* (Boston, 1720), p. 22.
83. Ebenezer Gay, *Ministers Are Men of Like Passions with Others*, p. 13.
84. Cotton Mather, *The Minister* (Boston, 1722), p. 21.
85. From England Nathaniel Mather wrote his young nephew Cotton, "by any means get to preach without any use of or help from your notes. When I was in New England, no man that I remember used them except one, and hee because of a speciall infirmity, the vertigo as I take it, or some spicie of it. Neither of your grandfathers used any, nor did your uncle here, nor doe I, though we both of us write generally the materialls of all our sermons." March 8, probably 1681/82, Mather Papers, Massachusetts Historical Society, *Collections*, 5th series, vol. VIII (1868): 34.
86. John Hancock, Commonplace Book, p. 96, HLH.
87. Increase Mather, "Autobiography," p. 353. Nathan Stone of Southborough was so dependent on notes for preaching that when he forgot his notes for a sermon he intended to deliver in Westborough, he was forced to borrow and preach one of Ebenezer Parkman's old sermons. Parkman, "Diary" 72: 44.
88. John Hancock, Commonplace Book, p. 300, HLH.
89. Marston Cabot, Diary, November 2, 1740, NEHGS; David Hall, Diary, April 26, 1741, MHS.
90. For example, on November 22, 1741 Nicholas Gilman reported: "a very full meeting in between meetings. Mr. Stevens read Mr. Edwards's sermon on the danger of the unconverted at the meeting house." Diary, NHHS.
91. Ibid., January 22, 1744.
92. Legacy of a Dying Father, p. 16, CL.
93. Edward Goddard, Autobiography, p. 10, AAS.
94. John Loring to Israel Loring, Hull, July 23, 1708, Loring Papers, GLS.
95. Reported by Israel Loring, Diary, May 5, 1749, GLS.
96. William Waldron to Richard Waldron, December 30, 1723, MHS.
97. Joseph Baxter, Ministerial Meetings, August 15, 1704, MHS.
98. See chapter V for a discussion of lay piety.

CHAPTER IV

1. Daniel Lewes, *Of Taking Heed to, and Fulfilling the Ministry* (Boston, 1720), pp. 1–2.
2. John Wise, quoted in John Hancock, Commonplace Book, p. 298. See also, ibid., p. 98.
3. Ibid., pp. 297, 303.
4. Joseph Baxter, Ministerial Meetings, p. 56, MHS.
5. Ibid., October 16, 1711, MHS.
6. Ebenezer Gay, *Ministers Are Men of Like Passions with Others*, p. 31.
7. In *The Faithful Shepherd*, David Hall argues that the second-generation ministers sought greater formal authority because they lacked the charisma of the founders (p. 181). See his chapters 8 ("The Second Generation") and 9 ("Beyond the Cambridge Platform") on early changes in clerical authority. In *American Puritanism: Faith and Practice* (Philadelphia, 1970), Darrett B. Rutman discussed the tendencies toward professional self-consciousness among the ministers in the early seventeenth century.
8. [Authors unknown], *A Pastor's Power* (1693), p. 13.
9. John Hancock, Commonplace Book, p. 208, HLH.
10. Samuel Sewall, "Diary" V: 452.
11. Perry Miller, *Jonathan Edwards*, p. 3. A lecture on the pastoral topic, "the preaching of the gospel is the means of the salvation of souls," is typical

of these eighteenth-century performances. Samuel Dexter, Diary, January 31, 1722/23, DHS.

12. Stephen Williams, Diary, May 16, 1741, LMPL.

13. Benjamin Colman to George Curwin, February 1, 1715/16, Curwin Papers, IV, AAS.

14. For example, John Hancock, minister of Lexington, Massachusetts, was frequently addressed as "Bishop." See Daniel Rogers, Diary, March 14, 1732 and October 13, 1738, NEHGS.

15. For examples of this misconception, see Perry Miller, *Jonathan Edwards*, p. 12, and Richard Warch, *School of the Prophets*, p. 58.

16. "Records of the Cambridge–Boston Association," in Massachusetts Historical Society, *Proceedings* 17 (1879–80): 266, 268, 270, 275. In general, information on the associations is extremely scarce. A few books of minutes of early ministerial meetings have survived. Ministers' diaries allow us to locate other early associations. But, for the most part, records of these meetings were not kept or have disappeared.

17. Joseph Baxter, Ministerial Meetings, p. 77, MHS.

18. This manuscript is in the Colman Papers at MHS. It has no date, but some of the phrases which Colman uses to describe New England Congregationalists suggest that it was written soon after his return from England. He calls the Congregationalists "Dissenters" and "United Brethren," two common English terms. The document was probably drafted in 1699 or 1700.

19. These and other documents on the Proposals of 1705 are printed in Williston Walker, *Creeds and Platforms of Congregationalism* ([no place], 1960, first published 1893), pp. 483-94.

20. Benjamin Colman, Proposals for Standing Councils—made to the Association of Ministers at Cambridge, First Monday of August 1705, Colman Papers, MHS.

21. The proposal reads, the standing council shall "consult, advise and determine all affairs that shall be proper matter for the consideration of an ecclesiastical council within their respective limits." Walker, *Creeds and Platforms,* p. 488.

22. Williston Walker argues that the lack of support from the civil government was the crucial factor in the failure of the proposals to become effective in Massachusetts. *Creeds and Platforms,* pp. 493–94.

23. In *Ratio Disciplinae,* Increase's son, Cotton, remarks simply, "there were some very considerable Persons among the *Ministers,* as well as of the Brethren" who opposed the Proposals, feeling that they would infringe upon the liberties of the individual congregations, p. 184.

24. Benjamin Colman to Robert Wodrow, January 23, 1719, in Massachusetts Historical Society, *Proceedings* 77 (1965): 114. An inaccuracy in Colman's description of the proposed structure of the standing councils is revealing. He told Wodrow, "Some of us laboured some years ago" to have the ministerial associations transformed into "so many standing councils" with the idea "that any difference in any of those churches should first be brought to them and decided by them." In the proposals the associations were not in themselves going to function as councils, for the councils would include laymen as well as ministers and would constitute separate deliberative bodies. Colman's error here is suggestive, however, of the intent of the proposals: the ministers wanted to exercise greater influence in the deliberations and judgments of councils.

25. Increase Mather, *Disquisition Concerning Ecclesiastical Councils* (Boston, 1716).

26. The manuscript is in the Mather Papers at AAS.

27. Answers, p. 5.

28. Ibid., p. 6.

29. Historians generally assume incorrectly that the defeat of the Proposals

crippled the association movement. Larzer Ziff, for example, refers to "the thwarted move toward association in Massachusetts," *Puritanism in America,* p. 281; and Perry Miller asserts in *Colony to Province* that by the time John Wise published *Churches Quarrel Espoused* (New York, 1713), "The Movement was dead," p. 288. But, in fact, there were many more associations in Massachusetts in 1713 than in 1705 (see below). Wise was reacting not to an abortive scheme but to a continuing process in Massachusetts ecclesiastical history.

30. Benjamin Colman was able to report in 1719 that "the ministers of every vicinity here form themselves into associations, to have their stated meetings for prayers and mutual advice to one another, and to all that please to apply unto them." Benjamin Colman to Robert Wodrow, January 23, 1719, Massachusetts Historical Society, *Proceedings* 77 (1965): 114.

A few years later Cotton Mather wrote, "the Country is full of *Associations,* formed by the Pastors in their several Vicinities, for the Prosecution of *Evangelical Purposes." Ratio Disciplinae,* p. 181.

31. It was one of the five associations that subscribed to the Proposals of 1705. Josiah Cotton, who was ordained in Providence, Rhode Island, in 1728, joined it. In 1730 the "Associated Pastors of Bristol County" wrote a letter to Benjamin Colman, Colman Papers, April 21, 1730, MHS.

32. Samuel Osborne to Benjamin Colman, November 17, 1729, Colman Papers, MHS. Osborne mentions that ministers in the area of nearby Yarmouth were considering forming another association.

33. The Plymouth Association Book, with records for the years 1721 to 1736, is preserved in the CL. During these years the association's meetings were attended by ministers from Middleborough, Norwell, Plymouth, North Bridgewater, South Scituate, Marshfield, and East Scituate.

34. This association is mentioned in a letter from Peter Thacher to Samuel Danforth in the Plymouth Association Book, following September 26, 1722. This may have been a successor to the Weymouth Association, which subscribed to the Proposals of 1705.

35. Samuel Dexter, Diary, March 9, 1724/25, DHS. John Whiting, Diary, June 16, 1724, AAS. In 1749 Jonathan Townsend of Needham was moderator of an association which probably included Dedham and Milton. Ebenezer Parkman, Diary 74: 156.

36. In 1742 the Boston Association consisted of twelve Boston ministers and two Charlestown ministers. The Cambridge group included ministers from Lexington, Weston, Newton, Waltham, Watertown, Medford, Bedford, and Cambridge. Alonzo H. Quint, "The Origin of Ministerial Associations in New England," *Congregational Quarterly* 2 (1860): 210.

37. Joseph Baxter's minutes of the meetings of the Sherborne Association from 1702 to 1719 are unusually thorough. The towns that are mentioned in these records are: Mendon, Marlborough, Medfield, Lancaster, Framingham, Woodstock, Sherborne, Wrentham, and Weston. The Mendon Association was formed in the house of Rev. Joseph Dorr sometime after he settled in Mendon in 1717. Shipton, *Harvard Graduates* V: 577. Between 1720 and 1750 the Marlborough Association included ministers from Shrewsbury, Westborough, Lancaster, Framingham, Hopkinton, Grafton, Southborough, Sudbury, Harvard, Lunenburg, Marlborough, Northborough, Rutland, Acton, Wayland, Stow, Boylston, Bolton, Holden, Oxford, and Sterling. Ebenezer Parkman, "Diary," passim.

38. The Hampshire Association is mentioned throughout Stephen Williams's Diary, LMPL and MHS. The records of the Hampshire Association are located in the Forbes Library in Northampton, Massachusetts. Between the years 1731 and 1747 the association's meetings were attended by ministers from the following towns: Springfield, Hatfield, Suffield (Connecticut), Longmeadow, West Springfield, Enfield (Connecticut), Northampton, Sunderland, Westfield,

Northfield, Deerfield, Brookfield, Somers (Connecticut), South Hadley, Shef-
field, Stockbridge, Winchester (New Hampshire), Amherst, Keene (New
Hampshire), Belchertown, Wilbraham, Brimfield, Southampton, and Bernards-
ton. Sometime before 1751 the association apparently divided into two bodies.
The records for 1748 to 1751 are missing; those that begin in 1751 are for the
"North Association of the County of Hampshire."

39. Clifford K. Shipton says a Salem association was founded in the home of
Benjamin Prescott in Salem in 1716 (*Harvard Graduates* V: 487). Perhaps
Prescott was simply reviving an earlier association. In his diary Joseph Gerrish
mentioned a meeting in 1717 attended by ministers from Beverly, Peabody,
Marblehead, Salem, and Danvers, MHS.

40. The Bradford Association records for 1719 to 1750 are in the Andover–
Newton Theological Seminary Library. The towns represented in this associa-
tion were Bradford, Haverhill, Andover, West Newbury, Byfield, Groveland,
Methuen, Plaistow, Georgetown, and Boxford.

41. Joseph Whipple mentioned a meeting on July 9, 1734 attended by
ministers from Hampton Falls and Kingston (Diary, MHS). In 1744 the association included ministers from Salisbury, Hampton Falls, Newbury, Amesbury,
Kensington, North Hampton, Kingston, and South Hampton. Quint, "Ministerial Associations," p. 210.

42. Quint, "Ministerial Associations," p. 211.

43. Joseph Torrey of South Kingston, Rhode Island, was a member of an
association in that region.

44. Plymouth Association Records, September 26, 1722, CL. See also December 4, 1722.

45. Bradford Association Records, June 1738, ANTS.

46. Plymouth Association Records, February 25, 1734/35, CL.

47. Cotton Mather, *A Warning to Flocks* (Boston, 1700), preface.

48. [Cotton Mather and others], *Proposals for a Trial of Candidates of the
Ministry* (Boston, 1702), p. 203.

49. In 1715 the Massachusetts General Court gave its blessing to the idea
that ministers should determine clerical qualifications by declaring that when
the court was forced to procure a minister for a recalcitrant town it should
seek a man who was recommended by three or more settled pastors. Sarah
Martin Reed, *Church and State in Massachusetts* (Urbana, Illinois, 1914).

50. [Samuel Osborne], *A Church of Christ Vindicated*, pp. 7–8. The Hampshire County Association followed seven rules in admitting men to the ministry. The candidate should: (1) read Greek and Hebrew; (2) assent to the
Westminster Confession or draw up an orthodox confession of his own;
(3) be "well skilled" in divinity; (4) be a full communion member of a
particular church; (5) practice good moral behavior; (6) declare he intended
to devote himself to the "publick and private" work of the ministry; (7)
commonplace or an assigned scriptural text. Hampshire Association Records,
October 3, 1732, FL.

51. Joseph Baxter, Ministerial Meetings, October 18, 1715, MHS. See also
Plymouth Records, December 3, 1724, CL.

52. This is not to say that councils did not continue to meet in Massachusetts. They played an important role in many religious controversies, but on
many occasions the associations handled problems that were legitimate subjects for councils.

53. Bradford Association Records, June 17, 1730, ANTS.

54. Ibid., October 17, 1733.

55. Ibid., October 11, 1748.

56. Ebenezer Parkman, "Diary" 71: 132–33.

57. Ibid.

58. Cotton Mather, *Ratio Disciplinae*, p. 181.

59. See Williston Walker, *Creeds and Platforms* for a full discussion of the Saybrook Platform and relevant documents, pp. 495–516.

60. Connecticut Records, V: 51, quoted in Walker, *Creeds and Platforms*, pp. 499–500.

61. Ibid., pp. 502–06.

62. Ibid., pp. 508–13. Like the Massachusetts associations those of Connecticut tended to divide into new bodies as the growth of new towns made meetings too large. So, for example, the Windham Association divided into a northern and a southern association. By 1726 there was also a northern (and presumably a southern) association for New London county. Windham Association Book, October 28, 1723; September 6, 1726, CH.

63. Fairfield East Consociation, Book of Records (1735/36–1813), October 17, 1738; October 2, 1739, CH.

64. Windham Association Book, August 1725, CH.

65. Ibid., August 29, 1727; September 6, 1726. The Windham Association tested the candidate's ability to defend orthodoxy and his knowledge of Latin and Greek, divinity, ecclesiastical history, and the chronology of the scriptures. It required that candidates be full communion members of a particular church and that they preach a sermon on an assigned text. Ibid., August 25, 1730.

66. Cotton Mather noted that although the ministers convention in Boston did not have decisive power, the meetings were comparable to regular synods. He asserted that the convention's advice "has proved of great use unto the Country." *Ratio Disciplinae*, pp. 176–77.

67. Thomas Prince, Diary, May 25, 1737, AAS. Had there been none before? Daniel Rogers mentions a convention sermon in 1737 by Joseph Baxter, Rogers, Diary, May 26, 1737, NEHGS.

68. Israel Loring, Diary, June 1, 1749, GLS.

69. Ebenezer Bridge, Diary, May 31, 1750, HLH. See also ibid., May 31, 1744 and May 26, 1748.

70. Windham Association Book, passim.

71. Ibid., May 18, 1736.

72. Ibid., October 2, 1725; October 14, 1729; August 25, 1730.

73. *The Records of the General Association of the Colony of Connecticut* (Hartford, 1888), p. 5.

74. Ebenezer Parkman, "Diary" 71: 197 (August 16, 1727). Parkman reported, "I take it to be a very excellent piece."

75. These lectures, which had been founded in 1691 in Robert Boyle's will, were intended to prove the Christian religion against "notorious infidels, viz. atheists, theists, pagans, Jews and Mohommedans." ("Robert Boyle," in *Encyclopaedia Brittanica*, 11th edition [Cambridge, England, 1910], IV: 355.) Colman's Bath lectures are discussed in Charles Burk Giles, "Benjamin Colman" (Ph.D. dissertation, University of California, Los Angeles, 1963).

76. Benjamin Colman, *A Humble Discourse of the Incomprehensibleness of God* (Boston, 1715), p. 52.

77. Benjamin Colman, *Practical Discourse on the Parable of the Ten Virgins* (London, 1707), p. 57.

78. Ebenezer Turrell, "An Account of a Society in Harvard College," in Colonial Society of Massachusetts, *Publications* 12 (1909): 227–31.

79. Samuel Willard to Josiah Cotton, Boston, May 4, 1702, Curwin Papers, III, AAS.

80. Samuel Willard to Josiah Cotton, Harvard College, May 1702, in Curwin Papers, III, AAS.

81. Benjamin Colman, draft of a letter to the Boston *Gazette*, 1743, in Colman Papers, MHS.

82. See, for example, William Waldron to Richard Waldron, February 24,

1723/24, MHS; Samuel Mather's notes on Collins's *Grounds and Reasons of the Christian Religion* in his commonplace book, AAS; and John Hancock, Commonplace Book, pp. 59, 62, HLH.

83. This was Edward Holyoke's description of John Barnard. Quoted by Perry Miller, *Jonathan Edwards*, p. 24.

84. For a discussion of this change, see Robert G. Pope, *The Half Way Covenent* (Princeton, 1969), and "New England Versus the New England Mind: The Myth of Declension," *Journal of Social History* (1970): 95–108.

85. J. Nelson to Benjamin Colman, May 20, 1699, Colman Papers, MHS.

86. Ebenezer Pemberton to Benjamin Colman, May 22, 1699, Colman Papers, MHS.

87. John Leverett to Benjamin Colman, May 14, 1699, and J. Nelson to Benjamin Colman, May 20, 1699, Colman Papers, MHS.

88. Oliver Noyes to Benjamin Colman, May 14, 1699, and J. Nelson to Benjamin Colman, May 20, 1699, Colman Papers, MHS.

89. John Higginson and Nicholas Noyes, letter to the authors of the Brattle Street "Manifesto" [no date], Colman Papers, MHS.

90. Nathaniel Saltonstall to Rowland Cotton, December 9, 1700, MHS.

91. Samuel Sewall, "Diary," December 9, 1699.

92. John Barnard, "Autobiography," p. 215.

93. Solomon Stoddard, *The Inexcusableness of Neglecting the Worship of God* (Boston, 1708). Increase Mather, *The Strange Doctrine Confuted* (Boston, 1708).

94. Clayton Hardin Chapman, "The Life and Influence of the Rev. Benjamin Colman" (Ph.D. dissertation, Boston University School of Theology, 1948), pp. 38–41.

95. Cotton Mather to Dr. J. Edwards, May 10, 1715, AAS.

96. John White, *New England's Lamentation* (Boston, 1734), p. 16. Historians generally agree that Arminianism became a significant theological force in New England sometime in the early eighteenth century. The standard account of the development of Arminianism is Conrad Wright, *The Beginnings of Unitarianism in America* (Boston, 1955). In *The Shattered Synthesis* (New Haven, 1973), James W. Jones argues that there was a tendency toward Arminianism in early Puritanism. The sources of Arminianism are also discussed by Perry Miller in *Colony to Province* and *Jonathan Edwards*, and by Joseph G. Haroutunian in *Piety Versus Moralism: The Passing of the New England Theology* (New York, 1932). The roots of Arminianism in New England are often associated with the seventeenth-century idea of preparation, a doctrine that is fully discussed in Norman Pettit, *The Heart Prepared* (New Haven, 1966).

97. Jonathan Edwards, quoted by Conrad Wright, *The Beginnings of Unitarianism in America*, p. 9.

98. John Hancock, Commonplace Book, p. 28, HLH.

99. John Michael Bumsted, "The Pilgrims' Progress: The Ecclesiastical History of the Old Colony, 1620–1775" (Ph.D. dissertation, Brown University, 1965), p. 147. In a study of the New England Congregational clergy between 1680 and 1740, Clifford K. Shipton notes that of some five hundred pastors who settled in these years only five left their posts in theological controversies. Shipton, "The New England Clergy in the 'Glacial Age'," in Colonial Society of Massachusetts, *Publications* 32 (1933–37): 50.

100. Benjamin Wright, et al., to Benjamin Doolittle, March 12, 1738/39, and Benjamin Doolittle, reply [no date], ANTS.

101. Nicholas Gilman, Diary, November 21, 1740, NHHS. It is interesting that a few months before Gilman had "perused" with approval Dr. Clark's "Grounds of Natural Religion and Moral Virtue." Diary, March 7, 1740.

102. Benjamin Colman to William Cooper, November 26, 1735; Colman to

William Williams of Hatfield, September 1, 1735; Colman to Cooper, December 30, 1735, Colman Papers, MHS.

103. When Cooper belittled the idea of the authority of local clergy and wrote Colman that he and his associates from Boston had indulged in "the daring crime of entering the see of Hampshire," Colman replied, as to your "writing *the see of Hampshire*, I dare not refrain from telling you that I despise the wit of it." He told Cooper, "You seem to feel within yourself, and especially in what you write, as much of Lordship, Jurisdiction and Diocese as anything they have said or done can give you a pretense for these reproaches upon them." William Cooper to Benjamin Colman, November 25, 1735; Colman to Cooper, November 26, 1735, Colman Papers, MHS.

104. Benjamin Colman to Stephen Williams, August 19, 1735; Colman to Cooper, August 19, 1735, Colman Papers, MHS.

105. Benjamin Colman to William Williams of Hatfield, September 11, 1735, Colman Papers, MHS.

106. Colman's desire for unity is apparent in several statements he made in this period. As much as he disapproved of Breck's doctrinal indiscretions and his interference with the ecclesiastical system of New England, Colman was most concerned that contention itself would hurt the ministry in New England. He agreed not to try to prevent his Boston colleagues from going to Springfield because "when I have judged right, I can't stand by it as I should against the eager fixed judgment of others whom I love and honor." Benjamin Colman to William Cooper, November 26, 1735, Colman Papers, MHS.

Colman had already been disturbed by recent events in Salem, where the church was divided in a bitter quarrel over the choice of a pastor. Early in the Breck episode, he wrote Stephen Williams in Longmeadow, "The discord at Salem, and from thence of late at Boston terrify me. Keep it as far from you as possible. We see the confusion and every evil work attending strife. Leave off the contention before it be muddled with." Colman believed that the best way out of such difficulties was through mutual understanding and forgiveness. Of the Breck case he said, "never was a snarl more easie to be wound up, if people will be just and righteous. But then there must be self-denials, which nobody cares for." Colman to Williams, August 12, 1735; Colman to William Cooper, December 30, 1735, Colman Papers, MHS.

107. Eliphalet Adams, *Work of Ministers*, p. 31.

108. Cotton Mather, *Maintenance of Ministers*, p. 10.

109. Thomas Paine, *Gospel Light*, p. 27.

110. John Tufts, *Anti-Ministerial Objections*, p. 38.

111. Solomon Williams, *The Glorious Reward* (Boston, 1730), p. 22.

112. Ebenezer Parkman, "Diary" 71: 211.

113. Solomon Williams, *Glorious Reward*, pp. 10–11.

114. William Shurtleff, *Gospel Ministers* (Boston, 1739), pp. 20–21.

115. Benjamin Colman, Preface to Thomas Symmes, *Ordination Sermon* (Boston, 1722).

116. Larzar Ziff describes this development as follows: "The clergy, who initially had stood in something of an organic relationship to their villages, as the chosen teachers and leaders of a cooperative band of the faithful, were separating into a class distinct from them" (*Puritanism in America*, p. 198). On the seventeenth-century background to this development, see David Hall, *The Faithful Shepherd*, Chapters 8–12.

117. Thomas Foxcroft, *Ministers, Spiritual Parents*, p. 26.

118. William Shurtleff, *The Labor that Attends the Gospel Ministry* (Boston, 1727), p. 30.

CHAPTER V

1. Edward Goddard, Autobiography, p. 10, AAS.

2. Solomon Hancock, recorded in John Hancock, Commonplace Book, p. 89, HLH.

3. Henry Flynt, Meditations [in his Diary], HLH. Throughout Flynt's Diary are other, similar expressions.

4. John Barnard, "Autobiography," p. 178.

5. John Barnard, *Examinations and Meditation*, p. 155, MHS.

6. Ibid., p. 1.

7. Ibid., p. 5.

8. Other examples of lay piety can be found in ministers' accounts of their visits to dying parishioners, many of whom showed deep religious awareness in composing their thoughts. See, for example, Ebenezer Parkman, "Diary" 72: 100–01. Ministers also gave notice to lay piety in biographies of particularly religious citizens, such as William Cooper's sermon on John Coney, *The Service of God Recommended to the Choice of Young People* (Boston, 1726).

9. Israel Loring, "Memorial to Elder John Loring"; John Loring to Caleb Loring, November 19, 1710; and John Loring to Israel Loring, December 8, 1707, Loring Papers, GLS.

10. William Parkman to John Parkman, June 22, 1722, Parkman Miscellaneous Papers, AAS.

11. Ebenezer Parkman, "Diary" 73: 129; Samuel Sewall, "Diary" V: 473.

12. Benjamin Colman, Proposals for Standing Councils, Colman Papers, MHS.

13. Jonathan Edwards to Thomas Foxcroft, February 19, 1749/50, BLY.

14. Cotton Mather described the duties of the deacons as follows: "We have our *Deacons*, that stand engaged what they can, to free our *Ministers* from secular Disturbances and Avocations, to look after the *Outward Concerns* and *Supports* of the Ordinances, and to dispose of the *Church Stock* for the Relief of such as it belongs unto." Cotton Mather, *Companion for Communicants* (Boston, 1690), p. 163.

15. "Cambridge Platform," in Williston Walker, ed., *Creeds and Platforms*, p. 212.

16. Williston Walker, ed., *Creeds and Platforms*, p. 212n. David D. Hall agrees with this explanation for the seventeenth-century decline of the office. See *The Faithful Shepherd*, p. 95.

17. Joseph Baxter, Ministerial Meetings, June 10, 1718, MHS.

18. This phrase is from Ebenezer Parkman, "Diary" 72: 357.

19. When Ebenezer Parkman had to leave a church meeting early and some of the laymen indicated that they intended to continue the deliberations, Parkman pointed out, "It hasn't been known that a Church can act (as a Church) without the pastor." Parkman, "Diary" 71: 214–16. Elisha Marsh of Westminster, Massachusetts, held that "his vote and one other constituted a majority in church or parish meetings." Shipton, *Harvard Graduates* X: 301.

20. The same tendency to limit the role of laymen in ecclesiastical affairs is also apparent in contemporary developments in the structure of church councils. See chapter IV.

21. Cotton Mather, *The Minister* (Boston, 1722), pp. 41–42.

22. Azariah Mather, *Gospel Minister*, p. 14. See also Daniel Lewes, *Fulfilling the Ministry* (Boston, 1720), p. ii; Solomon Stoddard, *Presence of Christ* (Boston, 1718), p. 19; Nathaniel Appleton, *Isaiah's Mission* (Boston, 1728), pp. 9–10; William Shurtleff, *Gospel Ministry* (Boston, 1727), pp. 7–8; Thomas Clap, *Greatness of the Ministry*, p. 2.

23. Samuel Sewall to Benjamin Colman, Medford, September 12, 1721, Colman Papers, MHS.

24. Edward Goddard, Autobiography, pp. 54–60, AAS.
25. Ibid., pp. 32–37, AAS.
26. Ebenezer Parkman, "Diary" 72: 338.
27. Joseph Baxter, Ministerial Meetings, October 18, 1715, MHS.
28. Roger Wolcott, A Narrative of the Troubles in the Second Church in Windsor, CHS, pp. 6, 18, 19.
29. *New England Courant*, August 28, 1721.
30. Ibid., March 12–18, 1721/22.
31. Ibid., September 25, 1721.
32. Ibid., February 12–18, 1721/22.
33. Ibid., January 15–22, 1721/22.
34. Ibid., July 16–23, 1722.
35. Ibid., December 10–17, 1722.
36. January 29–February 4, 1721/22.
37. Ibid., August 21, 1721. It should be noted that the *Courant* did not include all of the ministers in its condemnation. On occasion the paper praised clergymen who refused to interfere in nonreligious matters. The *Courant* congratulated Joseph Sewall of Old South Church for his restraint. "If you would all take Example by the Rev. Mr. S-L [Sewall]," the *Courant* told the ministers, "and let Innoculation and State Affairs alone, there would not be so much Hagling and Contention as there is." Ibid., January 15–22, 1721/22. During the early months of the epidemic, both Joseph Sewall and Thomas Prince preached conventional jeremiads, calling the people to repent their sins. Thomas Prince, Sermon Notes, October 26, 1721–January 21, 1721/22, BPL. Joseph Sewall, Sermon Notes, August 20–December 24, 1721, BPL.
38. Ibid., September 10–17, 1722.
39. Ibid., February 5–12, 1721/22.
40. Sarah Gill, Diary, Summer and December 11, 1743, BLY.
41. Edward Goddard, Autobiography, pp. 9–12, AAS.
42. William Waldron to Richard Waldron, December 2, 1723, MHS.
43. Timothy Edwards to Anne Edwards, September 12, 1729, Edwards Papers, ANTS.
44. See, for example, Joseph Baxter, Ministerial Meetings, August 15, 1704, MHS.
45. Cotton's letter to his wife, Joanna, expresses the dismay of a minister who had lost his parish. I have resolved, he said, "to cry night and day to God to have pity on me, and, if possible, to dispose that as soon as you are returned home, I may have some retiring place out of the noise of this babel." He signed himself, "thine in depths of affliction." John Cotton to Joanna Cotton, April 19, 1698, Miscellaneous Bound Manuscripts, MHS.
46. Ebenezer Parkman, Commonplace Book, MHS.
47. [John Tufts], *Anti-Ministerial Objections* (Boston, 1725), p. 3.
48. Josiah Cotton, Memoirs, p. 110, MHS.
49. Fitch, *Plea for the Ministers*, p. 9. Tufts, *Anti-Ministerial Objections*, p. 16.
50. Cotton Mather to Thomas Hollis, August 1, 1720, AAS.
51. Bradford Association, October 20, 1724, ANTS.
52. Cotton Mather, *Maintenance of Ministers* (Boston, 1700), p. 4.
53. John Tufts, *Anti-Ministerial Objections*, p. 26.
54. David Hall, Diary, October 28, 1741, MHS.
55. Ibid., June 14, 1745, MHS.
56. John Tufts, *Anti-Ministerial Objections*, pp. 6–7.
57. Cotton Mather, *Maintenance of Ministers*, p. 11.
58. Increase Mather, *Discourse Concerning Maintenance*, p. 4.
59. John Tufts, *Anti-Ministerial Objections*, p. 16.

162 NOTES TO PAGES 107–113

60. Azariah Mather, *Gospel Minister*, p. 29. See also Ebenezer Pemberton, *Plea for the Ministers*, p. 28; and Cotton Mather, *Maintenance of Ministers*, p. 14.

61. John Tufts, *Anti-Ministerial Objections*, p. 28.

62. Shipton, "New England Clergy of the 'Glacial Age,'" Colonial Society of Massachusetts, *Publications* 32 (1933): 50.

63. Parkman, "Diary" 71: 144.

64. In the years 1722, 1727, and 1733, respectively, the average salaries of teachers were 44, 45, and 55 pounds per annum. In the same years ministers' starting salaries averaged 87, 86, and 116 pounds per annum. Figures on teachers' salaries are from Robert Middlekauf, *Ancients and Axioms* (New Haven, 1963), p. 117; those on ministers are based on salary figures in Shipton, *Harvard Graduates*.

CHAPTER VI

1. Samuel Dexter, Diary, September 30, 1732, DHS.

2. Joseph Baxter, Ministerial Meetings, p. 40, MHS.

3. Samuel Sewall to Stephen Sewall, August 20, 1716, Curwin Papers, volume I, AAS.

4. Samuel Sewall to his brother, March 6, 1703/04, Curwin Papers, volume I, AAS.

5. William Waldron to Richard Waldron, June 15, 1724, Library of Congress photostat at MHS.

6. Christopher Sergeant, Commonplace Book, Obesrvations on the Year 1727, MHS.

7. William Bradbury to Josiah Cotton [no date], in Josiah Cotton, Memoirs, p. 180, MHS.

8. Jeremiah Bumstead, Diary, October 30, 1727, AAS.

9. Samuel Dexter, Diary, October 29, 1727, DHS.

10. Ibid., October 29, 1727, and following, DHS.

11. Ebenezer Parkman, "Diary" 71: 201–02, 207–09. On the night of October 29, 1727, Parkman had reported "after 10 O'Clock at night, the sky clear, and the air cold, there was a very terrible earthquake" (p. 200).

12. Stephen Williams, Diary, August 19, 1717, LMPL.

13. Jonathan Edwards to Benjamin Colman, May 19, 1737, Colman Papers, MHS. See also Samuel Dexter, Diary, May 15, 1723, DHS.

14. The standard survey of the subject is Edwin Scott Gaustad, *The Great Awakening in New England* (New York, 1957). At the present writing, the most influential interpretation of the revival appears in Richard L. Bushman, *From Puritan to Yankee: Character and the Social Order in Connecticut 1690–1765* (Cambridge, Massachusetts, 1967). Bushman argues that the intensity of the Great Awakening was a result of tensions New Englanders experienced while indulging themselves in the pursuit of wealth and in conflicts with the state. He claims that revivalism, which stressed God's grace rather than human laws, released men from their sense of guilt and obligation to the old moral code. The argument is intriguing, but highly conjectural insofar as it purports to described the actual psychological condition of New Englanders who "experienced" divine grace during revival meetings. A psychohistorical analysis of some individuals who underwent conversion during the Awakening would greatly improve our knowledge of the psychology of the revival.

15. Stephen Williams, Diary, February 22, 1715/16, LMPL. In a letter to his sister, Mary, Jonathan Edwards reported that thirteen persons had become full members of their father's church during the revival and that "there comes commonly a Mondays above thirty persons to speak with father about the condition of their souls." May 10, 1716, Edwards Papers, ANTS.

16. Jonathan Edwards to Benjamin Colman, May 19, 1737, Colman Papers, MHS.

17. Eleazar Wheelock to Mrs. Wheelock, Southold, Long Island, April 26, 1740; Eleazar Wheelock to Stephen Williams, Lebanon, Connecticut, May 22, 1740, DC.

18. William Williams to Benjamin Colman, July 1, 1740, Colman Papers, MHS.

19. Benjamin Colman, notes on Whitefield's visit to Boston, Colman Papers, MHS.

20. Benjamin Colman to Harris, Watts, Neal, and Guyse (in London), October 3, 1740, Colman Papers, MHS.

21. Ebenezer Parkman, "Diary" 72: 132.

22. Nicholas Gilman, Diary, October 1, 1740, NHHS.

23. Stephen Williams, Diary, September 23–October 22, 1740, passim, LMPL.

24. For example, see Ebenezer Parkman to Gilbert Tennent, March 2, 1740/41, in Parkman, Commonplace Book, MHS.

25. Ebenezer Parkman to Jonathan Edwards, December 1741, in Parkman, Commonplace Book, MHS.

26. Henry Flynt, Diary, December, 1740–January 1740/41, HLH.

27. Stephen Williams, Diary, January 15, 1740/41, LMPL.

28. Nicholas Gilman, Diary, May 5, 1741; April 8, 1742, NHHS.

29. Marston Cabot, Diary, June 7, 1741; August 16, 1741, NEHGS.

30. David Hall, Diary, March 7, 1740/41; April 26, 1741; January 1, 18, 1741/42; August 16, 1742, MHS.

31. Jonathan Edwards to Eleazar Wheelock, Northampton, June 9, 1741; David Jewett to Eleazar Wheelock, New London, July 4, 1741, DCL.

32. Stephen Williams, Diary, July 7–9, 1741, LMPL.

CHAPTER VII

1. William Shurtleff to Ebenezer Parkman, Portsmouth, December 4, 1741, Parkman Commonplace Book, MHS.

2. See, for example, Nicholas Gilman, Diary, May 18, 1742, NHHS.

3. Ibid., March 12, 1741.

4. John Lee to Eleazar Wheelock, April 20, 1741, East Lyme, Connecticut, DCL.

5. The word "enthusiast" in this chapter refers to those ministers and laymen who believed that their actions were directed by the spirit of the Lord. I prefer this term to "New Light" because on fundamental issues relating to the ministry "New Lights" as well as "Old Lights" condemned enthusiasm. Many enthusiasts became Separatists or Baptists, but others, such as Nicholas Gilman, remained within the Congregational fold. For a discussion of the development of enthusiasm into Separatism, see C. C. Goen, *Revivalism and Separatism* (New Haven, 1962). Goen's definition of "enthusiasm" is useful here. He says, " 'Enthusiasm' may be defined as belief in immediate inspiration by divine or supernatural power; it leads to acting on impulses thought to come directly from the Holy Spirit. In extreme cases it may lead to a sort of frenzied possession." *Revivalism and Separatism*, p. 20. See also William G. McLoughlin, *Isaac Backus and the American Pietistic Tradition* (Boston, 1967).

6. Nicholas Gilman, Diary, November 17, 20, 1741; January 29, March 4, 14, 1741/42, NHHS.

7. Chester Williams to Jonathan Edwards, February 14, 1741/42, BLY.

8. David Hall, Diary, October 25, 1741; February 7, 1742/43, MHS.

9. Nicholas Gilman, Diary, June 23, 1741; April 5, 1743, NHHS.

10. Ibid., July 25–31, 1743, NHHS.

11. John Cleaveland, Diary, March 4, 1745/46, EI.

12. Daniel Rogers, Diary, October 29, 1748, NEHGS; and Israel Loring, Diary, November 23, 1748, GLS.

13. Richard Woodbury to William Parsons, May 23, 1744, in Gilman Notes, MHS.

14. Henry Flynt, Spiritual Account, April 8, 1742, HLH.

15. John Cleaveland, Diary, February 5, 1741/42, EI.

16. Jonathan Parsons to Ebenezer Turrell, Lyme, November 8, 1740, MHS.

17. Abigail Cleaveland to John Cleaveland, Canterbury, December 9, 1746, Cleaveland Papers, EI.

18. Joseph Cleaveland to John Cleaveland, Canterbury, December 1746, Cleaveland Papers, EI.

19. Ebenezer Cleaveland to John Cleaveland, March 11, 1746/47, Cleaveland Papers, EI.

20. Even the religious radicalism of the enthusiasts was somewhat muted when they attempted to found churches of their own. The Separatists continued to emphasize God's immediate presence in the world, but they did seek to exercise a degree of formal control over preaching. Although they believed that an internal call to the ministry was a prospective pastor's most important qualification, they did approve of human learning and founded a college in New London, Connecticut, in 1742. (The Connecticut legislature soon closed it.) They also believed that men should "subject the exercise of their talents to church control." Goen, Revivalism and Separatism, pp. 63, 174. On Separatist preaching, see Goen, pp. 174–80.

21. Benjamin Colman to George Whitefield [1740], Colman Papers, MHS.

22. Samuel Dexter, Diary, October 23, 1740, DHS.

23. Stephen Williams to Eleazar Wheelock, Longmeadow, July 18, 1740, DCL.

24. Stephen Williams, Diary, January 23, 1741/42; June 12, April 27, 1741, LMPL.

25. In Revivalism and Separatism, C. C. Goen notes that almost all of the Congregationalists opposed lay preaching. "Even among the most zealous friends of the revival," he says, "no one approved of them except a few erratic hotheads," pp. 57–58.

26. Israel Loring, Diary, November 23, 1748, GLS.

27. Parkman, "Diary" 73: 80.

28. Nicholas Gilman, Diary, November 8, 9, 1743, NHHS.

29. Declaration of the Association Ministers of Boston, June 30, 1742, in Colman Papers, MHS.

30. David Hall, Diary, October 7, 1748, MHS.

31. Ebenezer Parkman, "Diary" 72: 160.

32. Ibid., 72: 196–97.

33. Stephen Chase, Angels of the Churches (Boston, 1748), p. 6.

34. Jonathan Edwards, The Church's Marriage (Boston, 1746), pp. 13–14.

35. Jonathan Edwards, Christ the Great Example (Boston, 1750), p. 22.

36. William Rand, Ministers Should have a Sincere Love (Boston, 1742), p. 21.

37. Charles Chauncy, Ministers Exhorted (Boston, 1744), p. 42; William Rand, Ministers' Love (Boston, 1742), p. 22. See also ibid., p. 14, and David Hall, Faithfulness in Gospel Ministers (Boston, 1745), p. 19.

38. In Connecticut the Congregationalists sought to strengthen their order by passing a strict set of laws regarding itinerant preaching. Ministers who preached in other men's parishes without invitation from the settled pastor

could lose their legal right to a maintenance, and laymen who preached without invitation were subject to civil punishment. (See Goen, *Revivalism and Separatism*, pp. 59–60.)

39. Joseph Fish, *Love to Christ* (Newport, 1747), pp. 37–38.

40. John Graham, *Such as Have Grace* (Boston, 1746), p. 11.

41. Samuel Willard, *The Minister of God Approved* (Boston, 1743), p. 31.

42. Nathaniel Appleton, *The Usefulness and Necessity of Gifts* (Boston, 1746), p. 27.

43. Samuel Porter, *A Sermon Preach'd at Douglass* (Boston, 1748), p. 18.

44. Jonathan Edwards, *The True Excellency of a Minister* (Boston, 1744), p. 14. On the minister's need for grace, see also, ibid., p. 11; John Graham, *The Sufficiency of a Worm to the Work of an Angel* (Boston [1746]), p. 10; Ebenezer Gay, *Ministers Insufficiency for Their Important Work* (Boston, 1742), p. 22; John Porter, *Superlative Love to Christ* (Boston, 1748), passim.

45. John Porter, *Superlative Love to Christ* (Boston, 1748), p. 27.

46. John Graham, *Such as Have Grace* (Boston, 1746), pp. 8, 37.

47. Ibid., pp. 11, 46.

48. Ibid., p. 14.

49. Charles Chauncy, *Ministers Exhorted* (Boston, 1744), p. 7.

50. Samuel Willard, *The Minister of God Approved* (Boston, 1747), p. 32.

51. Ellis Gray, *The Fidelity of Ministers* (Boston, 1742), p. 9.

52. Solomon Williams, *Gospel Ministers* (Boston, 1747), p. 30; see also Joseph Fish, *Love to Christ* (Newport, 1747), p. 34.

53. John Hancock, *The Danger of an Unqualified Ministry* (Boston, 1743), p. 19, and passim.

54. Ward Cotton, *Ministers Must Make Full Proof of Their Ministry* (Boston, 1747), p. 9.

55. John Porter, *Superlative Love*, p. 26. See also Andrew Eliot, *A Sermon . . . at His Ordination* (Boston, 1742), p. 15; and John Graham, *Such as Have Grace*, p. 11.

56. Samuel Porter, *Sermon Preach'd at Douglass*, p. 20.

57. See Appendix.

58. Bradford Association Records, April 20, 1725, July 15, and October, 1729, ANTS. There are innumerable cases throughout these records where meetings were cancelled for similarly minor reasons.

59. Parkman, "Diary" 74: 174.

60. Jonathan Parsons, *A Minister's Care* (Boston, 1741), p. 13.

61. Jonathan Edwards, *Christ the Great Example*, p. 16.

62. Thomas Barnard, *Tyranny and Slavery* (Boston, 1743), p. 15, 22.

63. John Graham, *Sufficiency of a Worm*, p. 28.

EPILOGUE

1. Some of the most important books and articles which find connections between the Great Awakening and the American Revolution are Alan Heimert, *Religion and the American Mind* (Cambridge, Massachusetts, 1966); Perry Miller, "From the Covenant to the Revival," in *Nature's Nation* (Cambridge, Massachusetts, 1967); Richard L. Bushman, *From Puritan to Yankee;* William G. McLoughlin, *Isaac Backus and the American Pietistic Tradition;* and McLoughlin, "The Role of Religion in the Revolution," in Stephen G. Kurtz and James H. Hutson, eds., *Essays on the American Revolution* (Chapel Hill, 1973).

2. In *Ideological Origins of the American Revolution* (Cambridge, Massachusetts, 1967) and *The Origins of American Politics* (New York, 1968), Bernard Bailyn discusses the influence of the libertarian ideology in America. In

The Ordeal of Thomas Hutchinson (Cambridge, Massachusetts, 1974), he describes an American leader who sought unsuccessfully to emulate English models of authority in America. Jack P. Greene's views on the Revolution are set forth in numerous historiographic essays. One of the most useful is "An Uneasy Connection: An Analysis of the Preconditions of the American Revolution," in Kurtz and Hutson, eds., *Essays on the American Revolution.*

3. Bernard Bailyn, "Political Experience and Enlightenment Ideas," *American Historical Review* (January 1962): 351.

4. See Alice Baldwin, *The New England Clergy and the American Revolution* (Durham, 1928).

5. In his essay, "Jonathan Edwards and the Great Awakening," Perry Miller argues that the Awakening experience led Edwards to develop a view of the good political leader as a man who "has the job of accommodating himself to the realities of human and, in any particular situation, of social experience," in *Errand into the Wilderness* (Cambridge, 1956), p. 164. The parallels between ecclesiastical and political change are also suggested by Richard Bushman when he asserts that by 1765 Connecticut's political leaders were "looking for new methods of ordering society when human loyalties would be forthcoming voluntarily or not at all" (*Puritan to Yankee*, pp. ix–x).

BIBLIOGRAPHY

The principal primary and secondary works used in this study are listed in the notes. In lieu of concluding with an extensive bibliographic essay, I have included comments on the sources in the text and footnotes. As an indication, however, of the rich store of unpublished sources used in this study and available to other scholars who may wish to explore the religious history of this period, there follows a list of manuscripts that contributed to my understanding of the topic.

UNPUBLISHED MANUSCRIPTS

Adams, Eliphalet. Annotated Almanac, 1717, MHS.
[Anonymous]. Answers to the . . . Proposals, Mather Papers, AAS.
[Anonymous]. Legacy of a Dying Father Bequeathed to his Beloved Children: or Sundry Directions in Order unto a Well Regulated Conversation, 1693–94, CL.
Ashley, Jonathan. Correspondence with Father Jean-Baptiste de Saint-Pe, 1748–53, CL.
Ballantine, John. Diary, 1737–74, AAS. (This is a typewritten copy of the original, which is in the Westfield Atheneum.)
Barnard, Edward. Account Book, CL.
Branard, John. Meditations and Self Examinations, 1716–19, MHS.
Barnard, Thomas. List of Presents, 1708–19, CL.
Baxter, Joseph. Commonplace Book, HL.
Baxter, Joseph. Notes on Ministerial Meetings, 1702–19, MHS.
Belcher, Joseph. Notebook, MHS.
Bradford Association of Ministers. Records, 1719–73, ANTS.
Bridge, Ebenezer. Diary, 1749–92, HLH.
Bumstead, Jeremiah. Interleaved Almanacs, 1722–27, 1729–33, AAS.
Burt, John. Interleaved Almanacs, 1737–39, AAS.
Byles, Mather. Letter Books, NEHGS.
Cabot, Marston. Diary, 1740–45, NEHGS.
Chamberlain Manuscripts, BPL.
Cleaveland, John. Papers, EI. (Includes diaries for 1742, 1746, and 1749.)
Colman, Benjamin. Bath Sermons, 1699, HLH.
———. Papers, two volumes, MHS.
Cooper, William. Interleaved Almanacs, 1715, 1716, 1723, 1725, 1754, MHS.
Cotton, Josiah. Memoirs, MHS.
Crosswell, Andrew. Letterbook, MHS.
Curwin Manuscripts, AAS.
Dexter, Samuel. Diary, 1721–52, DHS.
Dunster, Isaiah. Diary, 1747, EI.
Edwards, Jonathan. Catalogue of His Books, BLY.
———. Diary or Account Book, 1733–57, BLY.
———. Letters, BLY.

————. Miscellaneous Manuscripts, ANTS.
————. Miscellanies, BLY.
Edwards, Timothy. Account Books, BLY.
————. Diary and Account Book, 1711–24, BLY.
Eells, Nathaniel. Letters to Joseph Fish, BLY.
Emerson, John. Diaries, 1743, 1746, 1754, AAS.
Flynt, Henry. Diary, 1724–42, HLH.
Flynt, Josiah. Sermon Book, HLH.
Gee, Joshua. Commonplace Book, in John Davis Manuscripts, MHS.
Gerrish, Joseph. Diary, 1717–19, MHS.
Gill, Sarah. Diary, 1743–45, BPL.
Gilman, Nicholas. Diary, 1740–44, NHHS.
————. Papers, MHS.
Goddard, David. Diary, 1741, AAS.
Goddard, Edward. Autobiography, AAS.
Hall, David. Diary, 1740–89, MHS.
Hancock, John. Commonplace Book, HLH.
Hull, Joseph. Journal, 1724, AAS.
Loring, Israel. Papers, GLS. (Collection includes Loring's Diaries for 1748–50, 1753, 1753–57, 1757–59, 1762–65).
Mather, Cotton. Letters, AAS.
————. Letters, BPL.
Mather, Increase. Interleaved Almanacs, 1660, 1668, 1680–84, 1688, 1693, 1695, 1697, 1698, 1702, 1704–06, 1717, 1721, AAS.
Mather, Samuel. Collections Against the Church of England, AAS.
————. Commonplace Books, AAS.
May, John. Diary, AAS.
Miscellaneous Bound Manuscripts, MHS. (This collection includes many ministers' letters.)
Odlin, Elisha. Interleaved Almanac, 1729, AAS.
Parkman, Ebenezer. Commonplace Book, MHS.
————. Miscellaneous Papers, 1709–81, AAS.
Plymouth Association Book, 1722–36, CL.
Prince, Thomas. Interleaved Almanac, 1736–37, MHS.
————. Logs of Sea Voyages, MHS.
————. Sermon Notes, 1718–22, BPL.
Remington, Jonathan. Annotated Almanacs, 1730, 1732, 1733, AAS.
Rogers, Daniel (of Exeter, New Hampshire). Interleaved Almanacs, 1730–85, NEHGS.
————. Interleaved Almanac, 1731, AAS.
Sargeant, Christopher. Commonplace and Account Book, MHS.
Sewall, Joseph. Diary, 1707, BPL.
————. Sermon Notes, 1719–21, BPL.
————. Some Thoughts and Meditations Drawn from Places of Scripture, BPL.
Smith, William. Diaries, 1728, 1738–39, 1741, 1749, 1751, 1754, 1755, 1759, 1761–63, 1765–68, 1771, 1777–78, MHS. (The 1728 volume contains a series of anecdotes, rather than diary entries.)
Stevens, Joseph. Commonplace Book, NEHGS.
Stone, Nathan. Papers, MHS.
Symmes, Thomas. Diary, AAS. (Though catalogued as a diary for 1696, this is really a commonplace book.)
Townsend, Jonathan. Diary, DHS. (Extracts copied into Gregory Townsend, Expense Book.)
Townsend, Jonathan, Jr. Diary, DHS. (Extracts copied into Gregory Townsend, Expense Book.)

Waldron, Richard. Papers, NHHS.
Waldron, William. Letters to Richard Waldron, 1722–29, MHS. (This collection at MHS includes photostats of some ten letters at the Library of Congress.)
Wheelock, Eleazar. Papers, DCL.
Whipple, Joseph. Interleaved Almanacs, 1731–34, 1736, 1737, MHS.
Whiting, John. Diary, 1724, AAS.
Wigglesworth, Samuel. Account Book, 1709–68, NEHGS.
Williams, Stephen. Annotated Almanacs, 1714, 1727, AAS.
————. Autobiography, BPL.
————. Diary, LMPL.
————. Diary, MHS. (MHS has a photocopy of portions of Williams's diary at the Library of Congress.)
Williams, William (of Hatfield). Diary, 1723, AAS.
———— (of Weston). Annotated Almanacs, 1710, 1716, 1752, 1753, 1758, AAS.

INDEX

Adams, Eliphalet, 34, 89
Adams, John, 35, 56
Admonishments, 53–55, 152n.52
Allin, John, 31, 36
American Revolution, 139–41
Anglican Church, 81, 135, 138; opposed by Puritans, 2–4; influence of, on innovations in Congregational ordination, 30, 37–39; influence of, on informal Congregational hierarchy, 68–69; possible source of Colman's ordination, 83; popularity of, among Brattle Street Church's founders, 84–85. *See also* Archbishop John Tillotson
Anglicization. *See* Anglican Church; Arminianism; Court persuasion; Elegance; Gentility
Anticlericalism, 97–102
Appleton, Nathaniel, 33; visited by George Whitefield, 115; on importance of grace, 132
Arminianism, 8, 81, 85–88
Avery, John, 45
Awakening of 1735, 113

Baptism, changes in, 66–67
Barnard, John (carpenter), reflects lay piety, 93-94
Barnard, John (minister), 23, 78, 79, 83, 93; accepts "Calvinistical Scheme," 21
Barnard, Thomas, 136
Barrett, Samuel, 124
Baxter, Joseph (doctor), 22
Baxter, Joseph (minister), 110; discusses catechizing, 47–48; on pastoral visits, 51; on admonishments, 54; on unattentive congregations, 63; on ministers' importance, 65; on value of ministerial associations, 70, 75

Berkeley Fellowships, 19
Bible: read in original tongues, 14; familiar to "grown folks," 52; basis of sermons, 56
Boston Association, opposes James Davenport, 129
Bradbury, William, 111
Bradford Association, 73, 75, 105
Bradford, Simon, "whistles Greek," 14
Brattle, Thomas, 84
Brattle, William, 32
Brattle Street Church, 6, 9, 59, 79, 82–84
Breck, Robert, involved in controversy over his settlement, 86-88
Brett, Silas, 132
Brewer, Daniel, 25
Bridge, Ebenezer, 43, 54, 78
Bridge, Matthew, 132
Bridge, Thomas, 25
Bridgham, James, 44
Brude, Stephen, has vision, 123
Bulfinch, Adino, 22
Burr, Isaac, 124
Burt, John, 21, 45

Cabot, Marston: loses four children, 42; catechizes, 48; reports on revival in Thompson, Connecticut, 117
Callender, John, 29
Calvin, John, 2
Calvinism. *See* Doctrine; Puritanism
Cambridge–Boston Association, 69–70, 73
Cambridge Platform, 28–29; on ordination, 32; on ruling elders, 96–97
Carpenter, Ebenezer, 43, 45
Catechizing, 47–49, 151n.34
Chaplains, 22
Chase, Stephen, 130
Chauncy, Charles, 17; opposes tests of ministers' faith, 133

171

THE JOHNS HOPKINS UNIVERSITY PRESS
This book was composed in Linotype Caledonia text type, and Century Expanded
Bold and Goudy Text Outline display type, by Keith Press from a design by
Susan Bishop. It was printed on 60-lb. Warren 1854 regular paper and bound
by The Maple Press Company.

LIBRARY OF CONGRESS CATALOGING IN PUBLICATION DATA
Youngs, John William Theodore, 1941–
  God's messengers.
  "Frank S. and Elizabeth D. Brewer prize essay of the American Society of Church History."
  1. Congregational churches in New England–Clergy. 2. Clergy—New England. 3. New England—History—Colonial period, ca. 1600–1775. I. Title.
BX7136.Y68   253'.0974   76–8544
ISBN 0–8018–1799–4